Annual Update: Top Governmental and Not-for-Profit Accounting and Auditing Issues Facing CPAs

By Lynda Dennis, Ph.D., CPA, CGFO

T0338254

Notice to readers

Annual Update: Top Governmental and Not-for-Profit Accounting and Auditing Issues Facing CPAs is intended solely for use in continuing professional education and not as a reference. It does not represent an official position of the Association of International Certified Professional Accountants, and it is distributed with the understanding that the author and publisher are not rendering legal, accounting, or other professional services in the publication. This course is intended to be an overview of the topics discussed within, and the author has made every attempt to verify the completeness and accuracy of the information herein. However, neither the author nor publisher can guarantee the applicability of the information found herein. If legal advice or other expert assistance is required, the services of a competent professional should be sought.

**You can qualify to earn free CPE through our pilot testing program.
If interested, please visit https://aicpacompliance.polldaddy.com/s/pilot-testing-survey.**

ISBN 978-1-119-74275-3 (Paper)
ISBN 978-1-119-74307-1 (ePDF)
ISBN 978-1-119-74305-7 (ePub)
ISBN 978-1-119-74309-5 (oBook)

Course Code: **746640**
TGNP GS-0420-0A
Revised: **March 2020**

V10018984_061120

Table of Contents

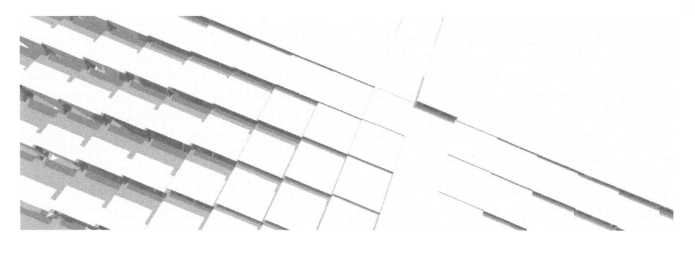

Chapter 1

GASB Statement No. 87, *Leases*

Learning objectives

- Identify how GASB Statement No. 87, *Leases,* affects accounting and reporting of leases by state and local governments acting as lessees.

- Identify how GASB Statement No. 87 affects accounting and reporting of leases by state and local governments acting as lessors.

- Recognize key terms identified in GASB Statement No. 87.

- Recognize how GASB Statement No. 87 affects accounting and reporting of lease modifications and terminations, subleases, and leasebacks by state and local governments.

- Determine the areas of GASB Statement No. 87 representing challenges for preparers of state and local government financial statements.

Major areas of inquiry

GASB issued GASB Statement No. 87, *Leases*, in June 2017, effective for financial statements for periods beginning after December 15, 2019. GASB issued Statement No. 87 to make accounting and reporting of leases consistent with GASB Concepts Statement No. 4, *Elements of Financial Statements*, and to update lease accounting for the approaches considered by the Financial Accounting Standards Board (FASB) and International Accounting Standards Board (IASB).

Both preparers and auditors of state and local government financial statements have had a number of questions relating to the requirements of GASB Statement No. 87 as well as how to effectively implement the requirements of the standard. A number of these questions relate to the following:

- When is GASB Statement No. 87 applicable?
- How do the requirements of GASB Statement No. 87 affect accounting and financial reporting of leases by lessees and lessors?
- What additional disclosures are required by lessees and lessors?
- What is the impact on financial reporting in the first year of implementation?
- How may GASB Statement No. 87 affect the financial condition of state and local governments?
- What are the implementation challenges for state and local governments and their auditors?

Background

Accounting for and financial reporting of leases by business entities and/or state and local governments has been the subject of much discussion by the relevant accounting standards-setting bodies since the early 1960s. In 1979 the National Council on Governmental Accounting (NCGA) published Statement 1, *Governmental Accounting and Financial Reporting Principles,* which stated that FASB Statement of Financial Accounting Standards (SFAS) No. 13, *Accounting for Leases* (published in 1976) was applicable to governmental units. Over the next 20 years, the FASB, NCGA, and GASB made relatively minor changes to lease accounting and financial reporting requirements.

In 2006, FASB and the IASB started a joint project to reexamine their guidance for leases which was the basis for the requirements in GASB Statement 62. The FASB and IASB project and the issuance of GASB Concepts Statement No. 4, *Elements of Financial Statements*, presented the GASB with an opportunity to reconsider lease accounting. In 2010, GASB issued GASB Statement No. 62, *Codification of Accounting and Financial Reporting Guidance Contained in Pre-November 30, 1989 FASB and AICPA Pronouncements,* which incorporated into the GASB literature all statements and interpretations of FASB.[1] In 2011, GASB initiated pre-agenda research on leases that initially only focused on monitoring the developments of the FASB and IASB project.

In April 2013, GASB added a leases project to the current technical agenda in response to the significant changes to lease accounting being proposed by FASB and IASB. The GASB Board approved a Preliminary Views—*Leases*, in November 2014 and conducted outreach to stakeholders during and after the comment period. Also, during the comment period, a field test was conducted where participants were asked to apply the provisions of the Preliminary Views to some or all of their leases as either a lessee or a lessor.

After consideration of respondent comments and testimony on the proposals in the Preliminary Views, the board issued an exposure draft, *Leases*, in January 2016. Again, GASB conducted outreach to stakeholders during and after the comment period for the exposure draft.

A task force was assembled to provide feedback to GASB on issues discussed by the board as well as on the Preliminary Views, Exposure Draft, and final statement. Also, during this time, the Governmental Accounting Standards Advisory Council provided feedback to the board on key issues. After deliberating comments to the exposure draft, the board approved GASB Statement No. 87 for issuance in mid-2017.

---

[1] Opinions of the Accounting Principles Board and Accounting Research Bulletins of the AICPA's Committee on Accounting Procedure were also incorporated into GASB literature with GASB Statement No. 62, *Codification of Accounting and Financial Reporting Guidance Contained in Pre-November 30, 1989 FASB and AICPA Pronouncements*.

Knowledge check

1. What is the objective of GASB Statement No. 87?

   a. To make accounting for leases by state and local governments consistent with the accounting for leases by business entities.
   b. To make accounting and reporting of leases consistent with GASB Concept Statement No. 4 and to update lease accounting for the approaches considered by FASB and IASB.
   c. To establish accounting and reporting requirements for lessors.
   d. To establish accounting and reporting requirements for lessees.

Applicability of GASB Statement No. 87

GASB Statement No. 87 establishes standards of accounting and financial reporting for leases by lessees and lessors and is effective for fiscal years beginning after December 15, 2019. A *lease* is a contract conveying control of the right to use another entity's nonfinancial asset (as specified in the contract) for a period of time in an exchange or exchange-like transaction.

Certain leases and contracts are not accounted for under the requirements of GASB Statement No. 87. Leases for the following are not within the scope of the statement:

- Intangible assets, including rights to explore for or to exploit natural resources such as oil, gas, and minerals and similar nonregenerative resources; licensing contracts for items such as motion picture films, video recordings, plays, manuscripts, patents, and copyrights; and, licensing contracts for computer software.[2]
- Biological assets, including timber, living plants, and living animals
- Inventory
- Underlying asset financed with outstanding conduit debt, unless both the underlying asset and the conduit debt are reported by the lessor.

Contracts[3] relating to the following are also not within the scope of GASB Statement No. 87:

- Service concession arrangement as defined in paragraph 4 of Statement No. 60, *Accounting and Financial Reporting for Service Concession Arrangements*
- Supply contracts, such as power purchase agreements.

GASB Statement No. 87 also makes distinctions between short-term leases and other leases.

Knowledge check

2. Which would be accounted for as a lease under the requirements of GASB Statement No. 87?

    a. Lease with the right to explore offshore for and oil and gas reserves.
    b. Contract to purchase fuel from a regional power company.
    c. Lease of forest land for the purpose of harvesting timber.
    d. Lease of buses to be used in providing public transportation.

---

[2] In a sublease transaction, GASB Statement No. 87 does apply to the intangible right-to-use assets that are created by the original leases of tangible underlying assets.

[3] While contracts for services are not within the scope of GASB Statement No. 87, contracts having both a lease component and a service component are within the statement's scope.

Terms and their application

GASB Statement No. 87 includes a number of terms that are defined and then expanded upon throughout the statement. These definitions represent those used in the statement even though they may have different meanings in other contexts. For example, the definition of a lease in GASB Statement No. 87 includes contracts if the contract meets the definition of a lease. Also, the legal definition of a lease (in any state) is likely not the same as the definition of a lease for purposes of GASB Statement No. 87.

Lease

A contract that conveys control of the right to use another entity's nonfinancial asset (the underlying asset) as specified in the contract for a period of time in an exchange or exchange-like transaction.

As used in the definition of a lease, a *nonfinancial asset* is the underlying asset and is not a financial asset as defined in GASB Statement No. 72, *Fair Value Measurement and Application, as* amended. Examples include land, buildings, vehicles, and equipment.

When determining if a contract conveys the right to control the use of the underlying asset, a government should assess whether it has both of the following:

- Right to obtain the present service capacity from use of the underlying asset as specified in the contract and
- Right to determine the nature and manner of use of the underlying asset as specified in the contract.

Under the definition of a lease, leases of nonfinancial assets at amounts well below the fair value of the underlying asset would not likely meet the definition of an exchange or exchange-like transaction. For example, a government leasing one of its buildings on its own land to the local Chamber of Commerce for one dollar a year for 20 years is neither an exchange nor exchange-like transaction. As such, it does not meet the definition of a lease and is not required to be accounted for as such under GASB Statement No. 87.

Lease term

The period during which a lessee has a noncancelable right to use an underlying asset (referred to as the noncancelable period), plus the following periods, if applicable:

- Periods covered by a lessee's option to extend the lease if it is reasonably certain, based on all relevant factors, that the lessee will exercise that option
- Periods covered by a lessee's option to terminate the lease if it is reasonably certain, based on all relevant factors, that the lessee will not exercise that option
- Periods covered by a lessor's option to extend the lease if it is reasonably certain, based on all relevant factors, that the lessor will exercise that option
- Periods covered by a lessor's option to terminate the lease if it is reasonably certain, based on all relevant factors, that the lessor will not exercise that option.

Fiscal funding or cancellation clauses do not affect the least term unless it is reasonably certain the clause will be exercised. The ability of the government lessee to cancel a lease simply by not appropriating funds for the lease payment(s) does not change the noncancelable aspect of the lease.

Cancelable leases are those where (*a*) both the lessee and lessor have an option to terminate the lease without permission of the other party or (*b*) both parties have to agree to extend the lease. Cancelable leases are excluded from the scope of GASB Statement No. 87.

However, a lease may have both a noncancelable period and a cancelable period. In these circumstances, the period of time for which the lease is cancelable is excluded from the lease term. For example, a lease for office space has a five-year term after which the lease converts to a month-to-month lease. During the rolling month-to-month cancelable period, either the lessee or lessor may opt to terminate the lease without permission of the other party. The lease term in this example, for purposes of applying the requirements of GASB Statement No. 87, is five years.

Key point
A lease must convey control of the right to use the lease asset throughout the lease term. Control includes the right to obtain the present service capacity of the lease asset as well as the right to determine the nature and manner of use of the lease asset.

At the commencement of the lease the lessee and lessor should assess all factors relevant to the likelihood either party will exercise any termination options. Consideration should be given to whether the factors are based on the contract, underlying asset, or market or if they are government specific. Consideration of multiple interrelated factors may be necessary. GASB Statement No. 87 lists the following factors lessees and lessors should consider:

- A significant economic incentive
  - Examples include contractual terms and conditions for the optional periods that are favorable compared with current market rates
- A significant economic disincentive
  - Such as costs to terminate the lease and sign a new lease which could include
    - Negotiation costs
    - Relocation costs
    - Abandonment of significant leasehold improvements
    - Costs of identifying another suitable underlying asset
    - Costs associated with returning the underlying asset in a contractually specified condition or to a contractually specified location
    - Substantial cancellation penalty
- History of exercising options to extend or terminate
- Extent to which the asset underlying the lease is essential to the provision of government services.

GASB Statement No. 87 also enumerates when lessees and lessors should reassess the lease term. The lease term should be reassessed by both the lessee and lessor if one or more of the following occur:

- Lessee or lessor elect to exercise an option even though it was previously determined that it was reasonably certain the lessee or lessor would not exercise the option

- Lessee or lessor elects not to exercise an option even though it was previously determined that it was reasonably certain the lessee or lessor would exercise the option
- An event specified in the lease contract that requires an extension or termination of the lease takes place.

Short-term lease

Lease that, at the commencement of the lease term, has a maximum possible term under the lease contract of 12 months or less. This includes any option to extend regardless of the probability of the option being exercised. The *maximum possible term* under a cancellable month-to-month or year-to-year lease is the noncancelable period including any notice period.

Lessees recognize short-term lease payments as an expense/expenditure (outflow of resources) based on the payment provisions of the lease contract. The lessee should recognize an asset if payments are made in advance or a liability for rent due if payments are to be made subsequent to the reporting period. The lessee should not recognize an outflow of resources during any rent holiday period

A lessor should recognize short-term lease payments as revenue (inflows of resources) based on the payment provisions of the lease contract. The lessor should recognize a liability if payments are received in advance or an asset for rent due if payments are to be received subsequent to the reporting period. The lessor should not recognize an inflow of resources during any rent holiday period.

Key point
Upon the effective date of GASB Statement No. 87, leases will no longer be accounted for as operating or capital leases. State and local governments will account for leases as right to use assets having either a short or long lease term.

Knowledge check

3. In addition to the noncancelable period stated in a lease contract, which would also be considered part of the lease term?

   a. Periods covered by a lessor's option to terminate the lease if it is reasonably possible, based on all relevant factors, that the lessor will not exercise that option.
   b. Periods covered by a lessor's option to extend the lease if it is reasonably possible, based on all relevant factors, that the lessor will exercise that option.
   c. Periods covered by a lessee's option to extend the lease if it is reasonably possible, based on all relevant factors, that the lessee will exercise that option.
   d. Periods covered by a lessee's option to terminate the lease if it is reasonably certain, based on all relevant factors, that the lessee will not exercise that option.

Overview of requirements of GASB Statement No. 87

GASB Statement No. 87 establishes a single model for lease accounting based on the principle that leases are financings of the right to use an underlying asset. In most cases, implementation of this statement will result in governmental lessees and lessors accounting for the same lease transaction in a way that mirrors how the other party accounts for it. This section provides an overview of the major and most relevant accounting and reporting requirements for lessees and lessors required by GASB Statement No. 87. Readers are cautioned to read the actual statement in its entirety (including the Background and Basis for Conclusions sections) to understand all of the requirements of the statement. GASB Statement No. 87 is available at www.gasb.org.

In August 2019, GASB issued Implementation Guide 2019-3, *Leases*, to assist state and local governments in applying the requirements of the standard. Information as to how to acquire Implementation Guide 2019-3 is available at www.gasb.org.

Requirements for lessees

Leases other than short-term leases and leases and contracts that transfer ownership

A lessee should recognize a lease liability and an intangible right-to-use lease asset (a capital asset hereinafter referred to as the lease asset) at the commencement of the lease term. Exceptions to this are

- short-term leases (discussed previously), and
- contracts transferring ownership of the lease asset to the lessee at the end of the lease contract (discussed later in this chapter).

Lease liability

At inception, the lessee should measure the lease liability at the present value of payments expected to be made during the lease term. Measurement of the lease liability should include the following, if required by a lease:

- Fixed payments
- Variable payments that depend on an index or a rate initially measured using the index or rate as of the commencement of the lease term
- Variable payments that are fixed in substance (not based on future performance or usage)[4]
- Amounts reasonably certain of being required to be paid by the lessee under residual value guarantees
- Exercise price of a purchase option if it is reasonably certain the lessee will exercise that option

---

[4] Variable payments based on future performance of the lessee or usage of the underlying asset should be recognized as expenses (outflows of resources) in the period in which the obligation for the payments is incurred.

- Payments for penalties for terminating the lease, if the lease term reflects the lessee exercising either
  - an option to terminate the lease or
  - a fiscal funding or cancellation clause
- Any lease incentives (discussed later in this chapter) receivable from the lessor
- Any other payments reasonably certain of being required based on an assessment of all relevant factors

All future minimum lease payments should be discounted using the interest rate the lessor charges the lessee, which may be the interest rate implicit in the lease. If the interest rate cannot be readily determined by the lessee, the lessee's estimated incremental borrowing rate (an estimate of the interest rate that would be charged for borrowing the lease payment amounts during the lease term) should be used. Lessees are not required to apply the guidance for imputation of interest in paragraphs 173–187 of Statement 62 but may do so as a means of determining the interest rate implicit in the lease.

In subsequent financial reporting periods, the lessee should calculate the amortization of the discount on the lease liability and report the amount as interest expense/expenditure (outflow of resources) for the period. Any payments made should be allocated first to the accrued interest liability and then to the lease liability.

Knowledge check

4. Which would **not** be included in the initial measurement of a lease liability?

   a. Fixed payments.
   b. Variable payments that are fixed in substance.
   c. Exercise price of a purchase option if it is probable the lessee will exercise that option.
   d. Lease incentives due from the lessor.

The lessee is required to remeasure the lease liability at subsequent financial reporting dates if one or more of the following changes have occurred at or before that financial reporting date. In addition, any such changes[5], individually and in the aggregate, should be expected to significantly affect the amount of the lease liability since the previous measurement.

- Change in the lease term
- An assessment of all relevant factors indicates the likelihood of a residual value guarantee being paid has changed from reasonably certain to not reasonably certain, or vice versa
- An assessment of all relevant factors indicates the likelihood of a purchase option being exercised has changed from reasonably certain to not reasonably certain, or vice versa
- Change in the estimated amounts for payments already included in the measurement of the lease liability (except for changes in an index or rate used to determine variable payments)
- Change in the interest rate the lessor charges the lessee, if used as the initial discount rate

---

[5] Changes arising from amendments to a lease contract are accounted for as lease modifications and terminations that are discussed later in this chapter.

- A contingency, upon which some or all of the variable payments to be made over the remainder of the lease term are based, is resolved such that the payments now meet the criteria for measuring the lease liability as discussed previously.

A remeasured lease liability should also be adjusted for any change in an index rate, or other rate, used to determine variable payments if the change in such rate is expected to significantly affect the amount of the liability. By itself, a change in an index or other rate used to determine variable payments does not require remeasurement of a lease liability. Remeasurement of a lease liability is also not required, nor is reassessment of the discount rate required, solely due to a change in the lessee's incremental borrowing rate.

However, the discount rate should also be updated as part of the remeasurement in certain circumstances. When remeasurement of a lease liability is required and changes in the discount rate are expected to significantly affect the amount of the lease liability (either individually or in the aggregate), the discount rate should be updated if one or both of the following changes occur:

- There is a change in the lease term
- An assessment of all relevant factors indicates the likelihood of a purchase option being exercised has changed from reasonably certain to not reasonably certain, or vice versa.

If the discount rate is required to be updated (based on the provisions noted previously) the discount rate should be updated using the revised interest rate the lessor charges the lessee at the time of such update. The lessee's estimated incremental borrowing rate at the time the discount rate is updated should be used if the lessor's interest rate cannot be readily determined.

Lease asset

Initially a lease asset is measured as the sum of the following:

- Amount of the initial measurement of the lease liability
- Lease payments made to the lessor at or before commencement of the lease term, less any lease incentives received from the lessor at or before commencement of the lease term
- Ancillary initial direct costs necessary to place the lease asset into service
  - Any initial direct costs considered debt issuance costs under paragraph 12 of GASB Statement No. 7, *Advance Refundings Resulting in Defeasance of Debt*, should be recognized as expenses/expenditures (outflows of resources) in the period in which they are incurred.

A lease asset should be amortized in a systematic and rational manner over the shorter of the lease term or the useful life of the underlying asset. However, if a lease includes a purchase option the lessee is reasonably certain to exercise, the lease asset should be amortized over its useful life unless the underlying asset is nondepreciable (land for example). Amortization is reported as amortization expense (an outflow of resources) which may be combined with depreciation expense relating to capital assets for financial reporting purposes.

When a lease liability is remeasured and adjusted, the corresponding lease asset generally should be adjusted by the same amount. However, if the change reduces the carrying value of the lease asset to zero, any excess remeasurement adjustment amount should be reported as a gain or loss in the statement of activities or statement of revenues, expenses, and changes in net position.

Key point

To minimize the potential for significant gains or losses resulting from remeasurement of the lease liability, lessees may wish to consider amortizing the lease asset in an amount equal to the amortization of the lease liability (principal portion). Assuming there is no difference between the initial lease asset and initial lease liability, such an amortization method would result in the carrying value of the lease asset being equal to the carrying value of the lease liability. GASB Statement No. 87 requires the amortization method to only be "systematic and rational."

The presence of impairment indicators (described in paragraph 9 of GASB Statement 42, *Accounting and Financial Reporting for Impairment of Capital Assets and for Insurance Recoveries*) with respect to the underlying asset may result in a change in the manner or duration of use of the lessee's right-to-use asset. Such a change may indicate the service utility of the lease asset is impaired. The length of time during which the lessee cannot use the underlying asset or is limited to using it in a different manner, should be compared to its previously expected manner and duration of use to determine whether there is a significant decline in service utility of the lease asset. If a lease asset is impaired, the amount reported for the lease asset should be reduced first for any change in the corresponding lease liability. Any remaining amount should be recognized as an impairment using the requirements of GASB Statement No. 42.

Leases in governmental funds

Leases expected to be paid from general government resources should be accounted for and reported on a basis consistent with governmental fund accounting principles. In the period such a lease is initially measured, an expenditure and other financing source should be reported at an amount equal to the lease liability. Subsequent lease payments from governmental funds should be accounted for consistent with principles for debt service payments on long-term debt. That is, the lease payment should be reported as expenditures for principal and interest.

Disclosures

For other than short-term leases[6], a lessee should disclose the following relating to its lease activities (these items may be grouped for purposes of disclosure):

- General description of its leasing arrangements, including
  - basis, terms, and conditions on which variable payments not included in the measurement of the lease liability are determined

---

[6] GASB Statement No. 87 does not require disclosure of any information relating to short-term leases other than recognizing payments as expenses/expenditures, advance payments of rent as assets, and payments due subsequent to the reporting period as liabilities.

- existence, terms, and conditions of residual value guarantees provided by the lessee not included in the measurement of the lease liability
- Total amount of lease assets, and the related accumulated amortization, disclosed separately from other capital assets
- Amount of lease assets by major classes of underlying assets, disclosed separately from other capital assets
- Amount of expenses/expenditures (outflows of resources) recognized in the reporting period for variable payments not previously included in the measurement of the lease liability
- Amount of expenses/expenditures (outflows of resources) recognized in the reporting period for other payments, such as residual value guarantees or termination penalties, not previously included in the measurement of the lease liability
- Principal and interest requirements to maturity, presented separately, for the lease liability for each of the five subsequent fiscal years and in five-year increments thereafter
- Commitments under leases before the commencement of the lease term
- Components of any loss associated with an impairment (the impairment loss and any related change in the lease liability).

A lessee also should provide relevant disclosures for the following transactions (these lease transactions are discussed later in this chapter), if applicable:

- Sublease transactions
- Sale-leaseback transactions
- Lease-leaseback transactions

A lessee is not required to disclose collateral pledged as a security for a lease (under paragraph 113 of Statement 62) if the collateral is solely the asset underlying the lease.

Knowledge check

5. Which is **not** required to be disclosed by the lessee relating to its leasing arrangements?

   a. Commitments under leases after the commencement of the lease term.
   b. General description of its leasing arrangements.
   c. Amount of lease assets by major classes of underlying assets, disclosed separately from other capital assets.
   d. Principal and interest requirements to maturity, presented separately, for the lease liability for each of the five subsequent fiscal years and in five-year increments thereafter.

Requirements for lessors

Leases other than short-term leases and leases and contracts that transfer ownership
A lessor should recognize a lease receivable and a deferred inflow of resources at the commencement of the lease term. The following are exceptions to this:

- Short-term leases (discussed previously in this chapter)
- Contracts transferring ownership of the lease asset to the lessee at the end of the lease contract (discussed later in this chapter)
- Leases of assets that are investments (discussed below) and
- Certain regulated leases (disclosed below).

Initial direct costs incurred by the lessor should be reported as expenses/expenditures (outflows of resources).

Leases of assets that are investments

The provisions of GASB Statement No. 87 do not apply to the recognition and measurement of leases where the underlying asset is recognized as an investment (as defined in GASB Statement No. 72) by the lessor. In such cases, the lessor reports the underlying asset at fair value as required in GASB Statement No. 72.

Certain regulated leases

Lessors should not apply the requirements of GASB Statement No. 87 relating to a lease receivable, the corresponding deferred inflow of resources, and the underlying asset if a lease is subject to external laws, regulations, or legal rulings.[7] With respect to these "regulated leases," lessors disclose only certain unique information about the leasing arrangement if external laws, regulations, or legal rulings establish all of the following requirements:

- Lease rates cannot exceed a reasonable amount, with reasonableness being subject to determination by an external regulator.
- Lease rates should be similar for lessees that are similarly situated.
- Lessor cannot deny potential lessees the right to enter into leases if facilities are available, provided the lessee's use of the facilities complies with generally applicable use restrictions.

When a lease is a regulated lease, lessors should recognize revenue (inflows of resources) based on the payment provisions of the lease contract. In addition, lessors with one or more regulated leases are required to disclose the following about their regulated lease activities[8] (which may be grouped for purposes of disclosure), other than short-term leases:

- General description of its regulated lease agreements
- Extent to which capital assets are subject to preferential or exclusive use by counterparties under regulated lease agreements, by major class of assets and by major counterparty
- Total amount of revenues (inflows of resources such as lease revenue, interest revenue, and any other lease-related revenues) recognized in the reporting period from regulated lease agreements (if the amount cannot be determined based on the amounts displayed on the face of the financial statements)

---

[7] For example, the U.S. Department of Transportation and the Federal Aviation Administration regulate aviation leases between airports and air carriers and other aeronautical users.

[8] Other than short-term leases as defined in GASB Statement No. 87.

- Schedule of expected future minimum payments under regulated lease agreements for each of the subsequent five years and in five-year increments thereafter
- Amount of revenues (inflows of resources) recognized in the reporting period for variable payments not included in expected future minimum payments
- Existence, terms, and conditions of options by the lessee to terminate the regulated lease or abate lease payments if the lessor government has issued debt for which the principal and interest payments are secured by the lease payments.

Key point

In a regulated lease arrangement, external laws, regulations, or legal rulings establish rates and limit what a lessor can do in some circumstances. This lack of control imposed on the lessor creates a leasing arrangement significantly different from a non-regulated lease arrangement. The accounting and financial reporting requirements of GASB Statement No. 87 recognize these differences.

Lease receivable

At inception, the lessor should measure the lease receivable at the present value of payments expected to be received during the lease term. Amounts expected to be received should be reduced for any provision for estimated uncollectible amounts. Measurement of the lease receivable should include the following, if required by a lease:

- Fixed payments
- Variable payments that depend on an index or a rate initially measured using the index or rate as of the commencement of the lease term
- Variable payments that are fixed in substance (not based on future performance or usage)[9]
- Residual value guarantee payments that are fixed in substance (not based on future performance or usage)[10]
- Any lease incentives (discussed later in this chapter) payable to the lessee.

All future minimum lease payments should be discounted using the interest rate the lessor charges the lessee, which may be the interest rate implicit in the lease. Like lessees, lessors are not required to apply the guidance for imputation of interest in paragraphs 173–187 of Statement 62 but may do so as a means of determining the interest rate implicit in the lease.

---

[9] Variable payments based on future performance of the lessee or usage of the underlying asset should be recognized as revenues (inflows of resources) in the period to which the payments relate.

[10] Residual value guarantee amounts not fixed in substance should be recognized as a receivable and revenue (inflow of resources) if an agreed-upon guarantee payment is required and the amount can be reasonably estimated. Amounts to be received for the exercise price of a purchase option or penalty for lease termination should be recognized as a receivable and revenue (inflow of resources) when the options are exercised.

In subsequent financial reporting periods, the lessor should calculate the amortization of the discount on the lease receivable and report the amount as interest revenue (inflow of resources) for the period. Any payments received should be allocated first to the accrued interest receivable and then to the lease receivable.

Knowledge check

6. Which would **not** be included in the initial measurement of a lease receivable?

    a. Fixed payments.
    b. Variable payments that are fixed in substance.
    c. Exercise price of a purchase option if it is probable the lessee will exercise that option.
    d. Lease incentives due to the lessee.

The lessor is required to remeasure the lease receivable at subsequent financial reporting dates if one or more of the following changes have occurred at or before that financial reporting date. In addition, any such changes[11], individually and in the aggregate, should be expected to significantly affect the amount of the lease receivable since the previous measurement.

- Change in the lease term
- Change in the interest rate the lessor charges the lessee
- A contingency, upon which some or all of the variable payments to be received over the remainder of the lease term are based, is resolved such that the payments now meet the criteria for measuring the lease receivable as discussed previously.

A remeasured lease receivable should also be adjusted for any change in an index rate, or other rate, used to determine variable payments if the change in such rate is expected to significantly affect the amount of the receivable. By itself, a change in an index or other rate used to determine variable payments does not require remeasurement of a lease receivable.

However, the discount rate should be updated as part of the remeasurement in certain circumstances. When remeasurement of a lease receivable is required and changes in the discount rate are expected to significantly affect the amount of the lease receivable (either individually or in the aggregate), the discount rate should be updated if one or both of the following changes occur:

- There is a change in the lease term
- There is a change in the interest rate the lessor charges the lessee.

If the discount rate is required to be updated (based on the provisions noted previously) the discount rate should be updated using the revised discount rate.

---

[11] Changes arising from amendments to a lease contract are accounted for as lease modifications and terminations which are discussed later in this chapter.

Deferred inflow of resources

Initially, a lessor should measure the deferred inflow of resources corresponding to the lease receivable as follows:

- Amount of the initial measurement of the lease receivable
- Lease payments received from the lessee at or before commencement of the lease term relating to future periods (for example, the final month's rent), less any lease incentives (discussed later in this chapter) paid to, or on behalf of, the lessee at or before commencement of the lease term.

In subsequent periods, a lessor should recognize the deferred inflow of resources as revenue (an inflow of resources) in a systematic and rational manner over the term of the lease. When a lease receivable is remeasured, the corresponding deferred inflow of resources generally should be adjusted by the same amount.

Underlying asset

A lessor does not derecognize the asset underlying the lease. As such, a lessor should continue to apply other applicable guidance to the underlying asset, including depreciation and impairment. If the lease contract requires the lessee to return the asset in its original or enhanced condition, a lessor should not depreciate the asset during the lease term.

Under existing guidance in GASB Statement No. 62, some lessor governments derecognized underlying assets for sales-type or direct-financing leases. In many cases, these leases involved a transfer of ownership of the underlying asset to the lessee. GASB Statement No. 87 does not require lessors to determine the value of these previously derecognized underlying assets. For any previously derecognized assets, any residual asset included in the net investment in the lease under Statement 62 becomes the new carrying value of the underlying asset.

Leases in governmental funds

In financial statements of governmental funds, a lessor should recognize a lease receivable and a deferred inflow of resources to account for a lease. The deferred inflow of resources is initially measured at the initial value of the lease receivable, plus the amount of any payments received at or before the commencement of the lease term relating to future periods (for example, the final month's rent). In subsequent periods, a lessor should recognize the deferred inflow of resources as revenue (an inflow of resources), if available, in a systematic and rational manner over the term of the lease.

Disclosures[12]

For other than short-term leases[13] and certain regulated leases (discussed in a previous section of this chapter), a lessor should disclose the following relating to its lease activities other than leases of assets that are investments (these items may be grouped for purposes of disclosure):

- General description of its leasing arrangements, including the basis, terms, and conditions on which any variable payments not included in the measurement of the lease receivable are determined
- Total amount of revenues (inflows of resources such as lease revenue, interest revenue, and any other lease-related revenues) recognized in the reporting period from leases, if the amount cannot be determined based on amounts displayed on the face of the financial statements
- Amount of revenues (inflows of resources) recognized in the reporting period for variable and other payments not previously included in the measurement of the lease receivable, including revenues (inflows of resources) relating to residual value guarantees and termination penalties.

Lessors should disclose the following for all lease activities including leases of assets that are investments:

- Existence, terms, and conditions of options by the lessee to terminate the lease or abate payments if the lessor government has issued debt for which the principal and interest payments are secured by the lease payments.

A lessor also should provide relevant disclosures for the following transactions, if applicable:

- Leases of assets that are investments (discussed previously in this chapter)
- Certain regulated leases (discussed previously in this chapter)
- Sublease transactions (discussed later in this chapter)
- Sale-leaseback transactions (discussed later in this chapter)
- Lease-leaseback transactions (discussed later in this chapter)

If a lessor's principal ongoing operations consist of leasing assets to other entities, the government should also disclose (in addition to the disclosures noted previously) a schedule of future payments that are included in the measurement of the lease receivable. Future payments should be presented separately for principal and interest for each of the five subsequent fiscal years and in five-year increments thereafter.

---

[12] Disclosures relating to regulated leases are discussed in a previous section of this chapter.

[13] GASB Statement No. 87 does not require disclosure of any information relating to short-term leases other than recognizing payments as expenses/expenditures, advance payments of rent as assets, and payments due subsequent to the reporting period as liabilities.

Knowledge check

7. Which is required to be disclosed by the lessor relating to all of its leasing arrangements other than leases of assets that are investments and regulated lease arrangements?

   a. Amount of lease assets by major classes of underlying assets, disclosed separately from other capital assets.
   b. Total amount of revenues (inflows of resources such as lease revenue, interest revenue, and any other lease-related revenues) recognized in the reporting period from leases, if the amount cannot be determined based on amounts displayed on the face of the financial statements.
   c. Existence, terms, and conditions of options by the lessee to terminate the lease or abate payments if the lessor government has issued debt for which the principal and interest payments are secured by the lease payments.
   d. Future payments included in the lease receivable with principal and interest presented separately for each of the five subsequent fiscal years and in five-year increments thereafter.

Requirements for lessees and lessors

Contracts that transfer ownership

In certain circumstances, lease contracts are required to be accounted for as a financed purchase or sale of the underlying asset by the lessee and lessor, respectively. GASB Statement No. 62 required lessors to account for this and similar type leases as sales-type or direct-financing leases. Lessors should not restate the assets underlying their existing sales-type or direct-financing leases in the period of implementation. Any residual assets for those leases should become the carrying values of the underlying assets.

Circumstances requiring the lease to be accounted for as a financed purchase or sale include lease contracts that

- transfer ownership of the underlying asset to the lessee by the end of the contract, and
- do not contain termination options but may include a fiscal funding or cancellation clause that is not reasonably certain of being exercised.

Key point
Lessors are not required to derecognize a right-to-use capital asset leased to a lessee unless the lease contract transfers ownership to the lessee at the end of the contract. A lessor continues to report the underlying asset with all other tangible capital assets if the lease contract does not transfer ownership to the lessee. When a lease contract transfers ownership, the lessor and the lessee account for the lease contract as a sale and financed purchase, respectively.

Lease incentives

Lease incentives reduce the amount that a lessee is required to pay for a lease.

In the context of GASB Statement No. 87, *lease incentives* are

- payments made to, or on behalf of, the lessee, for which the lessee has a right of offset with its obligation to the lessor, or
- other concessions granted to the lessee.

A lease incentive is equivalent to a rebate or discount and includes

- assumption of a lessee's preexisting lease obligations to a third party,
- other reimbursements of lessee costs,
- rent holidays, and
- reduction of interest or principal charges by the lessor.

Lease incentives providing payments to, or on behalf of, a lessee are recognized based on when the incentives are to be provided. The various accounting treatments are discussed below.

- Incentives provided at or before the commencement of a lease term — include in initial measurement by directly reducing the amount of the lease asset.
- Lease incentive payments to be provided after the commencement of the lease term — reduce lease payments for the periods in which the incentive payments will be provided. The payments should be measured by lessees consistently with the lessee's lease liability and by lessors consistently with the lessor's lease receivable.
  - Fixed or fixed in substance lease incentive payments — include in initial measurement and any remeasurement
  - Variable or contingent lease incentive payments — do not include in initial measurement.

Leasehold improvements provided by the lessee would not be an incentive received from the lessor. However, some lease contracts may require the lessor to pay for leasehold improvements. Depending on the facts and circumstances of the lease arrangement, this situation may be an incentive payment to or on behalf of the lessee. For example, a lessor providing additional assets to the lessee without additional cost could be an incentive based on the facts and circumstances of the leasehold improvement.

Contracts with multiple components

Lease contracts may include both a lease component and a nonlease component, or a lease may involve multiple underlying assets. For example, a monthly lease payment for a copier may include the lease component as well as nonlease components for maintenance, copier supplies, and property insurance.

In these types of lease contracts, the government should account for the lease and nonlease components as separate contracts unless (*a*) prices for the individual components are not included in the contract or (*b*) the prices appear to be unreasonable. When prices appear unreasonable, professional judgment should be used to estimate the component prices using observable information (for example, readily available stand-alone prices[14]).

When leases involve multiple underlying assets with assets having different lease terms, the lessee and the lessor should account for each underlying asset as a separate lease component. In addition, the lessee should account for each underlying asset as a separate lease component if the underlying assets are in different major classes of assets for disclosure purposes. This requirement does not apply if separate asset prices are not provided in the lease contract or if prices provided are unreasonable.

Lessees and lessors should allocate the contract price to the different components using any prices for individual components included in the lease contract as long as they do not appear to be unreasonable. Some contracts provide discounts for bundling multiple leases or lease and nonlease components together in one contract. Those discounts may be taken into account when determining whether individual component prices do not appear to be unreasonable.

Multiple components are accounted for as a single lease unit when it is not practicable for the government to make estimates for price allocation. In such cases, the accounting for the unit should be based on the primary lease component within the unit. Circumstances in which it might not be practicable to make estimates for price allocation include the following:

- The lease may be uniquely designed for the leasing parties
- Specific provisions stipulated in certain lease contracts
- Other unique circumstances.

Knowledge check

8. Which is **not** a characteristic of a lease incentive?

   a. Lease incentives increase the amount a lessee is required to pay for a lease.
   b. Lease incentives are payments made to or on behalf of the lessee for which the lessee has a right of offset with its obligation to the lessor.
   c. Lease incentive payments provided after the commencement of the lease term are not included in the initial measurement.
   d. Lease incentive payments provided before the commencement of the lease term are included in the initial measurement.

---

[14] Stand-alone prices are those that would be paid or received if the same or similar assets were leased individually or if the same or similar nonlease components (such as services) were contracted individually.

Contract combinations

Contracts entered into at or near the same time with the same counterparty should be considered part of the same contract if either of the following criteria is met:

- Contracts are negotiated as a package with a single objective.
- The amount of consideration to be paid in one contract depends on the price or performance of the other contract.

Multiple contracts determined to be part of the same contract should be evaluated in accordance with the guidance for contracts with multiple components discussed previously.

Lease modifications

During the term of a lease contract various provisions may be amended which modify the lease contract. An amendment is considered a lease modification unless the lessee's right to use the underlying asset decreases. In these cases, the amendment is considered a partial or full lease termination.

Amendments resulting in a modification to a lease contract made during the financial reporting period should be accounted for as a separate lease by both the lessee and lessor if the following conditions are present:

- Lease modification gives the lessee an additional lease asset by adding one or more underlying assets that were not included in the original lease contract
- Increase in lease payments for the additional lease asset does not appear to be unreasonable based on (1) the terms of the amended lease contract and (2) professional judgment, maximizing the use of observable information.

A lessee should account for a lease modification by remeasuring the lease liability unless a modification is required to be reported as a separate lease as noted previously. The lease asset should be adjusted by the difference between the remeasured liability and the liability immediately before the lease modification. If the change reduces the carrying value of the lease asset to zero, any remaining amount should be reported in the statement of activities/statement of revenues, expenses, and changes in net position.

Unless a lease modification is required to be reported as a separate lease as noted previously, a lessor should account for a lease modification by remeasuring the lease receivable. The deferred inflow of resources should be adjusted by the difference between the remeasured receivable and the receivable immediately before the lease modification. To the extent the change relates to payments for the current period, the change should be recognized as revenue (inflow of resources) or an expense (outflow of resources) for the current period.

Key point
Lease amendments modify the terms of a lease contract. Examples of lease amendments include changing contract prices, lengthening or shortening the lease term, and adding or removing an underlying asset.

Lease terminations

The lessee and lessor should account for an amendment during the reporting period resulting in a decrease in the lessee's right to use the underlying asset as a partial or full lease termination.

A lessee generally should account for the partial or full lease termination by reducing the carrying values of the lease asset and lease liability and by recognizing a gain or loss for the difference. If the lease is terminated as a result of the lessee purchasing an underlying asset from the lessor, the lease asset should be reclassified to the appropriate class of owned asset.

A lessor should account for the partial or full lease termination by reducing the carrying values of the lease receivable and related deferred inflow of resources and by recognizing a gain or loss for the difference. If the lease is terminated as a result of the lessee purchasing an underlying asset from the lessor, the carrying value of the underlying asset should be derecognized and included in the calculation of any resulting gain or loss.

Subleases

Sublease transactions involve the following three parties:

- Original lessor
- Original lessee (becomes the lessor in the sublease)
- New lessee

Accounting and reporting by the parties to a sublease transaction is as follows:

- Original lessor
  - Continues to apply general lessor guidance
- Original lessee/new lessor
  - Accounts for original and sublease as lessee and lessor, respectively
    - Transactions should not be offset against each other
  - Includes sublease in disclosure of general description of lease arrangements
    - Lessor transactions relating to subleases should be disclosed separately from original lessee transaction
- New lessee
  - Applies general lessee guidance

Leaseback transactions

Leaseback transactions may involve a sale-leaseback transaction or a lease-leaseback transaction. Sale-leaseback transactions are accounted for as two separate transactions, whereas lease-leaseback transactions are accounted for as a net transaction.

Sale-leaseback transactions

A *sale-leaseback* transaction involves the sale of an underlying asset by the owner and a lease from the new owner of the asset back to the original owner. These transactions should qualify as a sale under paragraphs 287-319 and 321-323 of GASB Statement No. 62. If the transaction does not qualify as a sale, it is accounted for as a borrowing activity by the seller/lessee and a lending activity by the buyer/lessor.

In financial statements prepared using the economic resources measurement focus, the sale and lease portions of a sale-leaseback transaction should be accounted for as a sale transaction and a lease transaction. The difference between the carrying value of the capital asset sold and the net proceeds from the sale should be reported as a deferred inflow of resources or a deferred outflow of resources. These deferred resource flows are recognized in the statement of activities or the statement of revenues, expenses, and changes in net position in a systematic and rational manner over the term of the lease.

If the lease portion of the transaction qualifies as a short-term lease, any difference between the carrying value of the capital asset sold and the net proceeds from the sale should be recognized immediately. A seller-lessee should disclose the terms and conditions of sale-leaseback transactions in addition to other lease-related disclosures required of a lessee in GASB Statement No. 87. A buyer-lessor should provide the lease-related disclosures required of a lessor in GASB Statement No. 87.

Lease-leaseback transactions

A *lease-leaseback* transaction involves a lease asset where the original lessee leases the underlying asset to another party and who then leases it back to the original lessee. The leaseback may involve an additional asset or only a portion of the original asset. A lease-leaseback transaction should be accounted for as a net transaction and both parties should disclose the amounts of the lease and the leaseback separately in the notes to financial statements.

Intra-entity leases

Blended component units

When the lessee or lessor is included as a blended component unit of the primary government, the reporting requirements of GASB Statement No. 87 do not apply. Instead, when the lessor is a blended component unit, the debt and assets of the lessor should be reported as if they were the primary government's debt and assets.

With respect to leases with or between blended component units, for which eliminations are required, these eliminations should be made before the financial statements of the blended component units are aggregated with those of the primary government. The remaining cash payments between component units should be reported as inflows of resources and outflows of resources.

Discretely presented component units

Lease arrangements between the primary government and discretely presented component units (or between discretely presented component units) should be treated in the same as any other lease under the provisions of GASB Statement No. 87. However, related receivables and payables should not be combined with other amounts due to or due from discretely presented component units or with lease receivables and payables with organizations outside the reporting entity.

Leases between related parties

In the separate financial statements of the related parties, the classification and accounting should be the same as for similar leases between unrelated parties. An exception to this is in cases where it is clear the terms of the transaction have been significantly affected by the fact the lessee and lessor are related. In such cases, the classification and accounting should be modified as necessary to recognize the substance of the transaction rather than merely its legal form.

The nature and extent of leasing transactions with related parties should be disclosed. In financial statements for which an interest in an investee is accounted for using the equity method, any inflow of resources or outflow of resources (for example, gain or loss) on a leasing transaction with the related party should be accounted for in accordance with the principles set forth in paragraphs 202–210 of GASB Statement 62 and paragraph 77 of GASB Statement 72.

Financial reporting

Upon initial implementation

GASB Statement No. 87 is effective for periods beginning after December 15, 2019. When the requirements of the statement are first applied, changes resulting from these requirements should be applied retroactively by restating financial statements, if practicable, for all prior periods presented. Governmental entities presenting comparative statements in the year of implementation will need to restate all prior year statements presented.

If restatement for prior periods is not practicable, the cumulative effect of applying the requirements of GASB Statement No. 87, if any, should be reported as a restatement of beginning net position (or fund balance or fund net position) for the earliest period restated. The reason for not restating prior periods presented should also be disclosed. In the first period the requirements of the statement are applied, notes to the financial statements should disclose the nature of any restatement and its effect.

Leases should be recognized and measured using the facts and circumstances existing at the beginning of the period of implementation. If applied to earlier periods, leases should be recognized and measured using the facts and circumstances existing at the beginning of the earliest period restated. However, lessors should not restate the assets underlying their existing sales-type or direct-financing leases. Any residual assets for those leases should become the carrying values of the underlying assets.

Key point
The board believes reasonable efforts should be employed before a government determines restatement of all prior periods presented is not practicable. In the basis for conclusions section, paragraph 127 states inconvenient should not be considered equivalent to not practicable.

Implementation challenges

As can be seen from the previous sections, GASB Statement No. 87 has the potential to significantly affect state and local governments operations and financial condition. A summary of the practice areas most affected by GASB Statement No. 87 includes the following:

- Understand the requirements of the statement
- Communicate with elected officials and other stakeholders
- Identify existing leases
- Determine if identified leases terminate before the effective date of the statement
- Allocate human and financial resources
- Measure lease liabilities and lease assets
- Measure lease receivables and corresponding deferred inflows of resources
- Determine the effect of recording leases on financial condition, debt covenants, and debt limits

The issues relating to the initial implementation of GASB Statement No. 87 will vary from one government to the next depending on the type of leases involved, the complexity of existing lease arrangements, and the extent to which a government uses lease arrangements. Therefore, the following general discussion of implementation issues and how to mitigate them will affect state and local governments and their auditors differently.

Understand the requirements and communicate with elected officials and other stakeholders

Preparers and auditors of government financial statements will need to be familiar with the requirements of GASB Statement No. 87. In addition, it may be necessary to educate staff, elected officials, and other stakeholders.

Identify existing leases and determine if identified leases terminate before the effective date of the statement

Upon implementation, it is extremely important for state and local governments to identify all of their leasing arrangements. The process of identifying lease arrangements may be more challenging for governments with a decentralized lease function. Once leases have been identified, it will be necessary to determine which leases terminate prior to the effective date of the statement and which leases do not. In addition, all operating leases will need to be reviewed to determine if the initial term and expected renewals exceed 12 months. During the identification process, governments may wish to place a moratorium on entering into new lease arrangements or to require all new leases to be processed through the accounting or finance function.

Allocate human and financial resources

Much of the information needed to initially implement and annually apply the requirements of GASB Statement No. 87 will likely be the responsibility of a government's accounting and finance personnel. It is unlikely these personnel will have the time or staff needed to initially identify all existing lease arrangements. In subsequent years, governments may wish to consider a formal lease function to administer and monitor lease arrangements.

It may be necessary for some governments to hire contract staff to assist in identifying lease arrangements and in implementing the requirements of GASB Statement No. 87. It is imperative that a government budget adequate time and financial resources to obtain the information required to properly implement and annually apply the statement. Ideally, these amounts would be included in the annual budget for, at a minimum, the fiscal year in which the government will be required to implement GASB Statement No. 87.

Measure lease liabilities and lease assets

Lessees should recognize and measure lease contracts using the facts and circumstances existing at the beginning of the period the statement is implemented. Upon initial implementation of GASB Statement No. 87, a number of calculations will be necessary to determine the amounts to recognize as lease liabilities and lease assets. Each lease will need to be reviewed and evaluated to determine if any options exist in the lease and if it is reasonably certain the government will or will not exercise such options. In addition, lease agreements may or may not state the interest rate implicit in the lease which will require staff to make inquiries of lessors and/or to determine the government's estimated incremental borrowing rate.

Timing of any internally or externally prepared analyses or other information will need to be determined early in the initial implementation process and every year thereafter. The earlier this date can be determined the more time accounting and finance staff will have to prepare the information needed to properly implement GASB Statement No. 87.

Key point
Governments are required to use their estimated incremental borrowing rate if the rate the lessor charges the lessee or the implicit rate in the lease is not known. A government's estimated incremental borrowing rate may be different for lease assets accounted for in governmental activities than in business-type activities.

Measure lease receivables and corresponding deferred inflows of resources

Lessors should recognize and measure lease contracts using the facts and circumstances existing at the beginning of the period the statement is implemented. Lessors will need to review all existing operating, direct financing, and sales-type lease agreements to determine how they need to be accounted for and reported under the requirements of GASB Statement No. 87. Upon initial implementation a number of calculations may be necessary to determine the amounts to recognize as lease receivables and deferred inflows of resources for leases currently reported as operating leases. Each lease will need to be reviewed and evaluated to determine if any options exist in the lease and if it is reasonably certain the government will or will not exercise such options. In addition, lease agreements may or may not state the interest rate implicit in the lease which will take time to determine. This will likely prove challenging for lease arrangements previously accounted for as operating leases.

Determine the effect of recording leases on financial condition, debt covenants, and debt limits

Timing of any internally or externally prepared analyses or other information will need to be determined early in the initial implementation process and every year thereafter. The earlier this date can be determined the more time accounting and finance staff will have to prepare the information needed to properly implement GASB Statement No. 87.

Governments may also need to design and implement controls and update their information technology and financial management systems to effectively manage and report lease arrangements in years subsequent to initial implementation.

A governmental lessee may have a significant lease liability resulting from applying the requirements of GASB Statement No. 87 to short-term and other leases rather than the current accounting for leases as operating or capital leases. Additional debt and reporting interest expense may affect a government's compliance with debt limits and debt covenants. In these cases, financial statement preparers and their auditors will need to determine what effect, if any, implementation and ongoing application of GASB Statement No. 87 will have on the government's financial statements as soon as possible.

It is also possible lease-related amounts reported in the financial statements of a government may affect how a credit analyst views the government's credit risk. Governments may want to discuss the potential impact of the requirements of GASB Statement No. 87 with bond trustees and credit analysts, as well as their elected officials, as soon as possible.

Knowledge check

9. As discussed in this section what is **not** an implementation challenge state and local governments may face when implementing GASB Statement No. 87?

   a. Identify existing leases.
   b. Determining if identified leases terminate before the effective date of the statement.
   c. Effect of recording leases on total net position.
   d. Measure lease receivables and corresponding deferred inflows of resources.

Summary

This chapter discusses the requirements of GASB Statement No. 87 relating to accounting and financial reporting of leases by governmental lessees and lessors. The chapter discusses key terms established with GASB Statement No. 87 and provides an overview of the measurement, accounting, and reporting requirements for leases by lessees and lessors. Additionally, the chapter discusses the disclosures required by lessees and lessors relating to leases as well as potential issues associated with initial and subsequent measurement and reporting of lease-related transactions.

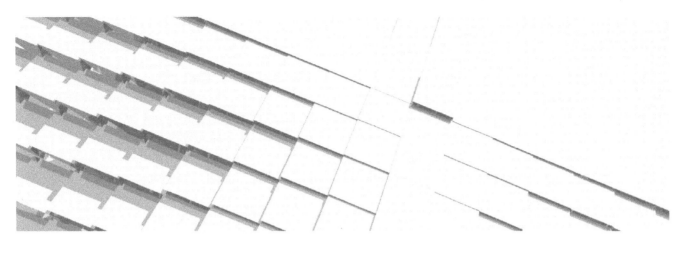

Chapter 2

Revenue Recognition by Not-for-Profit Entities

Learning objectives

- Identify the definitions of exchange transactions and contributions.

- Identify the difference in conditional, unconditional, and donor-restricted contributions.

- Identify the accounting for contributions of long-lived assets and cash and other assets restricted for the purchase of long-lived assets.

- Identify typical agency transactions of not-for-profit entities and determine the accounting for various types of agency transactions.

- Identify the concept of variance power and how it affects recognition of agency transactions.

- Differentiate exchange transactions and contributions for transactions commonly seen in not-for-profit entities.

Major areas of inquiry

Not-for-profit entities receive revenue from exchange and nonexchange transactions. For certain types of transactions such as contributions, grants, and membership dues, it may be difficult to determine whether the transaction is an exchange or a nonexchange transaction. Some contribution, grant, or membership dues transactions may represent both an exchange and a nonexchange transaction. Questions are continually raised by preparers and auditors of financial statements of not-for-profit entities relating to revenue recognition by not-for-profit entities. These questions include the following areas:

- Recognizing revenue from contributions with donor-imposed restrictions
- Determining whether a grant is a contribution or an exchange transaction
- Recognizing membership dues when part represents an exchange transaction and part represents a contribution

Overview

General

Revenues are generated from ongoing major or central operations; and FASB requires these transactions to be reported as increases in net assets without donor restrictions. Upon the effective date[1] of FASB ASU No. 2014-09, *Revenue from Contracts with Customers (Topic 606)*, revenues from exchange transactions are recognized when identified performance obligations are satisfied and classified as revenues and net assets without donor restrictions. On the other hand, gains typically result from transactions or events that are incidental or peripheral to the operations of the entity.

Judgment is often involved in determining if a transaction should be recognized as revenue or as a gain. Because of the diverse nature of not-for-profit entities, what is considered revenue in one not-for-profit entity might be considered a gain in another not-for-profit entity. For example, the year-round sale of clothes and household items donated to a not-for-profit entity would be considered revenue if such sales are a major source of revenue or a major activity for the entity. In another not-for-profit entity, such as a church, such sales and donations may be incidental or peripheral to the operations of the church and would be recognized as a gain.

Not-for-profit entities receive revenues from reciprocal transactions (exchange) and nonreciprocal transactions (contributions). In some cases, it may be difficult to determine if a transaction is an exchange transaction or a contribution, and this is an area where significant diversity in practice exists. FASB ASU No. 2018-08, *Not-for-Profit Entities, (Topic 958): Clarifying the Scope and the Accounting Guidance for Contributions Received and Contributions Made*, is intended to clarify and improve the accounting guidance for determining whether a transfer of assets (or reduction, settlement, or cancelation of liabilities) is a contribution or an exchange transaction.

Exchange transactions

Exchange transactions as noted in the FASB *Accounting Standards Codification*® (ASC) Master Glossary result from a *reciprocal transfer* (emphasis added) in which each party receives and sacrifices approximately commensurate value. In an exchange transaction, the potential public benefits are secondary to the potential direct benefits to the resource provider, and no restrictions are imposed by either party on the other. Exchange transactions are accounted for using the guidance in FASB ASC 606, *Revenue from Contracts with Customers*.

---

[1] Annual reporting periods beginning after December 15, 2017 for public business entities, including certain not-for-profits, and annual reporting periods beginning after December 15, 2018 for all other entities.

Typical transactions in a not-for-profit entity likely to represent exchange transactions giving rise to revenue include providing goods or services for a fee to

- members,
- clients,
- customers,
- patients, and
- other beneficiaries.

FASB ASC 606 requires an entity to recognize revenue to depict the transfer of goods or services to customers in an amount that reflects the consideration to which the entity expects to be entitled in exchange for those good or services. As such, an entity recognizes revenue when (or as) it satisfies a performance obligation by transferring a promised good or service to a customer (which is when the customer obtains control of that good or service).

To apply the requirements of FASB ASC 606, an entity should follow these five steps:

1. Identify the contract(s) with a customer.
2. Identify the performance obligations in the contract.
3. Determine the transaction price.
4. Allocate the transaction price to the performance obligations in the contract.
5. Recognize revenue when (or as) the entity satisfies a performance obligation.

Contributions

As defined in the FASB ASC Master Glossary, a contribution is an *unconditional transfer* (emphasis added) of cash or other assets, as well as unconditional promises to give, to an entity or a reduction, settlement, or cancelation of its liabilities in a voluntary nonreciprocal transfer by another entity acting other than as an owner. In a contribution transaction, the resource provider often receives value indirectly by providing a societal benefit although the benefit is not considered to be of commensurate value. Recall that in an exchange transaction, the potential public benefits are secondary to the potential direct benefits to the resource provider.

A not-for-profit entity may receive contributions with or without donor-imposed conditions and restrictions in various forms, including

- donations of financial assets;
- donations of nonfinancial assets;
- promises to give financial or nonfinancial assets in the future;
- grants (whole or in part);
- membership dues (whole or in part); and
- split-interest agreements (such as charitable lead or remainder trusts, pooled income trusts, perpetual trusts, and so on).[2]

---

[2] A detailed discussion of accounting and reporting for split-interest agreements is beyond the scope of this chapter.

In June 2018, FASB issued ASU No. 2018-08, *Not-For-Profit Entities (Topic 958): Clarifying the Scope and the Accounting Guidance for Contributions Received and Contributions Made*. The ASU clarifies when transactions should be accounted for as contributions subject to the requirements in FASB ASC 958, *Not-for-Profit Entities*, or as exchange transactions under FASB ASC 606. Additionally, the ASU provides guidance to determine when a contribution is conditional. This chapter has been updated to reflect the changes made to current practice upon the effective date of ASU No. 2018-08.

Amendments in the ASU are effective based on the type of entity involved in the transaction and whether the entity is acting in the capacity of a resource recipient or a resource provider. The various effective dates are as follows:

- Public business entities and not-for-profit entities that have issued, or are a conduit bond obligor for, securities traded, listed, or quoted on an exchange or over-the-counter market
  - Serving as a resource recipient
    - Annual periods beginning after June 15, 2018, including interim periods within those annual periods
  - Serving as a resource provider
    - Annual periods beginning after December 15, 2018, including interim periods within those annual periods
- All other entities
  - Serving as a resource recipient
    - Annual periods beginning after December 15, 2018, and interim periods within annual periods beginning after December 15, 2019
  - Serving as a resource provider
    - Annual periods beginning after December 15, 2019, and interim periods within annual periods beginning after December 15, 2020

Knowledge check

1. Which is **not** a characteristic of an exchange transaction?

    a. Reciprocal transfer.
    b. No restrictions are associated with an exchange transaction.
    c. Each party receives and sacrifices approximately commensurate value.
    d. Potential direct benefits to the resource provider are secondary to the potential public benefits.

Accounting for contributions[3]

General

According to the definition in FASB ASC 958, a contribution must be a voluntary transfer; however, the accounting for contributions is different from the accounting for other voluntary transfers (such as conditional transfers, agency transactions, and exchange transactions). It is necessary for a not-for-profit entity to assess the extent of discretion it has over the use of the assets it receives from a donor to determine how to account for the transaction.

Under generally accepted accounting principles (GAAP), a not-for-profit entity recognizes a contribution received if it has *discretion sufficient to choose the beneficiaries* of the assets. By itself, the *discretion to determine the timing* of the distribution to a specified beneficiary does not give a not-for-profit entity discretion sufficient to recognize a contribution.

Contribution revenues

By definition, contributions are unconditional. However, recognition of contribution revenue depends on whether the transfer of assets or promise to give is received with any of the following:

- *Donor-imposed conditions* (affect recognition of contribution revenue)
- *Donor-imposed restrictions* (affect classification of contribution revenue)
- Both donor-imposed conditions and restrictions (affect both the recognition and classification of contribution revenue)

From the preceding, it is apparent that only donors can place conditions on or restrict the use of their contribution. Management and those charged with governance can place neither conditions nor restrictions on the use of a donor's contribution. Formal actions of those charged with governance to self-impose limits on net assets result in a subclassification of net assets without donor restrictions defined as *board-designated net assets*. Contributions without donor-imposed restrictions or conditions are recognized as revenues or gains in the period received and as assets, decreases of liabilities, or expenses depending on the form of the benefits received.

As clarified in ASU No. 2018-18, an *unconditional promise to give* is a contribution and should be recognized when it is received. *Intentions to give* are not unconditional promises to give; therefore, they are not recognized as contributions because the individual or entity retains the ability to change its mind before assets are actually transferred to the not-for-profit entity. Bequests in a will are an example of intentions to give because the individual may change his or her mind about the bequest before he or she dies. When the probate court declares the will valid, the not-for-profit entity can recognize a contribution

---

[3] Nomenclature used in the Financial Accounting Standards Board (FASB) *Accounting Standards Codification*® (ASC) is "recipient," "recipient entity" or "recipient organization." For purposes of this section, "not-for-profit entity" is used in lieu of the nomenclature in the ASC.

unless the promise is conditional, in which case a contribution should not be recognized until the conditions are substantially met.

Conditional and restricted contributions

Conditional contributions

ASU No. 2018-08 defines *conditional contributions* as contributions that contain donor-imposed conditions. *Donor-imposed conditions* are donor stipulations (donors include other types of contributors, including makers of certain grants) that represent a *barrier* that must be overcome before the recipient is entitled to the assets transferred or promised. Failure to overcome the barrier gives the contributor a right of release of the assets it has transferred or gives the promisor a right of release from its obligation to transfer its assets. A contribution or promise to give is conditional if it has

- one or more barriers that must be overcome before a recipient is entitled to the assets transferred or promised *and*
- a right of return to the donor of assets transferred *or*
- a right of release of the promisor's obligation to transfer assets.

Donor-imposed conditions should be substantially met (or explicitly waived by the donor) before the receipt of assets or the promise to give assets is recognized as a contribution. ASU No. 2018-08 states that a probability assessment about whether a recipient is likely to meet a donor's stipulation is not a factor when determining whether an agreement includes a barrier. Transfers of assets that are conditional contributions are accounted for as "refundable advances" until the conditions have been substantially met or explicitly waived by the donor.

For a donor-imposed condition to exist, it must be determinable from the agreement, or another document referenced in the agreement, that barriers exist. In addition, such barriers must be overcome for the not-for-profit entity to be entitled to the transferred assets or future transfer of assets.

ASU No. 2018-08 states the agreement need not include the specific language "right of return" or "release from obligation." However, the agreement should be sufficiently clear to be able to support a reasonable conclusion about when a recipient would be entitled to the transfer of assets.

When donor stipulations do not clearly state whether both (*a*) one or more barriers exist and (*b*) the right to receive or retain payment or delivery of the promised assets depends on meeting those barriers, it may be difficult to determine if the contribution is conditional or unconditional. In such cases, the following might aid in making this determination:

- Review facts and circumstances surrounding the gift.
- If possible, communicate with the donor or his or her heirs.

If, after performing these procedures, the ambiguity cannot be resolved, the presumption under GAAP is that a promise to give is conditional if the stipulations are not clearly unconditional.

Indicators of barriers enumerated in ASU No. 2018-08 include the following:

- Measurable, performance-related barriers or other measurable barriers
  - Such barriers are often coupled with a time limitation.
  - Examples include achieving a specified level of service or a specific outcome (such as serving 1,000 meals per day, achieving a 70% graduation rate, or a matching/challenge grant).
- Limited discretion by the recipient on the conduct of an activity
  - Limited discretion is more specific than a donor-imposed restriction.
  - Restrictions limit the use of a contribution but do not necessarily limit how an activity is performed.
  - An example of limited discretion could include a requirement to expend funds only for allowable activities and costs as defined in the Uniform Guidance issued by the Office of Management and Budget.
- Stipulations related to the purpose of the agreement
  - Examples are programmatic in nature (such as requirements to prepare a report summarizing findings from a specific funded research project or expand a facility to serve more program beneficiaries).

ASU No. 2018-08 states that if the stipulation is not related to the purpose of the agreement (generally stipulations that are administrative or trivial), that stipulation is not indicative of a barrier. For example, a stipulation that an annual report must be provided by the donee to receive subsequent annual payments on a multiyear promise is not a barrier if the administrative requirement is not related to the purpose of the agreement.

In the absence of any apparent indication that a recipient is entitled only to the transferred assets or future transfer of assets if it has overcome a barrier, the agreement should not be considered to contain a right of return or release from obligation and should be deemed a contribution without donor-imposed conditions.

Some conditional promises may become unconditional in stages because they are dependent on several (or a series of) conditions or "milestones" rather than on a single condition. In such cases, those unconditional promises are recognized as contribution revenue in increments as each of the conditions is met.

For example, a donor may promise to give $1 for every $1 raised over the next year to a maximum of $25,000. As contributions are received from other donors, the conditions are met, and the promise would become unconditional in the amount of other such contributions. If, at its fiscal year-end, the not-for-profit entity has raised $10,000 of the maximum $25,000, it would recognize $10,000 in contribution revenue. Such revenues would be classified as net assets with donor restrictions because they are receivable at the end of the fiscal reporting period (restricted for time).

ASU No. 2018-08 allows a not-for-profit entity to elect a policy to report donor-restricted contributions that were initially conditional contributions, and for which the conditions and restrictions have been met in the same reporting period as the revenue is recognized, as support within net assets without donor restrictions. It is not necessary with this type of policy for a not-for-profit to adopt a similar policy for other donor-restricted contributions or investment gains and income, provided that the not-for-profit entity reports consistently from period to period and discloses its accounting policy. The requirement to have similar policies for investment gains and income relates only to when a not-for-profit elects to report donor-restricted contributions (which

---

were **not** initially conditional contributions) as support within net assets without donor restrictions when the restrictions are met in the same period that the revenue is recognized.

Knowledge check

2. When is contribution revenue recognized?

    a. At the time the donor imposes the condition(s).
    b. When conditions are substantially met or explicitly waived by the donor.
    c. Only when conditions are met in full.
    d. When conditions are likely to be met by the recipient.

Donor-restricted contributions

Donors may stipulate the use for a contributed asset that is more specific than broad limits resulting from the following:

- Nature of the not-for-profit entity
- Environment in which the not-for-profit entity operates
- Purposes specified in the entity's articles of incorporation, bylaws, or comparable documents for an unincorporated association

Some donors impose restrictions that are temporary in nature, for example, stipulating that resources be used after a specified date (time-based), for particular programs or services, or to acquire buildings or equipment (purpose-based). Other donors impose restrictions that are perpetual in nature, for example, stipulating that resources be maintained in perpetuity. Laws may extend those limits to investment returns from those resources and to other enhancements (diminishments) of those resources. Therefore, those laws would extend donor-imposed restrictions.

Additionally, *donor-imposed restrictions* may result from either

- an explicit stipulation, or
- circumstances surrounding the receipt of the contribution that make clear the donor's implicit restriction on the contributed assets.

Revenues from contributions with donor-imposed restrictions are reported as increases in net assets with donor restrictions. When donor-imposed purpose or time restrictions have been met, the net assets with donor restrictions are reclassified as net assets without donor restrictions in the period the time restriction lapses or the purpose restrictions are met.

Unconditional promises to give with payments due in future periods are typically reported as donor-restricted support unless explicit donor stipulations or circumstances surrounding the receipt of a promise make it clear the donor intended it to be used to support current-period activities. The rationale behind this accounting treatment is that the donor, by specifying future payment dates, indicates that his or her gift is to support activities in each period in which a payment is scheduled.

For example, a not-for-profit entity's brochure for the current-year operating fundraising campaign clearly indicates that contributions will be used to defray the cost of current-year activities. This message is prominently reiterated on the pledge card donors are required to sign. Donors are allowed to pay their pledge over a maximum of 12 months, which extends three months beyond the end of the current fiscal reporting period. Based on these circumstances surrounding the promises to give, it appears the intention is to support current-period activities. Therefore, the not-for-profit entity would report outstanding pledges from the current-year operating fundraising campaign as revenue without donor restrictions in the current fiscal reporting period.

Contributions of long-lived assets or gifts of cash or other assets restricted to acquire long-lived assets

A not-for-profit entity may receive contributions of long-lived assets (such as buildings, equipment, and so on), or gifts of cash or other assets restricted to acquire long-lived assets. In some cases, the *donor may not expressly stipulate how or how long* the long-lived asset must be used by the not-for-profit entity, or how to use any proceeds resulting from disposal of the asset(s).

ASU No. 2016-14 states that gifts of long-lived assets received without stipulations about how long the donated asset must be used should be reported as *contribution revenue without donor restrictions*. Gifts of cash or other assets restricted to acquire long-lived assets should initially be reported as *contribution revenue with donor restrictions*. When the asset is acquired and placed in service, the assets are released from restrictions by reclassifying net assets with donor restrictions to net assets without donor restrictions. If the donor has placed a time restriction on the use of the long-lived asset, net assets with donor restrictions are released over the life of the time restriction.

After implementation of ASU No. 2016-14, not-for-profit entities are no longer permitted to adopt a policy to imply a time restriction that expires over the useful life of certain long-lived assets. This prohibition relates to long-lived assets acquired with a gift of cash or other assets the donor restricted for the purpose of acquiring long-lived assets but did not stipulate how long such assets were to be used.

Contributed utilities

A not-for-profit entity may receive unconditional contributions of the use of electric, telephone, or other utilities, which are considered contributed assets rather than services under GAAP. GAAP require such contributions to be recognized at fair value as contribution revenue in the period in which the contribution is received and expenses in the period the utilities are used. If the promise to give utilities is for a specified period of time, the promise should be reported as contributions receivable and as donor-restricted support that increases net assets with donor restrictions. The amount recorded should be the fair value of the estimated utility services to be provided to the not-for-profit entity. In such cases, net assets with donor restrictions would be released as the utilities costs are incurred. Promises to give utilities that are not specified as to time are not specifically addressed in GAAP (FASB ASC 958-605). Therefore, a not-for-profit entity might conclude that such a promise is conditional and would therefore recognize revenue without donor restrictions as the utilities are used.

Agency transactions

Agency transactions most often occur in federated fundraising entities, community foundations, and institutionally related entities (such as college or university foundations supporting related colleges or universities, booster entities, clinics supporting hospitals, and so on). However, these transactions may also arise in circumstances when a not-for-profit entity conducts specific fundraising activities from which the entire net proceeds will be disbursed to a specific unrelated entity or individual.

The FASB ASC glossary defines an *agency transaction* as a *type of exchange transaction* in which a not-for-profit entity *acts as or on behalf of another party* (which may be a donor or donee) as an *agent*, a *trustee*, or an *intermediary*.

A not-for-profit entity is an agent and not a donee if it both

- accepts assets from a donor; and
- agrees to either
  - use the assets received on behalf of a beneficiary specified by the donor; or
  - transfer the assets, the return of investment of the assets, or both to a beneficiary specified by the donor.

On the other hand, a not-for-profit entity is a *donee* and should recognize a contribution received if the donor does not believe he or she is directing the gift to a specific beneficiary, which may be evidenced by the

- language used by the donor (broad generalizations versus specific identification of beneficiaries),
- representations of the not-for-profit entity during the solicitation of the gift, or
- actions surrounding the transfers.

The accounting for an agency transaction by the donor, the not-for-profit entity acting as the recipient entity, and the specified beneficiary is affected by whether the

- agency transaction *is a contribution,*
- not-for-profit entity (acting as the recipient entity) and the specified beneficiary are *financially interrelated,*
- agency *transaction is not a contribution, or*
- donor granted the not-for-profit entity acting as the recipient entity *variance power.*

Knowledge check

3. When is a not-for-profit entity an agent and **not** a donee?

    a. It only accepts assets from a donor.
    b. It only uses assets received on behalf of a beneficiary specified by the donor.
    c. It transfers the assets, the return of investment of the assets, or both to a beneficiary specified by the donor.
    d. All of the above.

Accounting for agency transactions that are contributions

Not-for-profit entity acting as the recipient entity

A not-for-profit entity helping donors make a contribution to another entity or individual is acting as an agent, as a trustee, or in an intermediary capacity. As such, the not-for-profit entity *does not recognize a contribution* when the assets are received, and it *does not make a contribution* when the assets are disbursed to the intended entity or individual. Rather, the not-for-profit entity *recognizes an asset and related liability when financial assets are received* from a donor and reduces the liability and the related assets when they are disbursed to the donor-specified beneficiary.

If a donor transfers nonfinancial assets rather than financial assets, the not-for-profit entity is *permitted, but not required,* to recognize an asset and related liability for the nonfinancial assets. However, the accounting for such transactions should be consistent from period to period and the related policy disclosed in the notes to the financial statements. Whether a donor transfers financial or nonfinancial assets, the not-for-profit entity should recognize any asset and liability at the fair value of the assets received from the donor.

Donor-specified beneficiary

The *specified beneficiary recognizes a contribution received* when the donor transfers the assets to the not-for-profit entity, offset by its rights to the assets held by the not-for-profit entity (acting as a recipient entity). Rights the beneficiary has to the assets held by the not-for-profit entity (acting as a recipient entity) may be recognized as

- an *interest in the net assets* of the not-for-profit entity acting as the recipient entity,
- a *beneficial interest* (that is, the beneficiary has an unconditional right to receive all or a portion of the specified cash flows from a charitable trust or other identifiable pool of assets), or
- a *receivable* when the beneficiary's rights in an unconditional promise to give are neither an interest in the net assets of the not-for-profit entity acting as the recipient entity nor a beneficial interest.

A *specified beneficiary should recognize an agency transaction* when either financial or nonfinancial assets are transferred by a donor to a not-for-profit entity (acting as a recipient entity). When the not-for-profit entity (acting as a recipient entity) disburses the assets, the specified beneficiary reduces its previously recognized rights to those assets.

Key point
A not-for-profit entity helping donors make a contribution to another donor-specified entity generally does not recognize a contribution when the assets are received, and it does not make a contribution when the assets are disbursed. Rather, the not-for-profit entity recognizes an asset and related liability when financial assets are received from a donor.

Financially interrelated entities

The relationship between the not-for-profit entity acting as the recipient entity and the specified beneficiary also affect the accounting for an agency transaction. Under GAAP, in circumstances when a not-for-profit entity (acting as a recipient entity) and a specified beneficiary are financially interrelated, the not-for-profit entity (acting as a recipient entity) is not a trustee.

A not-for-profit entity (acting as a recipient entity) is financially interrelated to a donor-specified beneficiary if one of the entities has both of the following characteristics:

- The *ability to influence the operating and financial decisions of the other*, which may be demonstrated by any of the following:
  - The entities are affiliates.
  - One entity has considerable representation on the governing board of the other entity.
  - The charter or bylaws of one entity limit its activities to those beneficial to the other entity.
  - An agreement between the entities allows one entity to actively participate in the policy-making processes of the other (for example, setting entity priorities, budgets, and management compensation).
- An *ongoing economic interest in the net assets of the other* (such as the residual right to another not-for-profit entity's ever-changing net assets resulting from an ongoing relationship).

Knowledge check

4. A not-for-profit entity is financially interrelated to a donor-specified beneficiary when either the not-for-profit entity or the beneficiary has

   a. The ability to influence the operating and financial decisions of the other.
   b. An ongoing economic interest in the net assets of the other.
   c. Both the ability to influence the operating and financial decisions of the other, and an ongoing economic interest in the net assets of the other.
   d. Neither the ability to influence the operating and financial decisions of the other, nor an ongoing economic interest in the net assets of the other.

Accounting for agency transactions when the parties are financially interrelated

Because the *not-for-profit entity* (acting as a recipient entity) is not a trustee when it is financially interrelated to the specified beneficiary, it should *recognize a contribution received when it receives either financial or nonfinancial assets* from the donor that are specified for the financially interrelated beneficiary. A *beneficiary that is not a state or local government should recognize its interest in the net assets of the not-for-profit entity* (acting as a recipient entity) adjusted for its share of the change in net assets using a method similar to the equity method of accounting. Beneficiaries that are state or local governments recognize such a relationship using component unit guidance established by GASB.

Accounting for agency transactions that are not contributions

Certain agency transactions (for example, between a donor, a not-for-profit entity [acting as a recipient entity], and a specified beneficiary) are not accounted for as contributions because the terms of the transfer or the relationship between the parties cause the transfer of assets to be *revocable, repayable, or reciprocal*. GAAP identify the following four types of transfers as those that are not contributions for either the not-for-profit entity (acting as the recipient entity) or the specified beneficiary:

1. Transfer of assets is *subject to the donor's unilateral right to redirect the use* of the assets to another beneficiary.
2. Transfer of assets is accompanied by the *donor's conditional promise* to give or is otherwise revocable or repayable.
3. *Donor controls* the not-for-profit entity (acting as the recipient entity) and specifies an unaffiliated beneficiary.
4. Transfer of assets is *reciprocal because the donor specifies itself or its affiliate as the beneficiary* of the assets transferred to the not-for-profit entity (acting as the recipient entity).

In the first three types of transfers, the transfer is *reported by the donor as an asset and as a liability by the not-for-profit entity* acting as the recipient entity. Accounting for the fourth type of transfer depends on whether the reciprocal transfer is an "equity transaction."

Equity transactions

An *equity transaction* is a transfer of assets to a recipient entity meeting all of the following characteristics:

- Donor *specifies itself or an affiliate as the beneficiary.*
- Donor and the not-for-profit entity acting as the recipient entity are *financially interrelated* entities.
- *Neither donor nor its affiliate expects payment* for the transferred assets; however, payment of investment return on the transferred assets may be expected.

If the fourth type of transfer is not an equity transaction, the accounting is the same as for the first three types of transfers. That is, the donor reports the transfer as an asset, and the not-for-profit entity acting as the recipient entity reports the transfer as a liability.

Accounting for the *fourth type of transfer when it* is *an equity transaction* depends on whether the donor or its affiliate is the specified beneficiary.

- *Donor as beneficiary* in an equity transaction:
  - *Donor* reports the assets transferred in the equity transaction as an *interest in the net assets* of the not-for-profit entity acting as the recipient entity.
  - *Not-for-profit entity acting as the recipient entity reports the assets transferred in the equity transaction* as a separate *line in its statement of activities.*
- *Affiliate of the donor as beneficiary* in an equity transaction:
  - Donor reports the assets transferred in the equity transaction as a *separate line in its statement of activities* (debit balance transaction).
  - *Not-for-profit entity* acting as the recipient entity reports the assets transferred in the equity transaction as a separate *line in its statement of activities* (credit balance transaction).
  - *Affiliate named as beneficiary* reports the assets transferred in the equity transaction as an interest in the net assets of the not-for-profit entity acting as the recipient entity.

Variance power

In addition to designating a specific entity or individual as a beneficiary, a donor may provide the not-for-profit entity the power to redirect the use of the transferred assets to another beneficiary. This power to redirect the use of the transferred assets may or may not be considered *"variance power."* A not-for-profit entity explicitly granted variance power has the ability to use the assets it receives from the donor to further its own purpose; from the date it accepts the assets. Therefore, variance power provides a not-for-profit entity with discretion sufficient to recognize a contribution received (despite the specification of a beneficiary by the donor).[4] The specified beneficiary should not recognize its rights to the financial or nonfinancial assets held by the not-for-profit entity as an asset if the not-for-profit entity has been granted variance power[5].

Variance power is defined in the FASB ASC glossary as

> The unilateral power to redirect the use of the transferred assets to another beneficiary. A *donor explicitly grants* [emphasis added] variance power if the recipient entity's [not-for-profit entity's] *unilateral power* [emphasis added] to redirect the use of the assets is *explicitly referred to* [emphasis added] in the instrument transferring the assets. Unilateral power means the recipient entity [not-for-profit entity] can override the donor's instructions without approval from the donor, specified beneficiary, or any other interested party.

Key point
For a not-for-profit entity to have the power to redirect transferred assets from the donor-specified beneficiary to another beneficiary, such power should be (1) explicitly granted by the donor, (2) unilateral, and (3) explicitly referred to in the instrument transferring the assets.

---

[4] A not-for-profit organization given variance power should not recognize a contribution received if the resource provider (such as a donor) specifies itself or its affiliate(s) as the beneficiary of the transferred assets. By their nature, these transactions are reciprocal in nature and therefore do not meet the definition of a contribution, even if variance power is granted at the time of the transfer.

[5] Beneficiaries that are state or local governmental entities recognize these interests using standards established by GASB.

Exchange transaction or contribution[6]

In some situations, it may be relatively easy to distinguish an exchange transaction from a contribution. For example, the sale of preschool educational materials to parents of preschool age children is clearly an exchange transaction. A donation of cash in direct response to an annual operating fundraising appeal is easily distinguished as a contribution.

However, classifying transactions as exchange transactions or as contributions may not always be clear-cut, thus requiring the *use of judgment* to determine if a reciprocal transaction (in which each party to the transaction receives and sacrifices commensurate value) has occurred. In making this determination, it is necessary to consider "commensurate value" from the *perspective of both the recipient entity and the resource provider.*

Types of revenues that may be difficult to determine if they are exchange transactions or contributions typically include

- membership dues; and
- grants, awards, and sponsorships.

Revenue recognition for, and the class of net assets affected by, an exchange transaction differs from the accounting for a contribution. Upon the effective date of ASU No. 2014-09, revenues from *exchange transactions* are recognized when identified performance obligations are satisfied and classified as revenues and net assets without donor restrictions. *Contributions*, including unconditional promises to give, are recognized as contribution revenues and classified as net assets with donor restrictions or net assets without donor restrictions when the resources or promises are received. Upon the effective date of ASU No. 2018-08, a transfer of assets that is a *conditional contribution* is accounted for as a refundable advance until the conditions have been substantially met or explicitly waived by the donor. Conditional promises to give are recognized when the conditions on which they depend are substantially met (that is, when the conditional promise becomes unconditional).

Some resource providers place restrictions on how the resources are to be used. If the resources provided represent exchange transactions, the restrictions on the use of those resources do not affect the classification of the revenues and net assets as without donor restrictions. However, as discussed earlier in this chapter, donor-imposed restrictions on contributions cause the contribution to be classified as net assets with donor restrictions.

---

[6] See A for a high-level overview of ASU No. 2014-09 and a discussion of how it affects current recognition of revenues from exchange transactions. See appendix B for an overview of Accounting Standards Update (ASU) 2018-08, Not-for-Profit Entities (Topic 958) *Clarifying the Scope and the Accounting Guidance for Contributions Received and Contributions Made.*

Revenues from grants, awards, and sponsorships

Foundations, government agencies, business entities, individuals, and other types of entities provide resources to not-for-profit entities in the form of grants, awards, or sponsorships. ASU No. 2018-08 clearly states the type of resource provider should not factor into the determination of whether the resource provider receives commensurate value in return for the transferred resources. A grant, award, or sponsorship may be an exchange transaction, a contribution, or a combination of both. Some of these transactions may also have characteristics of agency transactions.

Grants, awards, or sponsorships are contributions if the resource providers (grantors) do not receive commensurate value in exchange for the assets transferred or if the value received by the resource providers is incidental to the potential public benefit from the not-for-profit entity (grantee) using the assets transferred.

If grant activity is (a) planned and carried out by the not-for-profit entity (grantee), and (b) the not-for-profit entity (grantee) retains the right to the benefits of carrying out the grant activity, the grant would likely be a *contribution.* On the other hand, if a grant is made to a not-for-profit entity (grantee) by a resource provider (grantor) that (a) provides materials to be tested in the grant activity and (b) retains the right to any patents or other results of the activity, the grant would likely be an *exchange transaction.*

To determine whether a transaction is an exchange transaction or contribution, an entity should assess the relevant facts and circumstances. ASU No. 2018-08 also provides examples[7] to illustrate the following guidance in FASB ASC 958-605-15 for determining whether a transaction is an exchange or contribution.

1. A resource provider (grantor) is not synonymous with the general public. Benefits received by the public resulting from the assets transferred (that is grant funds or other resources) are not equivalent to commensurate value received by the resource provider.

   For example, a government agency providing a grant to a not-for-profit entity to offset the cost of providing flu shots to senior citizens provides far more benefit to the general public than the amount of the funds transferred under the grant. Because the flu is highly contagious, providing anyone with a flu shot is likely to decrease the potential spread of the flu. In the case of senior citizens, the flu may be far more serious than in younger populations which will increase the cost of medical care. Because many senior citizens qualify for Medicare and/or Medicaid, the cost of such care is funded by the federal and/or state governments. The cost of treating a senior citizen with the flu far exceeds the cost of the flu shot which benefits the public rather than the government agency funding the flu shot.

---

[7] Examples in the "Pending Content" in FASB ASC 958-605-55-13A-14I illustrate the guidance in Section 958-605-15 for determining whether a transaction is an exchange or a contribution. The analysis in each Example is not intended to represent the only manner in which the guidance could be applied, and the Examples are not intended to apply to only a specific illustration. Although some aspects of the Examples may be present in actual fact patterns, all relevant facts and circumstances of a particular fact pattern should be evaluated when applying the guidance in this Subtopic. The guidance in these Examples about distinguishing between contributions and exchange transactions applies to both a resource provider (for example, a corporate foundation, a corporation, or a not-for-profit) and a recipient.

2. Execution of a resource provider's (grantor's) mission or positive sentiment a donor feels does not constitute commensurate value received by the resource provider.
3. If the expressed intent asserted by both the recipient (grantee) and resource provider (grantor) is to exchange goods or services of commensurate value, then the transaction is indicative of an exchange transaction. If the recipient solicits assets from the resource provider without the intent of exchanging goods or services, then the transaction is indicative of a contribution.
   a. In reality, a grant agreement may not specifically express the intent of the parties.
   b. However, a number of federal and state grants are provided under the requirements of specific federal or state laws or regulations and often the enabling legislation is stated in the grant agreement.
   c. Reference to federal or state laws/regulations could be interpreted to represent the intent of the grantor/resource provider.
   d. By executing the grant agreement, the grantee is affirming the grantor's intent.
4. If the resource provider (grantor) has full discretion in determining the amount of the transferred assets, the transaction is indicative of a contribution. When both the recipient (grantee) and resource provider (grantor) agree on the amount of assets transferred in exchange for goods or services of commensurate value, the transaction is indicative of an exchange transaction.
   a. Typically, the grantor indicates the total amount available under a grant in the grant agreement. In a reimbursement grant, the grantee submits a reimbursement request to the grantor for approval which indicates the grantor/resource provider determines "the amount of the transferred assets."
   b. Determination of the amount of the requested reimbursement by the grantee does not negate the fact the grantor approves such request.
   c. Additionally, the grantor will not usually reimburse the grantee in total more than the total amount of the grant.
5. If penalties assessed on the recipient for failure to comply with the terms of the agreement are limited to the delivery of assets or services already provided and the return of the unspent amount, the transaction is indicative of a contribution. The existence of contractual provisions for economic forfeiture beyond the amount of assets transferred generally indicates the transaction is an exchange transaction.

Revenue recognition

Exchange transactions

Upon the effective date of ASU No. 2014-09, the *exchange transaction portion* of grants, awards, or sponsorships is *recognized when the related identified performance obligations are satisfied.* Amounts receivable under such grants reflect the portion of the transaction price allocated to the related performance obligation. The transaction price is the amount of consideration the not-for-profit entity expects to be entitled to upon satisfaction of all identified performance obligations.

However, the exchange transaction portion of amounts received in advance from a resource provider (grantor) may represent *a contract liability* if the not-for-profit entity (grantee) has not met the eligibility requirements or otherwise satisfied the identified performance obligations as of the end of its fiscal reporting period.

Grants, awards, and sponsorships may be restricted in purpose and time by the resource provider. Such *restrictions do not affect the classification of these resources as net assets without donor restrictions* when they represent an exchange transaction rather than a contribution.

Contributions

The *unconditional contribution portion* of grants, awards, and sponsorships is *recognized when the assets/services, or the promise to provide such assets/services, is received* as donor-restricted support or revenue without donor restrictions and classified as net assets with donor restrictions and net assets without donor restrictions, respectively. Amounts of grants, awards, and sponsorships representing unconditional contributions are recognized as contribution revenue at the earlier of the date received from, or promised by, the resource provider (grantor). Any grants, awards, and sponsorships representing conditional contributions, as defined in ASU No. 2018-08, are recognized as contribution revenue when the conditions have been substantially met or explicitly waived by the grantor/donor. In these circumstances, donor-restricted support would be recognized for any conditional contributions that also included donor-imposed restrictions.

Contribution revenues, by definition, do not represent a reciprocal transaction, which means the matching concept does not apply, and *deferral of contribution revenue is inappropriate under GAAP.* Therefore, for a grant, award, or sponsorship representing an unconditional contribution (or a conditional contribution for which the conditions have been substantially met or explicitly waived by the grantor/donor), the amount of contribution *revenue recognized upon execution of the related agreement is equal to the estimated future cash flows under the agreement.* Such contribution revenues are offset by a related receivable and allowance account if appropriate.[8] This accounting treatment may be confusing to leadership or management of a not-for-profit entity because the grant, award, or sponsorship agreement may restrict use of the resources in whole or part to a future period.

Amounts received in advance under a grant, award, or sponsorship agreement representing conditional contributions are recognized as a *refundable advance until the conditions have been substantially met or explicitly waived by the grantor or donor.* Such *liability* is reduced, and contribution revenue is recognized, as the conditions are substantially met or explicitly waived by the grantor or donor.

Key points
<ul><li>Grants, awards, or sponsorships that are unconditional contributions are recognized as contribution revenue at the earlier of the date received from, or promised by, the resource provider. The amount recognized is equal to the estimated future cash flows over the term of the related agreement.</li><li>Amounts received in advance under a grant, award, or sponsorship agreement representing conditional contributions are recognized as a refundable advance until the conditions have been substantially met or explicitly waived by the grantor or donor.</li></ul>

---

[8] If the grant, award, or sponsorship agreement is for more than 12 months, the contribution revenue should be measured using fair value (typically an income approach using estimated future cash flows under the agreement discounted to their present value as of the fiscal reporting date). Such amount will be offset by related receivable and discount accounts.

Revenues from membership dues

Dues may be provided by donors or by other individuals and *entities in return for tangible or intangible benefits* from their membership in a not-for-profit entity. As such, membership dues transactions may be a contribution, an exchange transaction, or both. Generally, whether the transaction is a contribution, an exchange transaction, or both *depends on whether the value the member receives is commensurate with the amount of dues paid.*

Regardless of whether or how often a member takes advantages of the benefits offered by membership in a not-for-profit entity, there is *generally some value to those benefits.* However, it is often difficult to measure the benefits a member receives and then determine if such benefits are commensurate with the dues paid by the member.

Indicators of membership dues as exchange transactions or contributions

The following indicators (based on FASB ASC 958) may be helpful in determining if membership dues are exchange transactions, contributions, or both. *None of the following indicators alone determines the classification* of membership dues; however, some indicators *may be more significant than others* depending on the facts and circumstances.

Indicators of membership dues as exchange transactions

- The membership solicitation materials indicate the dues provide economic benefits to members or to other entities or individuals designated by or related to members.
- Substantive member benefits (such as publications, admissions, reduced admissions, educational programs, and special events) may be available to nonmembers for a fee.
- Benefits provided by the not-for-profit entity are provided only to members.
- Benefits are provided to members for a defined period of time and additional payment of dues is required to extend benefits.
- The dues payment is fully or partially refundable if the member terminates his or her membership.
- Membership is available only to individuals meeting certain criteria (for example, members may be required to live in a certain area or possess a particular professional certification).

Indicators of membership dues as contributions[9]

- The membership solicitation materials indicate the dues provide benefits to the general public or to service beneficiaries of the not-for-profit entity.
- Member benefits are negligible.
- Benefits are provided by the not-for-profit entity to both members and nonmembers.

---

[9] If there are no significant benefits or duties connected with membership, membership development activities may be fundraising activities. In such circumstances, the costs of membership activities should be reported as fundraising expenses. Membership development is a joint activity if it involves soliciting revenues partly from exchange transactions and partly from contributions. To allocate these joint costs between fundraising and the exchange transaction, the purpose, audience, and content criteria should be met. If the purpose, audience, or content criteria are not met, the joint costs of membership development cannot be allocated and are, therefore, reported in full as fundraising expenses.

- Duration of the benefit period is not specified.
- The dues payment is not refundable if the member terminates his or her membership.
- Membership is available to the general public.

Key point
It is generally easier to determine if membership dues represent an exchange transaction or a contribution than it is to make the same determination for grants, awards, and sponsorships. Because the not-for-profit entity initiates and controls the dues solicitation process, it is better able to evaluate the indicators of whether membership dues represent exchange transactions or contributions.

Revenue recognition

Exchange transactions

The exchange transaction portion of membership dues, other than life membership dues, is *recognized as revenue when the identified performance obligations have been satisfied.* Not-for-profit entities may have one membership renewal date or multiple renewal dates that may or may not coincide with their fiscal reporting period. When membership periods do not coincide with the fiscal reporting period, the related identified performance obligations associated with membership may not be satisfied at the end of the current fiscal reporting period. In such cases, the amount of dues related to the performance obligations that are not satisfied at the end of the fiscal reporting period should be reported as *contract liabilities.*

- *Nonrefundable initiation and life membership fees* received in an exchange transaction should be accounted for under ASU No. 2014-09 based on the transaction price and the performance obligations identified in the initiation or life membership contract.

Contributions

The *unconditional contribution portion* of membership dues is *recognized when the dues amounts are received* as either donor-restricted support or revenues without donor restrictions and classified as net assets with donor restrictions or net assets without donor restrictions, respectively. This accounting treatment may be confusing to leadership or management of a not-for-profit entity because they may intend for the membership dues, in whole or part, to cover future operating and membership costs. Membership dues representing *conditional contributions,* if any, are recognized as contribution revenue when the conditions have been substantially met or explicitly waived by the member (donor, in this case).

Case study

Determine if the transaction in the following scenario should be accounted for as an exchange transaction or a contribution; and, if it is a contribution, whether the contribution is conditional. Please indicate what factor(s) led to your conclusion.

A local not-for-profit organized under IRC 501(c)(3) provides no- or low-cost day care for children of families meeting certain requirements relating to household income and size. Six months into the current year, the organization received a letter from the state Department of Children and Families informing them that their grant application to provide additional funds to operate one of their existing child care programs was approved.

The grant is a reimbursement grant for a maximum of $500,000 to cover the costs of allowable salaries and benefits of the staff working directly in the program. To be eligible for reimbursement, costs must conform to state procurement standards as well as the entity's own adopted procurement policies. Costs incurred without conforming to the state procurement standards are considered unallowable and will not be reimbursed. In the event the not-for-profit discontinues the program, reimbursement will be limited to the actual amounts spent rather than the grant amount approved.

As of year-end, the organization has incurred costs of $200,000, of which $150,000 has been reimbursed by the state, and $50,000 has been billed to the state and is currently outstanding.

Summary

This chapter discusses selected revenue recognition issues faced by not-for-profit entities. Specifically, this chapter reviews contributions and exchange transactions and discusses revenue recognition difficulties that may be associated with grants, awards, and sponsorships as well as membership dues. The chapter provides a discussion of conditional, unconditional, and donor-restricted contributions and the accounting for each. In addition, this chapter provides a detailed discussion of accounting for agency transactions by a not-for-profit entity, including the effects of variance power on these types of transactions. The chapter also discusses accounting for agency transactions when the not-for-profit entity acting as the recipient entity and the beneficiary are financially interrelated.

Practice questions

1. How does GAAP define an exchange transaction?

2. How does GAAP define contributions?

3. How is the contribution of a long-lived asset received without donor stipulations about how long it must be used, accounted for?

4. How does GAAP define variance power?

5. List three indicators that grants, awards, or sponsorships likely represent exchange transactions other than terms in the agreement.

6. List three indicators membership dues likely represent exchange transactions.

7. List three indicators membership dues likely represent contributions.

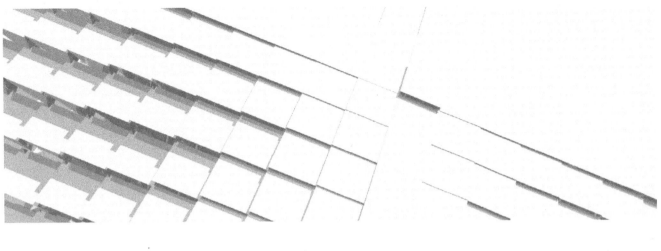

Chapter 3

Risk Assessment and Related Documentation

Learning objectives

- Identify the professional standards relating to the auditor's responsibility to assess and respond to the risk of material misstatement in the financial statements.

- Identify and apply risk assessment procedures.

- Identify and apply the types of further audit procedures and in what circumstances they may be appropriate.

- Identify the procedures to evaluate the sufficiency and appropriateness of audit evidence.

Major areas of inquiry

Professional standards state that the auditor should assess the risk of material misstatement in all financial statement audits. The auditor uses the results of this assessment in designing an audit strategy and an audit plan. Since the issuance of the risk assessment standards, the AICPA Technical Hotline has received a number of inquiries relating to the auditor's responsibilities with respect to its requirements. Additionally, risk assessment and the related documentation is an area highlighted in the 2019 *Areas of Focus* at https://www.aicpa.org/eaq.html.[1] The Peer Review Program routinely finds that many auditors perform their engagements without properly understanding their clients' risks. In the current peer review report, one of the most common deficiencies found was non-conformance with AU-C section 315, *Understanding the Entity and Its Environment and Assessing the Risks of Material Misstatement.*

The most frequent inquiries relating to the auditor's requirement to assess the risk of material misstatement include inquiries relating to the following:

- Risk assessment procedures
- Understanding internal control
- Assessing the risks of material misstatement
- Responding to the risk of material misstatement
- Linking results of the risk assessment process to the audit procedures
- Sufficiency and appropriateness of audit evidence

---

[1] The AICPA has developed an audit risk assessment tool to assist in identifying risks, including significant risks, that documents the planned response to those risks. It should be used as a supplement to existing planning tools and documentation systems. Use of the tool is recommended for use on audits of generally entities smaller in size and with less complex auditing and auditing issues. The tool is available at https://www.aicpa.org/eaq/aicpa-risk-assessment-resources.html.

Background

Audit risk is defined in professional standards as the risk the auditor may unknowingly fail to appropriately modify his or her opinion on the financial statements when they are materially misstated. As a concept, audit risk is a function of the following:

- Inherent risk
- Control risk
- Detection risk

The "risk of material misstatement" refers to inherent risk and control risk.

Inherent risk is the susceptibility of a *relevant assertion*[2] to a material misstatement (individually or in the aggregate) assuming there are not related controls. Factors influencing inherent risk include the following:

- Complexity of transaction or calculation (that is, derivative instruments)
- Susceptibility of tangible assets to theft (that is, cash, inventory, and so on)
- External circumstances giving rise to business risks (that is, economy, industry pressures)
- External or internal systemic issues related to several or all account balances, classes of transactions, or disclosures (that is, general decline in the entity's industry, lack of working capital)

Control risk is the risk a material misstatement (individually or in the aggregate) could occur in a *relevant assertion* and not be prevented or detected on a timely basis by the entity's internal controls. An entity manages its control risk primarily through an effectively designed and operated system of internal control. Because of the limitations inherent in any system of internal control, some control risk will always exist. Collectively, inherent risk and control risk represent the "risk of material misstatement." The entity, through its internal controls, is responsible for reducing control risk.

Detection risk is the risk the auditor will not detect a material misstatement (individually or in the aggregate) that exists for a *relevant assertion*. Because the auditor does not examine 100% of an account balance, class of transactions, or other factors,[3] detection risk cannot be reduced to zero. Therefore, detection risk is a function of the effectiveness of an audit procedure and its application by the auditor. Detection risk encompasses substantive analytical procedures and tests of details. The auditor is responsible for reducing detection risk.

In addition to audit risk, the auditor also has other risks that may arise in connection with an audit of an entity's financial statements. Such risks exist even though an audit may be done in accordance with generally accepted auditing standards (GAAS) and the auditor appropriately reports on the financial statements. Examples of these risks include the loss of or injury to the auditor's professional practice

---

[2] Relevant assertions are those having a meaningful bearing on whether an account is fairly stated. For example, valuation is generally a relevant assertion related to material inventories. See AU-C section 500, *Audit Evidence* (AICPA, *Professional Standards*), for guidance on how the auditor uses relevant assertions.

[3] Other factors include the possibility an auditor might select an inappropriate audit procedure, misapply an appropriate procedure, or misinterpret the results of an audit procedure.

resulting from litigation, adverse publicity, or other such events. A discussion of these risks is outside the scope of this chapter and this course.

Knowledge check

1. Which is **not** a component of audit risk?

   a. Industry risk.
   b. Control risk.
   c. Detection risk.
   d. Inherent risk.

Risk assessment and professional standards

AU-C section 200, *Overall Objectives of the Independent Auditor and the Conduct of an Audit in Accordance With Generally Accepted Auditing Standards* (AICPA, *Professional Standards*), defines the overall objectives of the auditor in conducting an audit of financial statements as being to

- obtain reasonable assurance about whether the financial statements as a whole are free from material misstatement, whether due to fraud or error, thereby enabling the auditor to express an opinion on whether the financial statements are presented fairly, in all material respects, in accordance with an applicable financial reporting framework; and
- report on the financial statements, and communicate as required by GAAS, in accordance with the auditor's findings.

Requirements and guidance specifically relating to the auditor's risk assessment process can primarily be found in the AICPA professional standards as follows:

- AU-C section 200
- AU-C section 315
- AU-C section 330, *Performing Audit Procedures in Response to Assessed Risks and Evaluating the Audit Evidence Obtained* (AICPA, *Professional Standards*)

The auditor should perform "risk assessment procedures" to assess the risk of misstatement at the *financial statement* and *relevant assertion levels*. Professional standards state the auditor should design and perform "further audit procedures" responsive to the assessed risks of material misstatement at the relevant assertion level. The nature, timing, and extent of further audit procedures are a matter of professional judgment.

Risk assessment procedures

Audit procedures used by the auditor to gain an understanding of the entity and its environment, including its internal control, are described in professional standards as "risk assessment procedures." The risk assessment procedures should include inquiries of management and others within the entity, analytical procedures, and observation and inspection.

Inquiries of management and others within the entity

When determining persons within the entity to whom inquiries might be directed, or the extent of those inquiries, the auditor should consider what information may be obtained from them that would be helpful in identifying risks of material misstatement. Auditors might find it effective to alternate the persons to whom they direct their inquiries from year to year.

Analytical procedures

When performing analytical procedures as risk assessment procedures, the auditor should develop expectations about plausible relationships expected to exist. The auditor should consider differences between expectations and recorded amounts (or unusual or unexpected relationships in any ratios calculated using recorded amounts) in identifying the risks of material misstatement. However, because such analytical procedures provide only a broad initial indication regarding material misstatements, the auditor should consider these results in conjunction with other information gathered in identifying the risks of material misstatement.

Observation and inspection

Typical audit procedures in this area include the following:

- Observation of entity activities and operations
- Inspection of documents, records, and internal control manuals
- Reading reports prepared by management, those charged with governance, and internal audit
- Visits to entity premises and plant facilities
- Tracing transactions relevant to financial reporting through the information system (may be performed as part of a walk-through)

Each of the aforementioned three specific risk assessment procedures need not be performed for all factors the auditor considers in obtaining the understanding of the entity and its environment, including internal control. Major factors[4] to consider in gaining an understanding of the entity and its environment include the following:

- Industry, regulatory, and other external factors
- Nature of the entity
- Objectives and strategies and the related business risks that may result in material misstatements in the financial statements
- Measurement and review of the entity's financial performance
- Internal control, including the selection and application of accounting policies

Obtaining an understanding of the entity and its environment is essential to performing an audit in accordance with GAAS. This understanding provides the framework the auditor uses in planning the audit and the context in which the auditor exercises professional judgment throughout the audit. Although professional standards define specific risk assessment procedures for the auditor to use in gaining an understanding of the entity and its environment, obtaining this understanding is a dynamic process encompassing gathering, updating, and analyzing information throughout the audit.

Tips to help comply with the requirements of AU-C section 315 and plan a successful audit include:

- Don't be afraid to ask the client questions to assist in understanding the client's industry and operating environment. In addition, keep eyes and ears open to better observe the client and get a feeling from their environment.
- Know the client's industry and transaction cycles including the significant accounts and transaction cycles. Having a large number of governmental and/or not-for-profit organizations as clients does not necessarily equate to an understanding of a specific governmental and/or not-for-profit organization.
- Identify client controls using the elements and principles in the COSO Framework to help identify possible missing controls. Remember, a control is any policy or procedure used to prevent or detect and correct a misstatement even an undocumented and/or informal control.
- Evaluate the design and implementation of the client's controls, which is not the same as testing a control for its operating effectiveness.[5]

The auditor also has a professional responsibility to specifically assess the risk of material misstatement due to fraud. In making this assessment, the auditor should also consider fraud risk factors relating to material misstatements due to (a) fraudulent financial reporting or (b) misappropriation of assets.

---

[4] See AU-C section 315, for specific items to consider within these categories.

[5] Adapted from *4 tips to identify audit client risks* by Tracy Harding guest blogger, on November 20, 2018. The full article can be found at https://blog.aicpa.org/2018/11/4-tips-to-identify-audit-client-risks.html#sthash.ay0OBdSN.dpbs.

Knowledge check

2. Which is **not** a risk assessment procedure?

   a. Substantive tests of details.
   b. Observation and inspection.
   c. Inquiries of management.
   d. Analytical procedures.

Understanding internal control

Risk assessment procedures are used by the auditor to

- obtain an understanding of internal control sufficient to evaluate the design of controls relevant to an audit of financial statements, and
- determine if they have been implemented.

Professional standards do not require the auditor to design audit procedures to detect deficiencies in an entity's internal control. However, as a result of the procedures performed in obtaining an understanding of the entity and its environment, including internal control, the auditor may note certain deficiencies in the design or operation of an entity's internal control. AU-C section 265, *Communicating Internal Control Related Matters Identified in an Audit* (AICPA, *Professional Standards*), addresses the auditor's responsibility to appropriately communicate to those charged with governance and management deficiencies in internal control that the auditor has identified in an audit of financial statements . A discussion of the requirements related to communicating internal control matters is outside the scope of this chapter and this course.

The auditor should obtain an understanding of the entity's five components of internal control as defined by the COSO as follows:

- Control environment
- Risk assessment
- Control activities
- Information and communication systems
- Monitoring

Obtaining an understanding of internal control includes evaluating the design of a control and determining if it has been implemented. This understanding applies to each component of internal control. When evaluating the design of a control, the auditor considers whether the control individually, or in combination with other controls, is effective in preventing, detecting, or correcting material misstatements.

The auditor also considers the design of a control when determining whether to consider its implementation. In this context, implementation means the control exists and the entity is using it. For example, testing properly designed controls for the effectiveness of implementation may be done when the auditor would like to reduce the extent of substantive procedures. On the other hand, if a control is improperly designed it would likely not be efficient or effective to consider its implementation.

Certain control activities, if present, are always relevant to the audit. These activities include control activities

- addressing significant risks;
- relevant to fraud risks;
- addressing risks for which substantive procedures alone do not provide sufficient appropriate audit evidence;

- addressing risks for which the auditor intends to rely on the operating effectiveness of controls in determining the nature, timing, and extent of substantive procedures; and
- over journal entries including those used to record nonrecurring, unusual transactions, or adjustments.

To determine whether control activities are relevant to the audit, the auditor may consider a number of factors including the following:

- Materiality and inherent risk
  - The auditor may focus on areas where the risk of material misstatement is likely to be higher.
- Understanding of other internal control components
  - Understanding what controls are present or absent in other components may mean the auditor needs to devote less or more attention to understanding control activities.
- Implementation of any new systems and the effectiveness of general IT controls
  - Deficiencies in its controls may affect the effective design and operation of application controls.
- Lack of segregation of duties
  - Because fewer employees limit the extent of segregation, the auditor may need a deeper understanding of controls performed by management.
- Legal and regulatory requirements
  - This may be more important in audits of not-for-profit and governmental entities.

Based on the aforementioned factors, the following control activities may be considered relevant to the audit.

- Control activities over the completeness and accuracy of information produced by the entity if the auditor intends to make use of it in designing and performing further audit procedures
- Control activities relating to operations or compliance objectives if they relate to data the auditor evaluates or uses in applying audit procedures
- Control activities over safeguarding assets to the extent they are relevant to the reliability of financial reporting
- Control activities, such as indirect controls, which are dependent on other controls

Knowledge obtained by the auditor in obtaining the understanding of internal control is used to

- identify types of potential misstatements,
- consider factors affecting the risk of material misstatement, and
- design tests of controls, when applicable, and substantive procedures.

Knowledge check

3. Which is **not** a component of internal control?

    a. An entity's hiring policies.
    b. The control environment.
    c. An entity's risk assessment process.
    d. An entity's information system.

Assessing the risks of material misstatement

Risks of material misstatement are assessed at the financial statement level and the relevant assertion level related to (*a*) account balances, (*b*) classes of transactions, and (*c*) disclosures (including the quantitative and qualitative aspects of such disclosures). These risks are identified by obtaining an understanding of the entity and its environment, including relevant internal controls. Once identified, the auditor relates these risks to *what could go wrong* at the relevant assertion level considering the magnitude and likelihood the risk could result in a material misstatement.

Additionally, the auditor should determine whether the identified risks relate to specific relevant assertions (related to account balances, classes of transactions, or disclosures) or whether they relate to the financial statements taken as a whole. Risks at the financial statement level may result from a weak control environment due, for example, to management's lack of competence. Weaknesses at a financial statement level are likely to be pervasive and may require an *overall response* by the auditor. For example, concerns about the integrity of management may be serious enough to cause the auditor to conclude the risk of management misrepresentation in the financial statements is such that an audit cannot be conducted.

The assessment of the risk of material misstatement at the relevant assertion level may change during the course of the audit as more audit evidence becomes available. For example, the auditor may obtain evidence of controls not operating effectively when performing tests of controls. Likewise, in performing substantive procedures, the auditor may detect misstatements in amounts or frequency exceeding those considered by the auditor in the risk assessment.

Key point
When audit evidence obtained from performing further audit procedures tends to contradict audit evidence on which the auditor based the risk assessment, the auditor should revise the risk assessment and should further modify planned audit procedures.

Significant risks

As part of the risk assessment process, the auditor should determine which identified risks are significant risks (that is, risks requiring special audit consideration). Significant risks may relate to nonroutine transactions[6] (that is, unusual or infrequent) and judgmental matters[7] (that is, estimates), as well as routine business transactions. In determining if a risk is a significant risk, the auditor should consider the following:

- Nature of the risk
  - Fraud risk
  - Related economic, accounting, or other developments
  - Complexity of transactions
  - Significant transactions with related parties
  - Degree of subjectivity in measuring financial information related to the risk
  - Significant nonroutine transactions including significant related party transactions
- Likely magnitude of the potential misstatement (including the possibility the risk might give rise to multiple misstatements)
- Likelihood of the risk occurring

The auditor should evaluate the design of an entity's controls related to significant risks (if not already done as part of the overall risk assessment process) as well as determine if any relevant control activities have been implemented. This information should provide adequate information for the auditor to develop an effective audit approach. A control deficiency exists if management has not implemented controls over significant risks. In such cases, the auditor should consider the implications for his or her risk assessment.

---

[6] The nature of nonroutine transactions inherently makes it difficult for an entity to implement effective controls. In addition, greater risks may arise due to (1) greater management intervention to specify accounting treatment, (2) greater manual intervention for data collection and processing, or (3) complex calculations or accounting principles.
[7] Judgment may be subjective or complex or may require assumptions about the effects of future events. In addition, accounting principles may be subject to differing interpretations in some cases (for example, estimates, revenue recognition, fair value measurements, and so on).

Responses to the risk of material misstatement and linking results of risk assessment to the audit procedures

Once the auditor has obtained an understanding of the entity and its environment (including internal control), assessed the risk of misstatement, and identified any significant risks, he or she responds to the assessed risks. The auditor responds to the assessed risks of material misstatement at the financial statement and relevant assertion level by determining overall responses and developing further audit procedures.

Overall responses to the assessed risk of material misstatement are those generally relating to the risk of material misstatement at the financial statement level. Accordingly, overall responses relate to the audit strategy for the current-period engagement. Examples of overall responses may include the following:

- Emphasizing the need to maintain professional skepticism in gathering and evaluating audit evidence
- Assigning more experienced staff
- Assigning staff with specialized skills or using specialists
- Providing more supervision
- Incorporating elements of unpredictability
- Performing some audit procedures at an interim date rather than year-end[8]
- Performing audit procedures at year-end rather than at an interim date

Further audit procedures

Further audit procedures are those whose nature, timing, and extent are determined in response to assessed risks of material misstatement at the relevant assertion level. As such, they affect the audit plan rather than the audit strategy for the current-period engagement. The purpose of further audit procedures is to test controls or to perform substantive tests. Selection of the procedures to be performed is based on the risk of material misstatement. Therefore, a higher assessment of risk will require more reliable and relevant audit evidence from substantive procedures.

Factors the auditor should consider in designing further audit procedures include the following:

- Significance of the risk[9]
- Likelihood a material misstatement will occur
- Characteristics of the account balance, class of transactions, or disclosure to which the risk relates

---

[8] Performing procedures at an interim date may be appropriate when the control environment is effective and the auditor has more confidence in internal control and the reliability of audit evidence generated internally by the entity.
[9] Professional standards state the auditor should design and perform substantive procedures for all relevant assertions related to each material account balance, class of transactions, or disclosure.

- Nature of specific controls used (that is, manual or automated)
- Whether the auditor expects to test the effectiveness of an entity's controls in preventing or detecting material misstatements[10]

Key point
Further audit procedures are those whose nature, timing, and extent are determined in response to assessed risks of material misstatement at the relevant assertion level. The purpose of further audit procedures is to test controls or to perform substantive tests.

Nature, timing, and extent of further audit procedures

The nature, timing, and extent of further audit procedures should be linked to the assessed risks of material misstatement at the relevant assertion level. Professional standards define nature, timing, and extent as follows:

- *Nature* of further audit procedures refers to their purpose and type.
- *Timing* refers to when audit procedures are performed or the date to which audit evidence applies.
- *Extent* refers to the quantity of the specific audit procedures to be performed.

Further audit procedures should take into consideration the reasons for the assessment of the risk of material misstatement at the relevant assertion level for *each*

- account balance,
- class of transactions, and
- disclosure.

Both (*a*) inherent risk associated with *each* account balance, class of transactions, and disclosure (that is, particular characteristics) and (*b*) whether the risk assessment takes into account control risk are included in this consideration. The risk of material misstatement due to the particular characteristics of an account balance, class of transactions, or disclosure (that is, inherent risk) is made without consideration of any related controls (that is, control risk). For example, when transaction amounts are calculated manually there may be a higher assessed level of risk that a material misstatement may occur, without consideration of any existing controls over the manual calculation, than if amounts were generated electronically. In this case, the auditor may conclude that substantive procedures alone may not provide sufficient appropriate audit evidence.

---

[10] Effective controls reduce, but do not eliminate, the risk of material misstatement. Therefore, tests of controls do not eliminate the need for substantive procedures.

Certain audit procedures may be more appropriate for some assertions than others. For example, in relation to expenses, tests of controls may be most responsive to the risk associated with the occurrence assertion, whereas substantive procedures may be most responsive for the completeness assertion.

Audit evidence about the accuracy and completeness of information generated by the entity's information system should be obtained when such information is used in performing audit procedures. In addition, the auditor should consider testing controls over the entity's preparation of such information if the auditor uses the information in performing analytical procedures.

Nature of further audit procedures[11]

The timing and extent of further audit procedures are only effective if the audit procedure itself is reliable and relevant to the specific risk. Therefore, the nature of an audit procedure is the most important consideration in the selection of further audit procedures. As noted already, the nature of further audit procedures refers to the purpose of the procedures and the type of procedure.

The purpose of further audit procedures is to test controls and perform substantive procedures.

Types of further audit procedures include the following:

- Inspection
- Observation
- Inquiry[12]
- Confirmation
- Recalculation
- Reperformance
- Analytical procedures

Tests of controls

"Tests of the operating effectiveness of controls" is not the same as *"obtaining audit evidence controls have been implemented."*

The auditor "obtains evidence of implementation" when performing risk assessment procedures. Many auditors obtain evidence controls have been implemented by performing a walk-through of the control process. There may be circumstances where the risk assessment procedures to evaluate the design of controls and to determine they are implemented may also provide evidence about their operating effectiveness. Consequently, such procedures would serve the dual purpose of obtaining evidence of implementation and testing the control for effectiveness.

---

[11] See AU-C section 330, *Performing Audit Procedures in Response to Assessed Risks and Evaluating the Audit Evidence Obtained* (AICPA, *Professional Standards*), for additional detailed guidance related to the nature of tests of controls and substantive procedures.

[12] Professional standards state the auditor should perform other audit procedures in combination with inquiries (that is, inspection, reperformance, and so on).

The nature of a particular control influences the type of audit procedure necessary to obtain audit evidence of its operating effectiveness. In "tests of controls," the auditor should obtain audit evidence the controls operate effectively, which includes obtaining audit evidence about

- how the controls were applied at relevant times during the audit period,
- consistency with which the controls were applied during the period,[13] and
- by whom or what means they were applied.

The auditor should design and perform tests of controls to obtain sufficient appropriate audit evidence about the operating effectiveness of relevant controls in the following circumstances:

- Auditor's risk assessment includes an expectation of the operating effectiveness of controls (that is, the auditor plans to rely on those controls that are *suitably designed to prevent/detect a material misstatement*[14] in the relevant assertion in order to reduce the nature, timing, and extent of substantive procedures).
- Substantive procedures alone do not provide sufficient appropriate audit evidence at the relevant assertion level (that is, entity transacts business using IT and no transaction documentation is produced or maintained other than through the IT system).
- Controls created to mitigate a significant risk (that is, the greater the risk of material misstatement, the more audit evidence the auditor should obtain indicating the mitigating controls are operating effectively).
- Controls the auditor tested for operating effectiveness in a prior audit period have changed and the auditor plans to rely on the controls in the current audit period because the controls continue to provide a basis for such reliance.
- Controls the auditor tested for operating effectiveness in the prior two audit periods have not changed and the auditor plans to rely on the controls in the current audit period because the controls continue to provide a basis for such reliance (that is, controls on which the auditor plans to rely should be tested for operating effectiveness at least once in every third year of an annual audit).

Key point
The nature of a particular control influences the type of audit procedure necessary to obtain audit evidence of its operating effectiveness. Therefore, the auditor should obtain audit evidence controls operate effectively when performing control tests.

Substantive procedures

Substantive procedures should be responsive to the related assessment of the risk of material misstatement at the relevant assertion level for *each* material

---

[13] When substantially different controls were used during the audit period, the auditor should consider each separately.

[14] It is not necessary to test controls that are not suitably designed or those that are suitably designed but not germane to amounts that could result in material misstatements in the relevant assertion.

- account balance,
- class of transactions, and
- disclosure.

Additionally, the auditor should plan substantive procedures to be responsive to the planned level of detection risk. Determination of substantive procedures most responsive to the planned level of detection risk is affected by whether audit evidence was obtained about the operating effectiveness of any related controls. Types of substantive procedures are as follows:

- *Tests of details* —More appropriate to obtain audit evidence regarding certain relevant assertions about account balances (that is, existence and valuation)
- *Substantive analytical procedures* — More appropriate to large volumes of transactions that tend to be predictable over time

In addition, professional standards state the auditor should perform substantive procedures in the following areas:

- *Financial statement reporting process* — Professional standards in this area states the auditor should include audit procedures related to
  - agreeing financial statements and the related notes to the underlying accounting records, and
  - examining material journal entries and other adjustments made during the financial statement preparation process.
- *Significant risks* — When only substantive procedures are to be performed for a significant risk, the audit procedures appropriate in this circumstance are
  - tests of details only, or
  - tests of details combined with substantive analytical procedures.

Tests of details should (*a*) be designed to be responsive to the assessed risk of material misstatement at the relevant assertion level and (*b*) provide sufficient appropriate audit evidence to achieve the planned level of assurance. The following may prove helpful in designing tests of details to provide relevant audit evidence and respond to the assertions noted as follows:

- Existence or occurrence
  - Select items to test from items included in a financial statement amount.
- Completeness
  - Select items from a source indicating items from the source would be included in the relevant financial statement amount.
  - Knowledge gained when obtaining an understanding of the business and its environment is helpful in selecting the nature, timing, and extent of audit procedures related to this assertion.

When designing analytical procedures, the auditor should consider the risk of management override of controls and evaluate if such override might have allowed adjustments to the financial statements to be made outside the normal period end financial reporting process. Adjustments made in these circumstances might have resulted in artificial changes to the financial statement relationships being analyzed using substantive analytical procedures. If undetected by the auditor, the artificial changes might cause the auditor to reach erroneous conclusions.

In designing substantive analytical procedures, the auditor should consider the following:

- Suitability of using substantive analytical procedures in light of the assertions (that is, analytical procedures might not provide sufficient appropriate audit evidence for existence and valuation assertions)
- Reliability of the data from which the expectation of recorded amounts or ratios is developed (that is, internal or external)
- Whether the expectation is sufficiently precise to identify the possibility of a material misstatement at the desired level of assurance
- Amount of any difference in recorded amounts from expected values that is acceptable

Knowledge check

4. Which is correct with respect to tests of controls?

    a. Tests of controls eliminate the need for substantive tests of details.
    b. Tests of controls must be performed on every audit engagement.
    c. Tests of controls provide evidence recorded amounts are correct.
    d. Tests of controls provide evidence of their operating effectiveness.

Timing of further audit procedures[15]

Tests of controls or substantive procedures may be performed at an interim date or at the end of the year. It is generally more effective to perform substantive procedures at or near the end of the year when the assessed risk of material misstatement is high. However, performing audit procedures at an interim date may help the auditor identify significant matters early in the audit process. Early identification of significant matters allows management to resolve them before the end of the period and also facilitates development of an effective audit approach to address the identified matters.

When considering the timing of the planned audit procedures, the auditor should consider the following:

- Control environment
- Availability of relevant information
- Nature of the risk
- Period or date to which the audit evidence relates

---

[15] See AU-C section 330 for additional detailed guidance related to the timing of tests of controls and substantive procedures.

Extent of further audit procedures[16]

Generally, the extent of audit procedures is directly related to the risk of material misstatement. An auditor determines the extent of an audit procedure using judgment and after considering the

- performance materiality,
- assessed risk of material misstatement, and
- degree of assurance the auditor plans to obtain.

Computer-assisted audit techniques may allow the auditor to greatly expand the extent of his or her audit procedures because they typically test an entire population instead of only a sample from the population. Data analytics provide the auditor with an opportunity to review and analyze a larger population of data to identify information used to support audit procedures. The AICPA's *Guide to Audit Data Analytics* provides guidance to auditors in the use of these techniques. With respect to performing risk assessment procedures, the Guide provides the following steps for use in planning, performing, and evaluating results of such techniques.

- Plan the audit data analytic.
- Access and prepare the data for purposes of the audit data analytic.
- Consider the relevance and reliability of the data used.
- Perform the audit data analytic.
- Evaluate the results and conclude on whether the purpose and specific objectives of performing the audit data analytic have been achieved.

Alternatively, the auditor may draw valid conclusions about a population using sampling techniques. There will be an unacceptable risk of the auditor's conclusion on a sample being different from one based on testing the entire population if

- sample size is too small,
- sampling approach or method of selection is not appropriate to achieve the specific audit objective, or
- follow-up on exceptions is not appropriate.

Evaluating the appropriateness of audit evidence

Throughout the audit, the audit evidence obtained may have caused the auditor to change the nature, timing, or extent of other planned audit procedures. Information significantly different from the information on which the risk assessments were based may also have come to the attention of the auditor, causing a reevaluation of the planned audit procedures.

Using the results of the audit procedures performed and the audit evidence obtained, the auditor evaluates whether the assessments of the risks of material misstatement at the relevant assertion level remain appropriate. Before the conclusion of the audit, the auditor should also evaluate whether audit

---

[16] See AU-C section 330 for additional detailed guidance related to the extent of tests of controls and substantive procedures.

risk has been reduced to an appropriately low level and whether the nature, timing, and extent of the audit procedures performed need to be reconsidered.

In evaluating the sufficiency and appropriateness of the audit evidence, the auditor might consider the following:

- Significance of the potential misstatement in the relevant assertion
- Likelihood a potential misstatement in a relevant assertion would have a material effect (individually or in the aggregate) with other potential misstatements in the financial statements
- Effectiveness of management's responses and controls to address the risks
- Experience gained during prior audits with respect to similar potential misstatements
- Results of audit procedures performed (including whether the procedures identified specific instances of fraud/error)
- Source and reliability of available information
- Persuasiveness of the audit evidence
- Understanding the entity and its environment, including its internal control

Determination of the sufficiency and appropriateness of audit evidence to support conclusions throughout the audit, and the opinion on the financial statements, is a matter of professional judgment. If the auditor concludes sufficient appropriate evidence has not been obtained with respect to a material financial statement assertion, he or she should attempt to obtain further audit evidence. The auditor should express a modified opinion (qualified or disclaimer of opinion) if he or she is unable to obtain sufficient appropriate audit evidence with respect to a material financial statement assertion.

Key point
Although tests of controls or substantive procedures may be performed at an interim date or at the end of the year, it is generally more effective to perform substantive procedures at or near the end of the year. The assessed risk of material misstatement is generally higher at or near the end of the year.

Summary

This chapter discusses the auditor's responsibilities under professional standards relating to the assessment of the risk of material misstatement. The chapter defines, explains, and provides examples of risk assessment procedures and further audit procedures. In addition, the chapter discusses how to link the risk of material misstatement to the nature, timing, and extent of further audit procedures. Concepts related to the nature, timing, and extent of further audit procedures are discussed in detail, including tests of controls and substantive procedures. With respect to substantive procedures, this chapter describes tests of details and substantive analytical procedures and when each is appropriate. Additionally, the chapter includes a discussion of the factors the auditor considers when evaluating the sufficiency and appropriateness of the audit evidence obtained throughout the audit engagement.

Practice questions

1. List the risk assessment procedures that professional standards state should be performed.

2. What are the two types of substantive procedures defined in professional standards?

3. What is audit risk?

4. What is a significant risk?

5. What is control risk?

6. What three things should the auditor consider when identifying significant risks?

7. What is inherent risk?

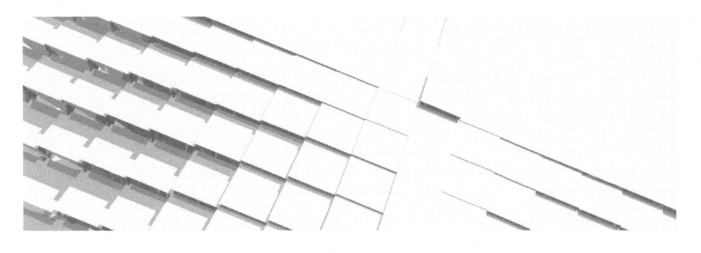

Chapter 4

GASB Statement No. 83, *Certain Asset Retirement Obligations*

Learning objectives

- Recognize the definition of key terms as defined in GASB Statement No. 83, *Certain Asset Retirement Obligations*.

- Identify external and internal events that determine the timing for recognition of an asset retirement obligation (ARO).

- Determine how to measure an ARO initially and in subsequent periods.

Major areas of inquiry

GASB issued Statement No. 83 in November 2016, effective for financial statements for periods beginning after June 15, 2018. GASB Statement No. 83 was issued to address accounting and financial reporting issues relating to AROs.

Both preparers and auditors of state and local government financial statements have questions regarding the requirements of the standard as well as how to effectively implement the requirements of the standard. A number of these questions relate to the following:

- How the requirements of GASB Statement No. 83 affect accounting and financial reporting of AROs
- How will the requirements of GASB Statement No. 83 affect previously reported AROs that were not measured in accordance with the requirements of GASB Statement No. 83
- How to measure AROs
- What are the financial reporting requirements in the first year of implementation
- What are the implementation challenges for state and local governments and their auditors

Background

Some governments have legal obligations to retire certain tangible capital assets at the end of their estimated useful lives. Prior to the issuance of GASB Statement No. 83, state and local governments were only required to report closure and postclosure costs associated with landfills as established in GASB Statement No. 18, *Accounting for Municipal Solid Waste Landfill Closure and Postclosure Care Costs*, as amended. GASB Statement No. 49, *Accounting and Financial Reporting for Pollution Remediation Obligations,* while requiring the reporting of pollution-related AROs at the time of retirement does not address reporting these obligations during periods prior to the retirement of the capital asset.

In December 2013, GASB approved pre-agenda research on the topic. Using the results of the pre-agenda research, GASB formally added the ARO project to its Technical Agenda in August 2014. A task force was assembled to provide feedback to GASB on issues discussed by the board as well as on the exposure draft that was issued in December 2015. Also, during this time, the Governmental Accounting Standards Advisory Council provided feedback to the board on key issues.

During the comment period, a field test of the proposed standard was conducted where participants were asked to apply the provisions of the exposure draft to their most recently issued financial statements on a pro forma basis. After deliberating comments to the exposure draft, the board approved GASB Statement No. 83 for issuance in late 2016.

Overview of GASB Statement No. 83

GASB Statement No. 83 addresses how state and local governments account for and report certain AROs. As such, it defines AROs and related key terms and provides guidance on measuring AROs and the related deferred outflow of resources for financial reporting purposes. In addition, GASB Statement No. 83 requires AROs to be adjusted at least annually for the effects of general inflation or deflation. The statement also requires a number of disclosures related to AROs that have been incurred but cannot be reasonably estimated, as well as AROs that have been incurred and are reasonably estimable.

AROs result from the normal operations of acquired or constructed tangible capital assets and are therefore different in nature than asset impairments and pollution remediation obligations.[1] GASB Statement No. 83 applies to legally enforceable liabilities associated with all of the following activities:

- Retirement of a tangible capital asset
- Disposal of a replaced part that is a component of a tangible capital asset
- Environmental remediation associated with the retirement of a tangible capital asset resulting from normal operation of the capital asset.

In addition, GASB Statement No. 83 applies to legally enforceable liabilities of a lessor in connection with the retirement of its leased property if those liabilities meet the definition of an ARO. However, GASB Statement No. 83 does not apply to the following:

- Obligations
  - arising solely from a plan to sell or otherwise dispose of a tangible capital asset
  - associated with the preparation of a tangible capital asset for an alternative use
  - for pollution remediation, such as asbestos removal, resulting from other-than-normal operation of a tangible capital asset
  - associated with maintenance, rather than retirement, of a tangible capital asset
- Cost of a replacement part that is a component of a tangible capital asset
- Landfill closure and postclosure care obligations, including those not covered by GASB Statement No. 18
- Conditional obligations to perform asset retirement activities.

Key point
AROs result from the normal operation of acquired or constructed tangible capital assets.

---

[1] A discussion of capital asset impairments and pollution remediation obligations is outside the scope of this chapter and this course.

Terminology

Paragraph 32 of GASB Statement No. 83 provides a number of definitions that can be found throughout the statement. These terms may have different meanings outside of the context of GASB Statement No. 83.

Asset retirement obligation — Legally enforceable liability associated with the retirement of a tangible capital asset.

Contamination — Event or condition normally involving a substance that is deposited in, on, or around a tangible capital asset in the form or concentration that may harm people, equipment, or the environment due to the substance's radiological, chemical, biological, reactive, explosive, or mutagenic nature.

Current value — Amount that would be paid if all equipment, facilities, and services included in the estimate were acquired at the end of the current reporting period.

Retirement of a tangible capital asset — Permanent removal of a tangible capital asset from service[2].

Key point
Terms identified in GASB Statement No. 83 may have different meanings outside the context of the statement. When working with engineers or other similar professionals to identify and measure AROs, it may be beneficial to discuss the meanings of the terms in the statement and the meanings of the terms outside the context of the statement.

Knowledge check

1. Which is **not** contemplated by the definition of *contamination* as defined in GASB Statement No. 83?

    a. An event or condition normally involving a substance.
    b. Substances may be deposited in, on, or around a tangible capital asset.
    c. Substances deposited may harm people, animals, equipment, or the environment.
    d. Substances deposited may harm people, equipment, or the environment.

---

[2] Retirement encompasses the sale, abandonment, recycling, or disposal in some other manner of a tangible capital asset. It does not encompass the temporary idling of a tangible asset.

Recognition of an ARO

State and local governments are required to recognize an ARO when the legally enforceable liability is incurred and can be reasonably estimated. ARO liabilities are recognized upon the occurrence of an external and internal obligating event resulting from the normal operation of a tangible capital asset. When an ARO is recognized, a corresponding deferred outflow of resources is also recognized.

External obligating events are one of the following:

- Approval of federal, state, or local laws or regulations
- Creation of a legally binding contract
- Issuance of a court judgment

Internal obligating events vary for contamination-related and noncontamination-related AROs. Completion of a plan to retire a tangible asset is not, by itself, an internal obligating event. Internal obligating events are as follows.

- *Contamination-related AROs*
  - The occurrence of contamination.
    - An example of contamination noted in GASB Statement No. 83 is nuclear contamination of a nuclear reactor vessel as a result of the normal operation of a nuclear power plant that is not in the scope of GASB Statement No. 49.
- *Non-contamination-related AROs*
  - Pattern of incurrence of the liability is based on the use of the tangible capital asset
    - Obligating event is placing the capital asset into operation and consuming a portion of the usable capacity by the normal operations of that capital asset (for example excavation of a coal strip mine and using a portion of the capacity of the coal strip mine).
  - Pattern of incurrence of the liability is not based on the use of the tangible capital asset
    - Obligating event is placing the capital asset into operation (for example placing a wind turbine into operation).
  - Tangible capital asset is permanently abandoned before it is placed into operation[3]
    - Obligating event is the permanent abandonment itself (for example, retirement of a tangible capital asset that is permanently abandoned during construction).
- *AROs related to acquired tangible capital assets*
  - Obligating event is the acquisition of the tangible capital asset (for example, acquisition date of a power plant acquired with an existing ARO).

---

[3] In these circumstances, an immediate outflow of resources is recognized rather than a deferred outflow of resources.

Initial measurement

The types of activities to be included in the measurement of an ARO should be based on relevant legal requirements that include relevant laws, regulations, contracts, or court judgments. For legal requirements resulting from laws and regulations, the federal, state, or local laws or regulations approved as of the financial reporting date should be used rather than the effective date of such laws and regulations.

The measurement of an ARO should be based on the best estimate of the current value of the outlays expected to be incurred in retiring the tangible capital asset. This estimate should be determined using all available evidence. A probability weighted approach is used when sufficient evidence is available or can be obtained at a reasonable cost. The most likely amount in a range of potential outcomes should be used when probability weighting cannot be accomplished at a reasonable cost. All other available evidence that can be obtained at a reasonable cost (including potentially higher or lower outcomes) should be considered when determining the amount of an ARO in this manner.

Exception for a minority owner[4]

When a nongovernmental entity is the majority owner of a tangible capital asset in which a government has a minority share (less than 50%), the nongovernmental majority owner typically reports an ARO in accordance with the guidance of another recognized accounting standards setter. In these cases, the initial measurement requirements of GASB Statement No. 83 do not apply to a government's minority share of the jointly owned tangible capital asset. Rather, the government's minority share of an ARO should be reported using the measurement provided by the nongovernmental majority owner or the nongovernmental minority owner having operational responsibility for the jointly owned tangible capital asset. The measurement date in these cases should be no more than one year and one day prior to the government's financial reporting date.

Key point
AROs are measured based on relevant laws or regulations approved as of the financial reporting date rather than the effective date of such laws and regulations.

Subsequent measurement

At least annually a government is required to adjust the current value of its ARO for the effects of general inflation or deflation and to evaluate all relevant factors relating to the estimated outlays associated with the ARO. Evaluation of the factors is required to determine if one or more of such factors is expected to

---

[4] Minority ownership in an undivided interest arrangement in which a government and one or more other entities jointly own a tangible capital asset (to the extent of each entity's ownership interest) and each joint owner is liable for its share of any ARO.

significantly increase or decrease the estimate outlays associated with the ARO. The ARO is required to be remeasured only when the evaluation indicates there is a significant change in the estimated outlays.

Factors that may lead to a significant change in the estimated outlays include (but are not limited to) the following:

- Price increases or decreases due to factors other than general inflation or deflation for specific components of the estimated outlays
- Changes in technology
- Changes in legal or regulatory requirements resulting from changes in laws, regulations, contracts, or court judgments
- Changes in the type of equipment, facilities, or services that will be used to meet the obligations to retire the tangible capital asset

When factors indicate a significant change in the estimated outlays, the carrying amount of the ARO should be increased or decreased in one of the following ways:

- For a liability that increases or decreases before the time of retirement of the tangible capital asset, the corresponding deferred outflow of resources is adjusted.
- For a liability that increases or decreases at or after retirement of the tangible capital asset (that is, the corresponding deferred outflow of resources has been fully recognized as outflows of resources), an outflow of resources or an inflow of resources should be recognized in the reporting period in which the increase or decrease occurs.

Exception for a minority owner

For a government with a minority share of an ARO, the subsequent measurement requirements of GASB Statement No. 83 relating to subsequent liability measurement and recognition do not apply. Instead, such a government should continue to report its minority share of an ARO using the measurement provided by the nongovernmental majority owner or the nongovernmental minority owner having operational responsibility for the jointly owned tangible capital asset. The measurement date in these cases should be no more than one year and one day prior to the government's financial reporting date.

Deferred outflows of resources associated with AROs

Upon initial recognition of an ARO, the corresponding initial deferred outflow of resources is measured at the same amount as the initial ARO. The deferred outflows associated with an ARO are reduced annually as an outflow of resources (expense). Reductions to the deferred outflow of resources should be determined in a systematic and rational manner over a period of time in one of the following ways:

- For a deferred outflow of resources initially reported at the beginning of a tangible capital asset's estimated useful life

- reduction of the deferred outflow of resources should be recognized as an outflow of resources over the entire estimated useful life of the tangible capital asset
- For a deferred outflow of resources initially reported after a tangible capital asset has been placed into operation, but before the end of its estimated useful life
  - reduction of the deferred outflow of resources should be recognized as an outflow of resources over the remaining estimated useful life of the tangible capital asset, starting from the point at which the deferred outflow of resources is initially recognized

Knowledge check

2. As noted in GASB Statement No. 83, which factor might **not** give rise to a significant change in the estimated outlays associated with an ARO?

   a. Price increases or decreases due to general inflation or deflation for specific components of the estimated outlays.
   b. Changes in technology.
   c. Changes in legal or regulatory requirements resulting from changes in laws, regulations, contracts, or court judgments.
   d. Changes in the type of equipment, facilities, or services that will be used to meet the obligations to retire the tangible capital asset.

ARO recognition and measurement in governmental funds[5]

Liabilities and expenditures for goods and services used for asset retirement activities should be recognized in governmental funds upon receipt of the goods and services (due and payable[6]). In some cases, governments may have accumulated resources in a governmental fund for eventual payment of AROs, which does not constitute an outflow of current financial resources. Therefore, such accumulated amounts should not result in recognition of an additional liability or expenditure in a governmental fund. Any facilities and equipment acquisitions associated with asset retirement activities should be reported as expenditures in the statement of revenues, expenditures, and changes in fund balance(s).

Funding and assurance provisions associated with AROs

In order to provide funding and assurance a government will be able to satisfy its AROs, some legal, regulatory, or contractual requirements may require them to set aside assets restricted for payment of an ARO. Restricted in this context has the same meaning as restricted net position as discussed in GASB

---

[5] GASB statements use the phrase "financial statements prepared using the current financial resources measurement focus". The phrase "governmental funds" is used in this chapter for brevity and clarity.

[6] GASB Statement No. 83 uses the phrase to the extent such amounts are normally expected to be liquidated with expendable available financial resources. The phrase "due and payable" is used in this chapter for brevity and clarity.

Statement No. 34, *Basic Financial Statements — and Management's Discussion and Analysis — for State and Local Governments*, as amended. That is, *restricted* refers to constraints that are

- externally imposed by
  - creditors, grantors, contributors
  - laws or regulations of other governments or
- "internally" imposed by law through constitutional provisions or enabling legislation.

When a government has set aside restricted assets for payment of an ARO, it should disclose this fact in accordance with the disclosure requirements established in GASB Statement No. 83 (discussed in the following section). Providing funding and assurance that a government will be able to satisfy its AROs does not satisfy or extinguish the related liabilities, nor should the assets restricted for payment of AROs be used to offset the related liabilities. Any costs associated with complying with funding and assurance provisions should be accounted for separately from the AROs.

Key point
Legal, regulatory, or contractual requirements may require a government to set aside assets restricted for payment of an ARO. Restricted in this context has the same meaning as restricted net position as discussed in GASB Statement No. 34.

Disclosures relating to AROs

Notes to the financial statements

Unless a government has a minority share of an ARO in an undivided interest arrangement, a government should disclose the following information about its AROs:

- General description of the AROs and associated tangible capital assets, as well as the source of the obligations (whether they are a result of federal, state, or local laws or regulations, contracts, or court judgments)
- Methods and assumptions used to measure the liabilities
- Estimated remaining useful life of the associated tangible capital assets
- How any legally required funding and assurance provisions associated with AROs are being met (surety bonds, insurance policies, letters of credit, guarantees by other entities, or trusts used for funding and assurance)
- Amount of assets restricted for payment of the liabilities, if not separately displayed in the financial statements
- If an ARO or portions thereof has been incurred by a government but is not yet recognized because it is not reasonably estimable, the government should disclose this fact and the reasons therefore.

Governments with a minority share of an ARO

A government with a minority share of an ARO should disclose the following information about its minority share:

- General description of the ARO and associated tangible capital asset, including
  - total amount of the ARO shared by the nongovernmental majority owner or the nongovernmental minority owner that has operational responsibility, other minority owners, if any, and the reporting government
  - reporting government's minority share of the total amount of the ARO, stated as a percentage
  - dollar amount of the reporting government's minority share of the ARO
- Date of the measurement of the ARO produced by the nongovernmental majority owner or the nongovernmental minority owner that has operational responsibility, if that date differs from the government's reporting date
- How any legally required funding and assurance provisions associated with the government's minority share of an ARO are being met (surety bonds, insurance policies, letters of credit, guarantees by other entities, or trusts used for funding and assurance)
- Amount of assets restricted for payment of the government's minority share of the ARO, if not separately displayed in the financial statements.

Key point
An ARO or portions thereof that has been incurred by a government but is not yet recognized because it is not reasonably estimable, the government should disclose this fact and the reasons therefor.

Knowledge check

3. Which is **not** required to be disclosed in the notes to the financial statements under the requirements of GASB Statement No. 83?

   a. General description of the ARO and associated tangible capital assets.
   b. Assets available for payment of ARO liabilities.
   c. Methods and assumptions used to measure the liabilities.
   d. How any legally required funding and assurance provisions associated with AROs are being met.

Financial reporting

Upon initial implementation

GASB Statement No. 83 is effective for periods beginning after June 15, 2018. When the requirements of the statement are first applied, changes resulting from these requirements should be applied retroactively by restating financial statements, if practicable, for all prior periods presented.

If restatement for prior periods is not practicable, the cumulative effect of applying the requirements of GASB Statement No. 83, if any, should be reported as a restatement of beginning net position (or fund balance or fund net position) for the earliest period restated. The reason for not restating prior periods presented should also be disclosed. In the first period the requirements of the statement are applied, notes to the financial statements should disclose the nature of any restatement and its effect.

Knowledge check

4. What is **not** required when the requirements of GASB Statement No. 83 are first applied?

    a. Changes resulting from the requirements should be applied retroactively by restating all prior periods presented.
    b. Cumulative effect of applying the requirements should be reported when restatement of prior periods is not practicable.
    c. Reasons for not restating prior periods when it is not practicable to do so.
    d. Cost of implementing the requirements in the first year of application.

Implementation challenges

As can be seen from the previous sections, GASB Statement No. 83 has the potential to significantly affect state and local governments. A summary of the practice areas most affected by GASB Statement No. 83 includes the following:

- Understanding the requirements of the statement
- Identifying tangible capital assets with asset retirement activities
- Allocating human and financial resources
- Measuring AROs
- Determining financial statement amounts and allocations
- Communicating with elected officials and other stakeholders

The issues relating to the initial implementation and ongoing application of GASB Statement No. 83 affect governments differently as the requirements vary based on the existence of and type of AROs. Therefore, the following general discussion of implementation issues and how to mitigate them will affect state and local governments and their auditors differently.

Understanding the requirements of the statement

Preparers and auditors of government financial statements will need to be familiar with the requirements of GASB Statement No. 83. In addition, it may be necessary to educate staff, elected officials, and other stakeholders.

Identifying tangible capital assets with asset retirement activities

Upon implementation, it is extremely important for state and local governments to determine what tangible capital assets are subject to the requirements of GASB Statement No. 83. Some examples of tangible capital assets that are typically subject to legal requirements requiring asset retirement activities include:

- Solid waste treatment facilities
- Solid waste percolation ponds
- X-ray equipment
- Fuel tanks
- Nuclear power plants
- Wind turbines

Once relevant tangible capital assets have been identified, it will be necessary to identify and document all external events resulting from laws, regulations, contracts, and court judgments requiring asset retirement activities. All internal obligating events will need to be identified and documented. Each subsequent year, it will be necessary to ensure that any additional external or internal obligating events have occurred or if any previously identified obligating events have changed.

Allocating human and financial resources

Much of the information needed to initially implement and annually apply the requirements of GASB Statement No. 83 will likely be the responsibility of a government's accounting and finance personnel. It is unlikely these personnel will have the expertise needed to measure the AROs in the year of implementation or in subsequent fiscal periods.

In-house or external consulting engineers or other professionals will be needed to identify the tangible capital assets subject to retirement activities as well as to provide information to measure the related AROs. The need for these services in the year of implementation, as well as in subsequent years, will require funding or redeployment of engineering or other professional staff. It is imperative that a government budget adequate time and financial resources to obtain the information required to properly implement and annually apply the statement. Ideally, these amounts would be included in the annual budget for, at a minimum, the fiscal year in which the government will be required to implement GASB Statement No. 83.

Measuring AROs

Upon initial implementation and each year thereafter, management and the engineers or other professionals will need to establish or review the asset retirement activities as well as the current value of these activities.

Timing of any internally or externally prepared reports will need to be determined early in the initial implementation process and every year thereafter. The earlier this date can be determined, the more time accounting and finance staff will have to prepare the information needed to account for and report the government's AROs.

Key point
Key decisions relating to AROs need to be made as soon as possible to ensure a government will be able to timely apply the requirements of GASB Statement No. 83.

Determining financial statement amounts and allocations

Bases used to allocate ARO-related amounts between governmental and business-type activities and between functions in the government-wide and fund level statements will need to be initially determined and reviewed each year thereafter for continued applicability and reasonableness. At a minimum, governments will need to ascertain the rationale used to allocate amounts is appropriate and consistent with the functions typically charged with any asset retirement activities.

Communicating with elected officials and other stakeholders

Because there is potential for a government to have a significant ARO liability, financial statement preparers and their auditors will need to determine what effect, if any, implementation and ongoing application of GASB Statement No. 83 will have on the government's financial statements as soon as possible. It is possible that ARO-related amounts reported in the financial statements of a government may affect how a credit analyst views the government's credit risk. Governments may want to discuss the potential impact of the requirements of GASB Statement No. 83 with bond trustees and credit analysts, as well as their elected officials, as soon as possible.

Knowledge check

5. As discussed in this section what is **not** an example of a tangible capital asset typically subject to legal requirements requiring asset retirement activities?

    a. Solid waste treatment facilities.
    b. X-ray equipment.
    c. Wind turbines.
    d. Fossil fuel power plants.

Summary

This chapter discusses the requirements of GASB Statement No. 83 relating to the measurement and reporting of AROs. The chapter discusses key terms established with GASB Statement No. 83 and provides an overview of the measurement, accounting, and reporting requirements for AROs. Additionally, the chapter discusses the required disclosures relating to AROs as well as potential issues associated with initial and subsequent measurement and reporting of AROs.

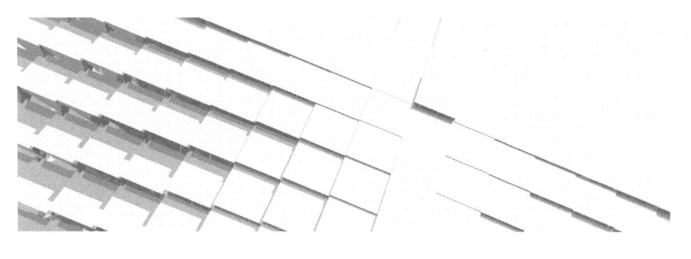

Chapter 5

Accounting for Special Events by Not-for-Profit Entities[1]

Learning objectives

- Identify the revenue recognition requirements relating to special events.

- Determine how to recognize costs relating to special events.

- Identify how to account for special event receipts representing both an exchange transaction and a contribution.

- Identify the various ways special events can be presented in the statement of activities.

---

[1] FASB issued ASU No. 2014-09, *Revenue from Contracts with Customers (Topic 606)*, in May 2014. See appendix A for a high-level overview of the standard and a discussion of the areas to which not-for-profit entities will likely need to apply the requirements of the standard.

Major areas of inquiry

Many not-for-profit entities hold special events as part of their fundraising activities. Special events are recorded depending on the particular facts and circumstances surrounding each special event. Generally accepted accounting principles (GAAP) allow several options for reporting special events on the statement of activities. Questions raised by preparers and auditors of financial statements of not-for-profit entities relating to accounting and reporting special events by not-for-profit entities include the following areas:

- Recognition of revenue from *special events*
- Accounting for special events *transactions crossing fiscal reporting periods*
- Determining the appropriate *financial statement presentation* of special events

Overview[2]

Not-for-profit entities conduct a variety of fundraising activities, including special social and educational events. These special events range from sophisticated formal dinner dances to parking lot chili cook-off competitions; however, in most cases, supporters and attendees of these events receive a *direct benefit* of some value.

Special events commonly sponsored by not-for-profit entities include the following:

- Breakfast, luncheon, or dinner events
- Dinner dances
- Silent and live auctions (separately or as part of a specific special event)
- Sports tournaments (such as golf, fishing, tennis, and so on)
- Track and field races and events
- Symposiums featuring recognized authors, actors, medical professionals, and so on
- Performing arts productions (such as theater, symphony, opera, and so on)
- Culinary events (such as cook-offs, food and beverage tasting, and so on)
- Days/nights at local attractions or other areas of interest

The *frequency* of a special event and the *significance* of the gross revenues and expenses determine how a not-for-profit entity will report special events in the statement of activities. Due to the diverse nature of not-for-profit entities, the same type of special event may be reported differently on the statement of activities by different not-for-profit entities.

---

[2] Revenue recognition issues related to contributions and selected exchange transactions are not within the scope of this chapter.

Revenue recognition[3]

Under GAAP, *revenues and expenses* are generated from *ongoing major or central operations* and *gains and losses* typically result from transactions or events *incidental or peripheral* to the operations of the entity. Similarly, *revenue is recognized when identified performance obligations have been satisfied and expenses are incurred* when an entity has substantially accomplished what it must do to be entitled to the benefits represented by the revenues and expenses. On the other hand, *gains and losses* involve no earning process; therefore, gains and losses are recognized when *realized or realizable* rather than being earned or incurred, respectively.

Judgment is often involved in determining if a special event should be recognized as revenue and expenses or as a gain or loss. When accounting for special events, a not-for-profit entity must first determine if the event is either

- an *ongoing major* event;
- *central to the operations* of the not-for-profit entity; or
- *incidental or peripheral to the operations* of the not-for-profit entity.

In the statement of activities, a special event that is ongoing or central to the operations of a not-for-profit entity is recognized as *donor-restricted support or revenue without donor restrictions*. GAAP defines ongoing major and central activities or events as those that

- are normally part of a not-for-profit entity's strategy and it normally carries on such activities; or
- generate gross revenues or incur expenses that are significant in relation to the not-for-profit entity's annual budget.

Special events incidental or peripheral to operations are recognized as a *net gain or loss* in the statement of activities. Net losses on special events are not required to be reported by functional classification in the statement of activities, notes to the financial statements, or analysis of expenses by their nature and function. GAAP define incidental or peripheral events as being either

- not an integral part of a not-for-profit entity's usual activities; or
- not significant in relation to a not-for-profit entity's annual budget.

---

[3] In June 2018, FASB issued ASU No. 2018-08, which is generally effective for annual periods beginning after December 15, 2018, for public entities and not-for-profit entities involved in certain public securities transactions. For all other entities, the requirements are generally effective for periods beginning after December 15, 2019. The ASU provides guidance to evaluate whether transactions should be accounted for as contributions (nonreciprocal transactions) within the scope of FASB Accounting Standards Codification (ASC) 958, *Not-for-Profit Entities*, or as exchange (reciprocal) transactions subject to other guidance and (2) determining whether a contribution is conditional. This chapter, where relevant, has been updated for ASU No. 2018-08. Please see appendix B for a high-level overview of the ASU and a discussion of how it may affect current practice.

Key point
A special event reported as revenue in one not-for-profit entity might be reported as a gain or loss in another not-for-profit entity.

Knowledge check

1. How are revenues and expenses of a special event that are incidental to the operations of a not-for-profit entity generally reported?

    a. Gross revenues and gross expenses.
    b. Gross revenues reduced by direct benefits to donors.
    c. As an extraordinary item.
    d. Net gain or net loss.

Reporting costs relating to special events

General

Special events may be conducted solely as fundraising activities or as "joint activities," which include fundraising activities as well as components of *program* or *management and general activities.* As discussed previously in this chapter, reporting costs associated with special events depends on whether it is a major, ongoing, or central event or incidental or peripheral to operations. However, the reporting of costs associated with special events also depends on whether the event is conducted as a joint activity.

Costs incurred in connection with special events are classified as any or all of the following:

- *Direct benefits received by donors* or attendees (such as meals, facility rentals, entertainment, and so on)
- *Direct costs* not specifically benefiting donors or attendees (such as invitations, postage, advertising, and so on)
- *Indirect costs* (such as staff time and expenses allocated to the special event)
- *Fundraising* expenses

Special events as joint activities

For special events that are joint activities, the *purpose, audience, and content criteria* should be met to allocate the costs of the event, other than the direct benefits received by donors or attendees, between fundraising and, as appropriate, program and management and general functions.[4] *If neither the purpose, audience, nor content criterion can be met, all costs of a special event, other than those representing direct benefits received by donors or attendees, should be reported as fundraising expenses.*

Knowledge check

2. Which is accurate relating to allocating costs associated with special events conducted as joint activities?

    a. The purpose, audience, and content criteria must be met.
    b. Only the purpose and audience criteria must be met.
    c. Only the purpose and content criteria must be met.
    d. The purpose, audience, and content criteria need not be met.

---

[4] A detailed discussion of joint activities, joint costs, and allocation of joint costs is beyond the scope of this chapter and this course. Additional information related to joint activities and joint costs can be found in the FASB *Accounting Standards Codification* (ASC) 958-720.

Special event as a joint activity example

A not-for-profit entity is required by its bylaws to hold a meeting of the board of directors open to all members at least annually. To facilitate this, the not-for-profit entity sponsors a dinner dance during which the business of the required annual meeting is conducted. The dinner dance is also open to the public and serves as a major fundraising activity for the not-for-profit entity. As such, planning and executing the special event involve a significant amount of time and effort on the part of volunteers and staff. Assuming the purpose, audience, and content criteria are met, the costs associated with the dinner dance are related and can be allocated to

- management and general activities;
- fundraising activities;
- direct costs (such as direct benefits and other direct costs of the dinner dance); and
- indirect costs for the staff time, and so on involved in organizing the dinner dance.

Direct costs and direct benefits to donors

Major, ongoing, or central special events

Direct and indirect costs of special events conducted as *joint activities meeting the purpose, audience, and content criteria* are recognized as special event costs (including direct benefits received by donors or attendees). Special event costs are required to be reported by their natural classification in the not-for-profit entity's analysis of expenses by their nature and function. For *joint activities not meeting the purpose, audience, and content criteria,* only costs associated with direct benefits to donors or attendees would be reported as special event costs. Any other direct costs are recognized as *fundraising expenses* (and expensed in the period incurred regardless of when the special event occurs) because the criteria to allocate joint costs are not met.

For special events conducted solely as *fundraising activities,* direct benefits received by donors or attendees are reported as special event costs. All other direct and indirect costs are reported as *fundraising expenses* when incurred.

Incidental or peripheral special events

Costs netted against receipts from special events that are *not joint activities* and that are incidental or peripheral to the operations of a not-for-profit entity should be *limited to direct costs* (including direct benefits). It is not appropriate to allocate indirect costs against receipts from special events that are incidental or peripheral to the operations of the not-for-profit entity.

However, if the purpose, audience, and content criteria are not met for special events that *are joint activities* and that are incidental or peripheral to the operations of a not-for-profit entity, accounting for the costs of the event is different. Costs netted against receipts from special events that are joint activities, *not meeting the purpose, audience, and content criteria,* should be *limited to direct benefits received by donors and attendees.*

Special events accounting and reporting considerations

Special events as exchange transactions and contributions

Pricing for a special event may be structured such that the amount charged to attend is approximately equal to the benefit received by the attendee — in other words it is an *exchange transaction*. Conversely, the amount charged may be in excess of the benefit received by the donor or attendee — in this case it is *part exchange transaction and part contribution.* In addition, those providing goods and services for a special event may provide them at no charge — resulting in *a contribution* — or at amounts less than the fair value of the related goods or services — that is *part exchange transaction and part contribution*.

When the receipts of a special event represent both an exchange transaction and a contribution, a not-for-profit entity may choose to bifurcate the receipts to reflect the duality of the transaction. The accounting for special events recognized as both an exchange transaction and a contribution is discussed in the following sections.

Exchange transaction portion

To the extent special event receipts represent an exchange transaction they are recognized as revenue when the identified performance obligations are satisfied or as a net gain or loss when realized or realizable. The portion of special event receipts relating to an exchange transaction is not recognized as revenue until the event is held and therefore would be reported as a contract liability until such time.

Contribution portion

Accounting for the portion of the receipts representing a contribution *depends on whether the contribution is unconditional or conditional.*

Unconditional contributions

For unconditional contributions, the contribution portion of the special event receipts is recognized when received or promised. The unconditional contribution portion of special event receipts received in advance of the event is reported as *donor-restricted support* (restricted for time until the event occurs) when received or promised. Unless purpose restrictions have been placed on the contribution, net assets with donor restrictions are released when the event is held and reclassified as net assets without donor restrictions.

Conditional contributions

FASB ASU No. 2018-08, *Not-for-Profit Entities (Topic 958): Clarifying the Scope and the Accounting Guidance for Contributions Received and Contributions Made*, requires a not-for-profit entity to determine whether a contribution is conditional on the basis of whether an agreement includes a barrier that must be overcome and either

- a right of return of assets transferred or
- a right of release of a promisor's obligation to transfer assets.

For a donor-imposed condition to exist, it must be determinable from the agreement or any other document referenced in the agreement. In addition, barriers exist that must be overcome for the not-for-profit entity to be entitled to the transferred assets or future transfer of assets. In cases of ambiguous donor stipulations, a contribution agreement including stipulations that are not clearly unconditional shall be presumed to be a conditional contribution.

ASU No. 2108-08 does not specifically state that an agreement between the not-for-profit entity and the donor is required to be in writing. However, the ASU does state "an agreement should be sufficiently clear to be able to support a reasonable conclusion about when a recipient would be entitled to the transfer of assets." The ASU also states the agreement need not include the specific language "right of return" or "right of release."

In some cases, a planned special event may not actually be held. For example, inclement weather may cause an outdoor event, such as a golf tournament or 5K run, to be canceled. As such, this possibility would represent a barrier the not-for-profit entity would need to overcome before recognizing the contribution portion of any funds received relating to the event. Such a barrier might not be considered to exist in certain circumstances. For example, if the event has been insured or if the not-for-profit promotes the event as being rescheduled in the event of inclement weather, there is no barrier to the event occurring. The determination of whether or not a barrier exists is a matter of judgment and is based on facts and circumstances.

When planning for special events, the not-for-profit entity typically will determine when, or if, a donor/sponsor would be entitled to a refund of any monies paid in advance of the special event (that is a right of return). Additionally, the not-for-profit entity will determine if a donor/sponsor would be relieved from a promise to attend/sponsor the event (that is a right of release) during the planning for the event. If there is a barrier to the special event occurring, the existence of such barrier and either of these circumstances indicate the not-for-profit entity sponsoring the special event would not be entitled to any monies paid in advance of the event until the barrier (that is holding the special event) is overcome.

Indicating that an event will be rescheduled in the event of inclement weather printed on event tickets, flyers mailed, advertisements, and the like may be sufficient to conclude a right of return does not exist. In this case, the transfer of assets is not conditional, and the not-for-profit would recognize a contribution without donor-imposed condition. The not-for-profit entity is entitled to the assets because there is only a barrier to overcome.

On the other hand, if a not-for-profit entity has a policy (formal or informal) of not pursuing donors or sponsors who promise to give or sponsor but do not pay, this may be sufficient to conclude a right of release exists. This right of release, coupled with the barrier of the event needing to occur, represents a contribution with donor-imposed conditions, and the not-for-profit entity is not entitled to the transferred assets until the barrier is overcome.

The portion of special event receipts relating to conditional contributions is not recognized as contribution revenue until the conditions have been substantially met (that is, the donor-imposed barrier has been overcome) or have been explicitly waived by the donor. Special event receipts received in advance relating to conditional contributions are recognized as *refundable advances* until any barriers specified in the agreement have been overcome.

Special event as exchange transaction and contribution example

A not-for-profit entity sponsors an annual golf tournament to provide funds for general operations. The not-for-profit is obligated to refund entrance fees if inclement weather does not allow the tournament to be held or requires the tournament to be rescheduled.

Of the $200-per-person refundable entrance fee, $80 represents the amounts paid to the golf course for greens and cart fees and $20 represents the cost of a box lunch provided to all golfers. The remaining $100 represents a contribution that is conditional upon the event being held. This condition represents a barrier, and the obligation to refund entrance fees represents a right of return of any funds advanced to the donor. As such, management has concluded this meets the requirements to be accounted for as a conditional contribution.

No specific performance obligations are identified in the contract other than playing golf and eating lunch on the date of the event. Accounting for the entrance fee as a bifurcated transaction is as follows:

Upon receipt of the entrance fee

Cash	$200		
Contract liability		$100	Greens/cart fees and lunch
Refundable advances		100	Contribution portion

When the tournament is held, and the golf course is paid

Contract liability	$100		
Special event revenues		$100	Greens/cart fees and lunch
Refundable advances	100		
Contribution revenue		100	Contribution portion
Direct benefits to donors	100		
Cash		100	Greens/cart fees and lunch

On the other hand, if the not-for-profit entity were to purchase event insurance or clearly communicate the entrance fees are nonrefundable for any reason, there is no barrier associated with the transfer of the assets provided by the donor. Therefore, the contribution portion of the receipt would be unconditional. Accounting for the $200 entrance fee as a bifurcated transaction in this case is as follows:

Upon receipt of the entrance fee

Cash	$200		
Contract liability		$100	Greens/cart fees and lunch
Support without donor restrictions		100	Contribution portion

When the tournament is held, and the golf course is paid

Contract liability	$100		
Special event revenues		$100	Greens/cart fees and lunch
Assets released from donor restrictions	100		Donor restricted
Assets released from donor restrictions		100	Without donor restrictions
Direct benefits to donors	100		Greens/cart fees and lunch
Cash		100	

Knowledge check

3. When no specific performance obligations are identified other than to hold an event, when is the exchange portion of special event receipts recognized?

    a. When the ticket to the event is purchased.
    b. When the promise to buy a ticket is given.
    c. When the special event is held.
    d. When the ticket purchaser attends the event.

Special events and donated items

Goods (such as gifts in kind) and services might be *contributed* to a not-for-profit entity for use in a special event, or vendors might offer to provide goods and services for the special event at *reduced rates*. Some goods and services necessary to the entity, coordination, and execution of a special event (such as advertising, audiovisual equipment use and operation, facility use, and so on) might be donated. On the other hand, other goods and services might be donated for use during the special event (such as door prizes, raffle prizes, auction items, and so on).

GAAP require gifts in kind that can be *used or sold* to be measured at fair value and recognized as *contributions when received or promised.* In the context of special events, *contributed services* would be recognized as revenue without donor support (offset as assets or expenses) if the services meet all of the following criteria:

- Require specialized skills
- Performed by individuals possessing those skills
- Would typically need to be purchased if not provided by contribution

To the extent that vendors offer goods and services at reduced rates, the difference between the fair value of the goods and services and the amount paid by the not-for-profit entity may be recognized as

---

revenue without donor restrictions. If the vendor offers the same types of goods and services at reduced rates for almost any entity's special events, there would be no difference in the fair value of the goods and services and the amount paid by the not-for-profit entity. In these cases, the difference in the fair value and the amount paid is in essence a trade discount. When determining fair value, the quality and quantity of the goods and services, *as well as any applicable discounts* the not-for-profit entity would have received (including any quantity discounts), are considered.

Donations of items for special events are *nonfinancial assets* representing conditional or unconditional contributions. A donated item would be a *conditional contribution* if the donor specifies the specific special event for which it is to be used (a barrier) and if the item is to be returned if the event is not held or the item is not used as specified (right of return). A not-for-profit entity is *permitted, but not required, to recognize conditional contributions that are nonfinancial assets*. All donated goods and services are recognized at their fair value on the date of the donation (that is, not the date they are used).[5]

A donor may simply specify that the not-for-profit entity use the donated item for its tax-exempt purpose if the event is not held. In these circumstances, the donated item is recognized as a *contribution without donor restrictions* as it is *unconditional*. (There is no barrier because the entity is able to use the donated item if the auction is not held.) As such, donor-restricted support (time restriction until the event occurs) would be recognized upon receipt of the item and offset with an asset such as "inventory" or "prepaid special event costs."[6] This asset account would be eliminated and recognized as "direct benefits to donors" if the donated item is used at the event.

If the item is not used at the event, the donor restriction is released and net assets with donor restrictions would be reclassified as net assets without donor restrictions. An element of program or management and general activities would be recognized when the donated item is used by the not-for-profit entity for its tax-exempt purpose.

> If items are donated for a specific special event in the same year the event is held, a not-for-profit entity might, as a practical matter, choose to recognize such donated items as contribution revenue when the event is held.

---

[5] If donated items are subsequently sold (such as in an auction), the difference between the amount received for those items and the fair value of the donated items when originally contributed to the not-for-profit entity is recognized as adjustments to the original contribution when the items are transferred to the buyer.

[6] The option to recognize or not recognize contributions that are nonfinancial assets is only relevant for *conditional contributions*. GAAP require recognition of unconditional contributions (financial or nonfinancial assets) when received or promised.

Knowledge check

4. Which is accurate relating to goods and services donated, without any donor-specified conditions, for a special event?

   a. Donated goods and services are not recognized until the event is held.
   b. Donated goods and services are recognized at fair value.
   c. Donated goods and services are recognized at the donor's cost, billing rate, or salary.
   d. Donated services need not meet the criteria for donated services to be recognized because the services relate to a special event.

Special events and fiscal reporting periods

In some cases, the planning for a special event occurs well in advance of the date the special event is held. Such activities may need to be accounted for in more than one fiscal reporting period.

Reporting revenues

For special event receipts accounted for as a bifurcated transaction, the portion of the receipts relating to an *exchange transaction* is not recognized as revenue until the identified performance obligations are satisfied. Therefore, the exchange transaction portion of special event receipts received in one year for an event to be held in the subsequent period should be reported as a contract liability.

Accounting for special event receipts that are *contributions*, in whole or part, depends on whether the contribution is conditional or unconditional. Special event receipts received in one year for an event to be held in the subsequent period relating to unconditional contributions should be reported as donor-restricted support (restricted for time) in the year they are received or promised. The portion of special event receipts related to conditional contributions is not recognized as contribution revenue until the conditions have been met (the barrier is overcome) or substantially met. Therefore, special event receipts received in one year for an event to be held in the subsequent period related to conditional contributions are recognized as *refundable advances* (that is, until the conditions have been met or substantially met — typically when the event is held).

Reporting costs

Direct and indirect costs

Direct and indirect costs of special events conducted as *joint activities meeting the purpose, audience, and content criteria* are recognized as special event costs (including direct benefits to donors or attendees). Direct and indirect costs incurred in one year for a special event to be held in the subsequent period are *reported as an asset* such as "prepaid expenses" or "prepaid special event costs."

For joint *activities not meeting the purpose, audience, and content criteria,* only costs associated with *direct benefits to donors or attendees* would be reported as an asset such as "prepaid expenses" or "prepaid special event costs." Any other direct costs are recognized as fundraising expenses when incurred because the criteria to allocate joint costs are not met. GAAP requires all fundraising costs be expensed in the period incurred. Therefore, there is no difference in accounting for fundraising costs incurred in one year for a special event to be held in the subsequent period and those incurred in the same period a special event occurs.

Direct and indirect costs of special events conducted solely as *fundraising activities* are reported as *fundraising expenses* and discussed further in the following section.

Fundraising costs

If a special event is conducted solely as a fundraising activity or it is a joint activity not meeting the purpose, audience, and content criteria, any costs not representing direct benefits to donors should be reported when incurred as fundraising expenses in the statement of activities. GAAP require all fundraising costs to be recognized as expenses when incurred, regardless of the period benefited. Recognition of direct and indirect costs for special events meeting the purpose, audience, and content criteria is discussed previously.

Key point
GAAP requires all fundraising costs to be reported as fundraising expenses on the statement of activities, regardless of when the benefits of such costs will be received. Practically speaking, fundraising costs can never represent prepaid expenses.

Reporting special events in the statement of activities

GAAP provides a number of options for reporting special events in the statement of activities. FASB provides three illustrations in *Accounting Standards Codification* (ASC) 958-220-55 using an example of a special event that is an ongoing and major activity conducted as a joint activity. As a joint activity, the event does not meet the audience criterion.

Following are three examples using the same reporting options in FASB ASC 958-220-55; however, the facts and circumstances are slightly different, and the special event meets the purpose, audience, and content criteria.

Additional facts reflected in the following examples are as follows:

- The event is conducted to recognize outstanding program participants and to raise money to support various programs.
- Price to attend the event is $100 per person and neither the ticket or promotional materials specify any specific performance obligations other than to hold the event and provide dinner.
- All promotional materials and tickets state amounts will be refunded if the event is not held.
- The event includes a dinner with a cost to the not-for-profit entity of $25 and a fair value of $30.
- Other direct costs of $15, unrelated to the direct benefits received by donors, are incurred to promote and conduct the event. Included in the $15 are payroll and payroll-related costs for staff time spent coordinating and organizing the event.
- Two-thirds of the joint costs are allocated to program and one-third is allocated to fundraising.
- For illustrative purposes, the following transactions, unrelated to the special event, occurred:

Contribution revenue without donor restrictions	$200
Program expenses	60
Management and general expenses	20
Fundraising expenses	20

Example 1 – Direct Benefits to Donors Netted with Event Revenue

Changes in net assets without donor restrictions:

Contributions		$	200
Special event revenue	$ 100		
Less: costs of direct benefits to donors	(25)		
Net revenues from special events			75
Contributions and net revenues from special events			275
Other expenses:			
Program[1]			70
Management and general			20
Fundraising[2]			40
Total other expenses			130
Increase in net assets without donor restrictions		$	145

Example 2 – Direct Benefits to Donors Included as Expenses

Changes in net assets without donor restrictions:

Contributions	$	200
Special event revenue		100
Contributions and net revenues from special events		300
Other expenses:		
Program[1]		70
Costs of direct benefits to donors		25
Management and general		20
Fundraising[2]		40
Total other expenses		155
Increase in net assets without donor restrictions	$	145

Example 3 – Bifurcation of Exchange Transaction and Contribution

Changes in net assets without donor restrictions:

Contributions		$	270
Special event revenue	$ 30		
Less: costs of direct benefits to donors	(25)		
Net revenues from special events			5
Contributions and net revenues from special events			275
Other expenses:			
Program[1]			70
Management and general			20
Fundraising[2]			40
Total other expenses			130
Increase in net assets without donor restrictions		$	145

[1] Includes $10 of joint costs allocated two thirds to program and one third to fundraising.

[2] Includes $5 of joint costs allocated two thirds to program and one third to fundraising.

Summary

This chapter discusses selected revenue and cost recognition issues relating to special events held by not-for-profit entities. The chapter includes a detailed discussion of how special event receipts are classified, based on whether they are ongoing major events or incidental or peripheral to the operations of a not-for-profit entity. Additionally, the chapter discusses how costs associated with special events are recognized, including those relating to special events conducted as joint activities. Special accounting and reporting issues associated with special events are also discussed in this chapter. Items included in the discussion are (*a*) special event receipts as exchange transactions and contributions, (*b*) donated goods and services relating to special events, and (*c*) special event activities that are incurred in one year with event held in the subsequent year. The chapter concludes with three illustrations of reporting revenue and costs associated with special events conducted as a joint activity and meeting the purpose, audience, and content criteria.

Practice questions

1. What criteria determine if a special event is accounted for as revenue?

2. What criteria determine if a special event is accounted for as a gain?

3. How are ongoing major and central activities defined under GAAP?

4. How are *incidental and peripheral activities* defined under GAAP?

5. If a major ongoing special event is conducted as a joint activity and the purpose, audience, and content criteria are not met, how are the costs associated with the event reported?

6. If a major ongoing special event is conducted as a joint activity and the purpose, audience, and content criteria are met, how are the costs associated with the event reported?

7. How are special event receipts received in one year for an ongoing major special event to be held in the subsequent year accounted for in a bifurcated transaction?

Chapter 6

Audit Sampling

Learning objectives

- Identify the responsibilities of the auditor when he or she decides to use audit sampling in performing audit procedures.

- Determine the difference between statistical and nonstatistical samples.

- Identify the types of techniques used to select items for a sample.

- Determine the factors affecting size of a sample for a substantive test of details.

- Determine the factors affecting the interpretation of sampling results.

Major areas of inquiry

Sampling in a financial statement audit relates to when audit procedures are applied to less than 100% of the items within an account balance or class of transactions. Professional standards require the auditor to obtain sufficient appropriate audit evidence to provide a reasonable basis for an opinion on the financial statements. Auditors often use sampling to improve audit efficiency when performing audit procedures designed to obtain such evidence.

Use of sampling in the application of audit procedures requires a significant amount of judgment on the part of the auditor. Proper use of sampling procedures, application of sampling techniques, and evaluation of sampling results continue to be areas found to be deficient in peer reviews, inspector general investigations, and other types of practice reviews. Sampling is another area where documentation is often found to be missing or inadequate. Calls received by the AICPA Technical Hotline about sampling relate primarily to the following areas:

- Statistical sampling
- Testing internal controls
- Sampling and substantive tests of details
- Sample size
- Selecting items for a sample
- Evaluating sample results

Overview

Often, the auditor is aware of account balances and transactions that may be more or less likely to contain misstatements. Conversely, the auditor may have no special knowledge about other account balances and transactions. This collective knowledge is used in planning the audit procedures to be performed, including the use and application of sampling. AU-C section 530, *Audit Sampling* (AICPA, *Professional Standards*), defines the professional standards associated with the use of sampling in a financial statement audit.

In addition, the AICPA has issued an Audit Guide, *Audit Sampling*,[1] to assist auditors in designing and performing sampling in a financial statement audit conducted in accordance with generally accepted auditing standards. This guide includes guidance on the application of sampling to tests of controls and substantive tests of details, including determining the sample size and evaluating sample results, as well as guidance on following nonstatistical and statistical audit sampling[2] approaches. Additionally, the guide summarizes applicable requirements and practices and delivers "how-to" advice for audit sampling. Case studies are included to illustrate the use of different sampling methods in real-world situations. The appendixes include sampling tables, testing considerations, and a comparison of the key provisions of the risk assessment standards.

Knowledge check

1. The AICPA Audit Guide, *Audit Sampling*, does **not** provide guidance in

    a. Assisting auditors in designing and performing sampling in a financial statement audit conducted in accordance with generally accepted auditing standards.
    b. Application of nonstatistical and statistical sampling techniques to tests of controls and substantive tests of details.
    c. Application of only nonstatistical sampling techniques to tests of controls and substantive tests of details.
    d. Determining the sample size and evaluating sample results.

---

[1] This guide is available from the AICPA at www.AICPAStore.com.

[2] Statistical sampling is an approach to sampling with the following characteristics:

   a. Random selection of the sample items.
   b. The use of an appropriate statistical technique to evaluate sample results, including measurement of sampling risk.

   A sampling approach lacking both of these characteristics is considered nonstatistical sampling.

AU-C section 530 addresses the following with respect to audit sampling:

- Definitions
- Sample size design, size, and selection of items for testing
- Performing audit procedures
- Nature and cause of deviations and misstatements
- Projecting the results of audit sampling
- Evaluating the results of audit sampling
- Extensive application material relating to sample design and size

Key point
AU-C section 530 does not require the use of sampling in a financial statement audit. However, when the auditor decides to use audit sampling in performing audit procedures, the requirements of AU-C section 530 apply.

Uncertainty and audit sampling

Audit risk includes uncertainties related to sampling (sampling risk) and to factors other than sampling (nonsampling risk). Sampling risk is the risk that the auditor's conclusions based on a sample might have been different if the entire population had been tested.[3] Nonsampling risk is all aspects of audit risk not due to sampling.[4] Adequate planning and supervision, as well as an effective quality control system in the audit firm, help reduce nonsampling risk to negligible levels.

Definitions

Terms used in this chapter are consistent with those used in AU-C section 530 and in the AICPA Audit Guide *Audit Sampling*. Auditors may use various terms in their application of audit sampling techniques as long as they understand the relationship of those terms to AU-C section 530 and to *Audit Sampling*. Following are selected terms defined in AU-C section 530 and not previously defined in this chapter:

Population — Entire set of data from which a sample is selected and about which the auditor wishes to draw conclusions

Sampling unit — Individual items constituting a population

Stratification — Process of dividing a population into subpopulations, each of which is a group of sampling units having similar characteristics

Tolerable misstatement — Monetary amount set by the auditor in respect of which he or she seeks to obtain an appropriate level of assurance that the monetary amount set by the auditor is not exceeded by the actual misstatement in the population. Tolerable misstatement is the application of performance materiality[5] to a particular sampling procedure. Therefore, it may be the same amount or a smaller amount than performance materiality. In either case, tolerable misstatement is a different concept than performance materiality, and audit documentation

---

[3] Sampling risk can lead to two types of erroneous conclusions:
   a. In the case of a test of controls, that controls are more effective than they actually are. Likewise, in the case of a test of details, that a material misstatement does not exist when, in fact, it does. The auditor is primarily concerned with this type of erroneous conclusion because it affects audit effectiveness and is more likely to lead to an inappropriate audit opinion.
   b. In the case of a test of controls, that the controls are less effective than they actually are. Likewise, in the case of a test of details, that a material misstatement exists when, in fact, it does not. This type of erroneous conclusion affects audit efficiency because it would usually lead to additional to establish whether his or her initial conclusions were incorrect.

[4] Examples of nonsampling risk include selecting audit procedures that are not appropriate to achieve the given objectives and failing to recognize a misstatement included in the documents examined by the auditor.

[5] Performance materiality is discussed in AU-C section 320, *Materiality in Planning and Performing an Audit* (AICPA *Professional Standards*). Performance materiality relates to financial statements as a whole, account balances, classes of transactions, or disclosures while tolerable misstatement applies to sampling procedures.

---

would need to reference performance materiality and tolerable misstatement in the proper contexts.

Tolerable rate of deviation — Rate of deviation set by the auditor in respect of which the auditor seeks to obtain an appropriate level of assurance that the rate of deviation set by the auditor is not exceeded by the actual rate of deviation in the population.

Key point
Audit risk includes uncertainties related to sampling (sampling risk) and to factors other than sampling (nonsampling risk). Adequate planning and supervision as well as an effective quality control system in the audit firm help reduce nonsampling risk to negligible levels.

Procedures not involving audit sampling

Not all audit procedures involve the use of audit sampling. Areas where audit sampling is not typically involved include the following:

- Inquiry and observation
- Analytical procedures (these procedures do not result in projecting results to a population)
- Procedures applied to every item in a population (often performed using computer-assisted audit techniques)
- Some tests of controls (automated application controls, analysis of controls to determine proper segregation of duties, analyses of the effectiveness of security and access controls, tests directed toward obtaining evidence regarding the operation of the control environment/accounting system)
- Tests of controls when extrapolation is not intended (test counts of client counts at a physical inventory count)
- Procedures that do not evaluate characteristics (walk-through of a system/control)
- Untested balances (acceptably low risk of material misstatement exists)
- Tests of automated information technology controls (testing of one or two of each type of transaction at a point in time and test general controls to provide evidence automated controls operated effectively during the audit period)

Procedures involving sampling and nonsampling

Auditors may use a combination of procedures, that may or may not involve sampling, when examining an account balance or a class of transactions. For example, when examining repairs and maintenance expense of $1m an auditor concludes that it is appropriate to examine all seven items exceeding tolerable misstatement and totaling $750,000 and then to use sampling to examine the remaining 100 items totaling $250,000. The auditor's decision to use sampling for the items not exceeding tolerable misstatement is based on tolerable misstatement and the assessment of the risk of material misstatement in the $250,000. The decision is not based on the percentage of the total balance of $1m that is individually examined (75%).

There are a number of approaches the auditor may take in the preceding situation relating to the $250,000 repairs and maintenance expense not examined individually. Some of these approaches include the following.

Approach one

Sufficient evidence exists; no additional procedures needed.

The auditor has already performed risk assessment procedures, considered related controls supporting a low level of assessed control risk, reviewed entries to the account noting nothing unusual, and performed analytical procedures suggesting the $250,000 recorded amount does not contain a material misstatement.

Approach two

Sufficient evidence exists; no additional procedures needed.

The auditor has not performed any procedures related to the accuracy of the $250,000 but determines any misstatement in the remaining items would be immaterial because the assessed risk of material misstatement in recorded purchases is assessed by the auditor to be low.

Approach three

Sufficient evidence does not exist; additional procedures needed. Audit sampling is indicated.

The auditor has already performed risk assessment procedures, considered related controls, reviewed entries to the account, and performed analytical procedures. Based on the results of these procedures, the auditor concludes additional evidence about the remaining 100 items totaling $250,000 is needed.

Approaches to audit sampling

AU-C section 530 provides guidance for planning, performing, and evaluating audit samples using both statistical and nonstatistical sampling techniques.

Both sampling approaches require the use of professional judgment in planning, performing, and evaluating an audit sample. However, judgment is also required in relating the audit evidence from the sample to other audit evidence when forming a conclusion about an account balance or class of transactions.

Statistical sampling is based on probability theory and allows the auditor to

- design an efficient sample.
- measure sufficiency of the audit evidence obtained.
- quantitatively evaluate sample results.

The application of statistical sampling in a financial statement audit necessitates the auditor to have training in designing samples (to meet statistical requirements) and selecting the items to be tested. However, these additional costs may be offset through increased audit effectiveness because the auditor uses probability theory to

- quantify sampling risk to an acceptable low level.
- increase reliability/confidence level (that is, decrease risk).

On the other hand, the auditor generally relies on professional judgment as well as statistical training and experience to determine a nonstatistical sample. Factors considered when determining the size of a nonstatistical sample need not be quantified as is necessary for a statistical sample. *Any sampling procedure that does not permit the numerical measurement of sampling risk is a nonstatistical sampling procedure.* Regardless of the rigor an auditor uses in randomly selecting items for a nonstatistical sample, it remains a nonstatistical sampling application.

A nonstatistical sampling approach may not be as effective as a statistical approach when the auditor's judgment significantly differs from accepted probability theory and sampling concepts. Additionally, a potential risk exists that the auditor may misuse or not have an appropriate understanding of statistical concepts.

Choice of sampling approach

A properly designed nonstatistical sample considers the same factors considered in a properly designed statistical sample (reliability/confidence level or risk, alpha and beta risk, and precision or sampling risk). Because of this, there is no conceptual reason to expect a nonstatistical sample to provide different assurance from a statistical sample of *comparable size* for the same sampling procedure. Simply stated, there will likely be no significant difference between the size of a statistically determined sample and the size of a nonstatistical sample.

In designing a statistical sample, the auditor identifies the factors considered in quantitative terms. This requires knowledge of statistical concepts and how they relate to the population being tested as well as knowledge of audit risk in a financial statement audit. The same factors in a nonstatistical sample are estimated using qualitative terms such as "none," "few," or "many." This leads to the primary difference in statistical and nonstatistical sampling — that sampling risk is quantitatively controlled with a statistical sample.

Because the design and evaluation of a sample do not determine the appropriateness of the audit evidence, the choice of a nonstatistical or statistical sample does not directly affect decisions about

- auditing procedures to be applied.
- appropriateness of the audit evidence obtained (with respect to individual items in the sample).
- actions that might be taken in light of the nature and cause of particular misstatements.[6]

A statistical sampling approach may be efficient if sampling software is available and the population is in an electronic format. On the other hand, if reliable detailed data is not available, nonstatistical sampling may be more efficient.

> ### Key point
>
> A properly designed nonstatistical sample considers the same factors considered in a properly designed statistical sample (reliability/confidence level or risk, alpha and beta risk, and precision or sampling risk). Simply stated, there will likely be no significant difference between the size of a statistically determined sample and the size of a nonstatistical sample.

Types of audit tests[7]

In planning the audit, the auditor determines the extent of the use of audit sampling and the account balances or class of transactions for which sampling will be used. The area in which audit sampling is planned will determine the type of audit test to be performed. Professional standards identify the following three types of audit tests:

- *Tests of controls* — These tests provide evidence about the *effectiveness* of the design, implementation, or operation of a control in preventing or detecting material misstatements in a financial statement assertion.

---

[6] Because a statistical sample is based on probability theory, no additional evidence would be obtained by simply expanding the size of such a sample. However, expanding the size of a nonstatistical sample may provide additional evidence.

[7] A detailed discussion of the statistical concepts associated with various types of tests is beyond the scope of this course. Please refer to the AICPA Audit Guide *Audit Sampling* for additional information.

- *Substantive tests* — These tests provide evidence about the *validity and propriety* of the accounting treatment of transactions and balances as well as misstatements.
- *Dual-purpose tests* — Such tests are designed to provide evidence about the operating effectiveness of a control as well as whether a recorded balance or class of transactions is materially misstated.

Tests of controls (also referred to as attribute sampling) provide evidence about the rate of deviation from a particular control (that is, the specific item for which the control is tested either complies or not with the established control). Determination of the sampling unit (invoice, billing, payroll check) is done in light of the control being tested.

A test of controls measures the rate of deviation from a control and is used in the auditor's assessment of control risk. *Deviations are given equal weight, regardless of the dollar amount involved in the transaction, when evaluating the results of a test of controls.* When the audit strategy includes relying on a control to reduce the nature, timing, or extent of any related substantive procedures, professional standards require the auditor to test the control for operating effectiveness.

Substantive tests (also referred to as variables sampling) allow an auditor to conclude with respect to dollars rather than the effectiveness of controls. These types of tests allow the auditor to determine how much an account balance or class of transactions may be misstated and whether it is a material misstatement. The following are the types of substantive tests:

- Tests of details of transactions and balances
- Analytical procedures

When using a dual-purpose test, the same sample selection method needs to be applicable for both purposes. The sample size for a dual-purpose test will generally be the larger of either a sample for tests of controls or substantive tests designed for the two separate purposes. Separate procedures will need to be performed on the common sample to reach separate control and substantive conclusions.

Knowledge check

2. Which is **not** a type of audit test as defined in professional standards?

    a. Tests of controls.
    b. Single-purpose tests.
    c. Tests of details of transactions and balances.
    d. Dual-purpose tests.

Sample size[8]

The sufficiency of audit evidence is related, among other factors, to the design and size of an audit sample. Sample size depends on both the objectives and the efficiency of the sample. That is, factors considered in the determination of a sample for a test of controls differ from those considered for a sample for a substantive test. The efficiency of a sample relates to its design (that is, one sample is more efficient than another if it achieves the same objectives with a smaller size sample) and, generally, careful design produces a more efficient sample.

Sample sizes for substantive tests — Tests of details

For substantive tests of details, sample size relates to the individual importance of the items examined as well as to the potential for material misstatement. The number of items in the population for which substantive tests are planned has little effect on the appropriate sample size (unless the population is very small) because substantive tests relate to monetary amounts. Factors influencing the size of a sample for a substantive test of details include the following:

- *Assessment of inherent risk* — A low assessed level of inherent risk results in a *smaller* sample size.
- *Assessment of control risk* — A low assessed level of control risk also results in a *smaller* sample size.
- *Assessment of risk related to other substantive procedures directed at the same assertion* — A low assessment of risk associated with other relevant substantive procedures results in a *smaller* sample size.
- *Tolerable misstatement for the specific account balance/class of transactions being tested* — A small amount of tolerable misstatement results in a *larger* sample size.
- *Expected size and frequency of misstatement* [9] — Smaller expected misstatements or lower frequency rates result in a *smaller* sample size.

In designing a sample for a test of details, the auditor considers *how much misstatement* might exist in the sample and whether misstatement, when combined with the results of other audit tests, could cause the financial statements to be materially misstated. In a financial statement audit, the most common statistical approaches to substantive testing are

- classical variables sampling.
- monetary unit sampling.

Tolerable misstatement for a sample is the maximum amount of misstatement the auditor is willing to accept for the particular account balance/class of transactions being tested. This is different from performance materiality — a planning concept related to the amount of misstatement in the financial

---

[8] A detailed discussion of determining sample size under the various situations for which it might be appropriate in a financial statement audit is beyond the scope of this course. Please refer to the AICPA Audit Guide *Audit Sampling* for additional information.

[9] This is also referred to as the estimated variance (error) in the population being tested.

---

statements taken as a whole that the auditor is willing to tolerate. Therefore, the financial statement audit needs to be planned such that tolerable misstatement, combined with all of the tests in the entire audit, will not exceed performance materiality for the financial statements taken as a whole. Therefore, the auditor would normally establish the amount of tolerable misstatement *for a specific audit procedure* at less than the amount of performance materiality for the financial statements.

Factors to be considered in setting tolerable misstatement include the following:

- *Expected total amount of factual and judgmental misstatements*[10] — Higher expected misstatements lead to tolerable misstatement being much lower than performance materiality.
- *Management's attitude regarding proposed adjustments* — When management is generally resistant to adjustments, tolerable misstatement needs to be much lower than performance materiality.
- *Number of accounts where amounts will be subject to estimation and will not be able to be determined with precision* — When a significant number of accounts will be estimated, tolerable misstatement needs to be much lower than performance materiality.
- *Locations, subsidiaries, or samples within an account where separate procedures are applied for each location but that will be aggregated in reaching audit conclusions* — Significant numbers of these situations indicate tolerable misstatement needs to be much lower than performance materiality.

In addition to tolerable misstatement, the auditor may also identify, for a given account balance/class of transactions, items, that due to their size or risk of misstatement, are considered individually significant items. Such items are separated from the population and tested separately. Based on the auditor's judgment, the remainder of the population may not be tested or may be tested using sampling.

Stratification is a technique that may be used to reduce the required sample size or to focus on risk areas. Individually significant items are removed from the population prior to stratification.

Sample sizes for tests of controls

When designing a sample for a test of controls, the auditor is concerned with assessing control risk too low or too high. Assessing control risk too low may result in overreliance on the control because the control deviation rate in the sample is less than the true deviation rate in the population. On the other hand, assessing control risk too high may result in under reliance on the control because the control deviation rate in the sample is higher than the true deviation rate in the population. The latter situation affects audit efficiency because the auditor may respond to the results of the test of controls by unnecessarily expanding the scope of the substantive tests. However, this would not affect audit effectiveness.

---

[10] See AU-C section 450, *Evaluation of Misstatements Identified During an Audit* (AICPA *Professional Standards*), for additional information.

The number of items in the population for which control tests are planned has little effect on the appropriate sample size[11] unless the population is very small (less than 200 sampling units).[12] Factors influencing the size of a sample for a test of controls include the following:

- *Assessed level of control risk* — Assurance or confidence level is the complement of control risk.
- *Assessment of risk of overreliance on controls* — This is generally set at a low level (10% or less based on the population, nature of transactions, and significance of control being tested) because a test of controls is the primary source of evidence about their effectiveness. Assurance or confidence level is the complement of the risk of overreliance. The lower the acceptable risk of overreliance, the *larger* the sample needed.
- *Tolerable deviation rate* — In tests of controls, this is the maximum rate of deviation from a control the auditor is willing to accept without altering the planned assessed level of control risk. A higher tolerable rate results in a *smaller* sample size.[13]
- *Expected population deviation rate (also known as the expected rate of occurrence)* — There is a direct relationship between the expected population deviation rate and sample size. As the expected rate nears the tolerable rate, more precise information is needed from the sample, and a *larger* sample size is needed.
- *Desired level of assurance provided by the test* — High levels of desired assurance result in *larger* sample sizes.

In determining the tolerable deviation rate for a specific control, the (*a*) planned assessed level of control risk, (*b*) degree of reliance to be placed on the control, and (*c*) significance of the control to the audit are considered. A very high tolerable deviation rate indicates the control's operating effectiveness will not significantly reduce the extent of the related substantive tests.

The expected population deviation rate would rarely equal or exceed the tolerable deviation rate. If in fact the auditor believes this to be the case, the assessed level of control risk needs to be increased and testing of the specific control omitted entirely. Factors used in estimating the expected population deviation rate include the

- results of prior-year tests (considered in light of current-year changes in controls),
- design of internal controls, and
- control environment.

In practice, some auditors set a fixed tolerable deviation rate for all tests of controls and vary the desired level of assurance (confidence level) for each separate control test. Other auditors set one level of

---

[11] For example, everything being equal (90% confidence level, 1% expected population deviation rate, and 10% tolerable deviation rate), the required sample size for a population of 100 is 33 items and the required sample size is 38 items for a population of 2,000 or more.

[12] Population size may have a small effect on sample size, depending on the sample parameters, when population size is between 200 and 2,000.

[13] For example, increasing the tolerable deviation rate from 5% to 10% results in an approximate 50% reduction in the size of the sample.

assurance for all tests of controls and assess the tolerable deviation rate for each separate control based on the planned assessed level of control risk.

Key point
The expected population deviation rate would rarely equal or exceed the tolerable deviation rate. If the auditor expects the population deviation rate to equal or exceed the tolerable deviation rate, the assessed level of control risk would need to be increased and testing of the specific control omitted entirely. This would be the case when controls are missing or improperly designed.

Selecting items for a sample

Sample items should be selected in such a way the sample can be expected to represent the population being tested whether a statistical or nonstatistical sampling approach is used. This means all items in the population for the entire period under audit have an equal opportunity of being selected, and this necessitates some form of random-based selection. The auditor uses judgment in determining the technique to use in selecting items for a sample and also considers the efficiency to be gained by choosing one selection technique over another.

Random-based selection techniques include the following:

- *Random sampling* — Every combination of sampling units has an equal probability of being selected.
- *Stratified random sampling* — Every combination of sampling units within each individual stratum has an equal probability of being selected.
- *Systematic sampling with one or more random starts* — After a random start, items are selected based on a uniform interval (calculated by dividing the number of units in the population being tested by the sample size).
- *Sampling with probability proportional to size (PPS)* — This method is used *only for substantive tests* utilizing monetary unit sampling in which items are selected for such a sample in proportion to their relative size (dollar amount).

Knowledge check

3. What does sample size depend on?

    a. Objectives of the sample.
    b. Efficiency of the sample.
    c. Objectives and efficiency of the sample.
    d. The dollar amount of the population being tested.

Evaluating the results of sampling

Overview

Whether a statistical or nonstatistical sampling approach is used, the auditor uses judgment in evaluating the results of tests of controls and substantive tests of details and reaching an overall conclusion thereon. Additionally, the auditor considers not only the quantitative aspects of misstatements and deviations but the qualitative aspects as well. Qualitative aspects typically considered include the

- nature and cause of the misstatement or deviation (that is, due to error or fraud, differences in principle or in application, misunderstanding of instructions, or carelessness) and
- possible relationship of the misstatement or deviation to other phases of the audit (fraud ordinarily requires a broader consideration of possible implications than simple errors).

Evaluating the results of substantive tests of details

AU-C section 530 requires the auditor to project misstatements noted in a sample to the population from which the sample was selected and add such amounts to other misstatements noted in any items examined 100%. A number of methods are available for the auditor to use in projecting the amount of misstatement from a sample to the population. Factors affecting the method selected to project the misstatement include

- method of sample selection,
- whether the sample was stratified or not,
- use of statistical sampling techniques, and
- the auditor's understanding of the magnitude and distribution of misstatements in the population.

Three common methods used to project sample errors to the population in a financial statement audit include the following:

1. Apply the misstated rate of dollar misstatements observed in the sample to the population.
   a. This method does not require an estimate of the number of sampling units in the population.
   b. For stratified samples, misstatement results for each stratum are projected separately to each stratum, and then the projected misstatement for each stratum is summarized to determine the overall projected misstatement.
2. Project the average difference between the audited and recorded amounts of each item in the sample to all items in the population.
   a. This method requires an estimate of the number of sampling units in the population.

3. Use of a point estimator for nonstatistical samples when sample selection approximated another type of selection.
   a. Use of the point estimator draws on monetary unit sampling techniques.
   b. The effect of tainting must be determined for each misstatement when using this method.

The auditor should ask management, on a timely basis, to record all misstatements accumulated during the audit, including those identified using sampling procedures, unless the auditor believes they are trivial. Total projected misstatement,[14] adjusted for misstatements corrected by the audited entity, should then be compared to tolerable misstatement for the account balance/class of transactions. When the total projected misstatement is less than tolerable misstatement, the auditor should consider whether there might be other undetected misstatements in the population, that might indicate a material misstatement exists.

Knowledge check

4. Factors affecting the method selected to project the misstatement from a substantive test of details sample do **not** include

   a. Whether the sample was stratified.
   b. Number of items in the sample.
   c. Method of sample selection.
   d. The auditor's understanding of the magnitude and distribution of misstatements in the population.

Evaluating the results of tests of controls

In a test of controls, the sample deviation rate (number of observed deviations divided by sample size) is the best estimate of the deviation rate in the population. When an unexpected deviation rate occurs (in a sample from a population, that was expected to be deviation free or to have a low incidence of deviation), the auditor should consider the nature and causes of the deviations and their incidence of occurrence. An unexpected deviation rate for a particular control may indicate other deviations in the population. If such unexpected deviations were observed in a *small sample*, it might be appropriate to extend the sample (such an extension would not be small)[15] if the combined deviation rate from both samples is expected to be sufficiently low to support the planned reliance on the control.

For a given test of controls, the auditor is concerned that the actual rate of deviation in the population does not exceed the tolerable rate in a sample. An unacceptably high level of sampling risk is generally

---

[14] Projected misstatements are the auditor's best estimate of misstatements in populations. Projecting misstatements involves projection of misstatements identified in audit samples to the entire population from which the samples were drawn. Total projected misstatement, including factual and judgmental misstatements, is the difference between the estimated account balance/class of transactions being tested and the recorded amount.

[15] A rule of thumb is to increase the sample by at least the number of items in the original sample.

---

indicated when the actual deviation rate for a tested control, plus the allowance for sampling risk, exceeds the tolerable rate. The same holds true when the actual deviation rate exceeds the expected deviation rate used to design the sample. In these cases, the auditor will need to increase the assessed level of control risk or consider whether to rely on the control at all.

When deviations in tests of controls are found, the auditor needs to determine if they represent control deficiencies, and if so their proper classification (that is, material weakness, significant deficiency, or simple control weakness). Deficiencies in the design or operating effectiveness of a tested control are indicated when they are identified as control deficiencies and when the deviation rate in the sample is greater than the expected deviation rate. Professional standards require the auditor to communicate certain control deficiencies to those charged with governance.

Key point
When deviations in tests of controls are found, the auditor needs to determine if they represent control deficiencies, and if so their proper classification (that is, material weakness, significant deficiency, or simple control weakness). Professional standards require the auditor to communicate significant deficiencies and material weaknesses in controls to those charged with governance.

Summary

This chapter discusses the use of sampling in a financial audit and the related professional standards. The chapter provides an overview of statistical and nonstatistical sampling techniques and the circumstances in which each is appropriate. Types of tests for which sampling procedures might be appropriate, tests of controls, and substantive tests are also discussed in this chapter. In addition, the chapter provides insight into the factors to be considered in the determination of sample size and the selection of items for a sample. This chapter also discusses how sample results are evaluated, including when sample results are to be projected to the related population and how to calculate the amount of misstatement.

Practice questions

1. What is sampling risk?

2. What are the two approaches to sampling?

3. How do the two approaches to sampling differ? How are they the same?

4. Name and describe two methods by which to select items for a sample.

5. List and describe the three types of audit tests used in a financial statement audit.

6. List three factors to consider when determining the sampling approach in a financial statement audit.

7. List three factors influencing sample size determination for a substantive test of details.

8. List three factors influencing sample size determination for a test of controls.

9. Name and describe two methods to project sample errors to the population tested with a substantive test of details.

10. Why is the auditor concerned with the actual rate of deviation in the population and the tolerable deviation rate in a sample for a test of controls?

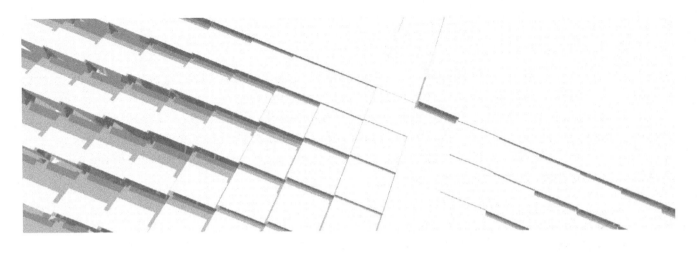

Chapter 7

The Financial Reporting Model for Not-for-Profit Entities

Learning objectives

- Identify the reasons FASB issued Financial Accounting Standards Update (ASU) No. 2016-14, *Not-for-Profit Entities (Topic 958): Presentation of Financial Statements of Not-for-Profit Entities*.

- Identify how ASU No. 2016-14 changed the financial statement reporting model used by not-for-profit entities.

- Determine the appropriate effective date by which not-for-profit entities are required to implement the requirements of ASU No. 2016-14.

- Identify areas not-for-profit entities need to consider upon initial implementation and subsequent application of the requirements of ASU No. 2016-14.

Major areas of inquiry

FASB issued ASU No. 2016-14 in August 2016. The amendments in the ASU make several improvements to current financial reporting requirements to address identified issues with the extant financial reporting model. Requirements of ASU No. 2016-14 are effective for calendar year 2018 or fiscal year 2019 financial statements and both preparers and auditors of not-for-profit entities have had a number of questions relating to initial implementation and ongoing application of the requirements of the ASU. These questions relate to the following:

- Applicability of ASU No. 2016-14
- How ASU No. 2016-14 changes the financial reporting model
- What effect ASU No. 2016-14 has on classes of net assets
- How to report the effect of ASU No. 2016-14 in the year of implementation
- What additional disclosures are required under ASU No. 2016-14
- What not-for-profit entities and their auditors can do to prepare for implementation of ASU No. 2016-14

Overview

In November 2011 FASB added a standards-setting project to its agenda relating to financial reporting by not-for-profit entities. The objectives of this project, "Not-for-Profit Financial Reporting: Financial Statements," included reexamining and updating existing standards to improve information in the financial statements and notes. Based on input from FASB's Not-for-Profit Advisory Committee and other stakeholders, the project focused on

- complexities relating to the use of three classes of net assets;
- deficiencies in the transparency and utility of information useful in assessing an entity's liquidity; caused by the use of the term *unrestricted net assets;*
- inconsistencies in the type of expense information provided; and
- having to prepare the indirect method reconciliation when using the direct method of presenting the statement of cash flows.

A Proposed ASU, *Not-for-Profit Entities (Topic 958) and Health Care Entities (Topic 954),* with a comment deadline of August 20, 2015, was issued in April 2015. The exposure draft requested responders to provide comments in 22 areas and 264 individuals or organizations responded, including the Financial Reporting Executive Committee and the Technical Issues Committee of the AICPA's Private Companies Practice Section.

Based on the comment letters and testimony by round table participants, FASB divided its redeliberations into two workstreams. The first workstream (Phase 1) reconsidered issues not dependent on other projects and improvements and resulted in the issuance of ASU No. 2016-14 in August 2016.

Issues involving reconsideration of the proposed changes that, for various reasons, need more time to resolve are in the second workstream (Phase 2). As of the date this course was written, work on Phase 2 had been deferred until further research is complete or until the FASB addresses the issues relating to all entities at a later point in time.

The amendments in ASU No. 2016-14 are intended to make immediate improvements to address the following areas:

- Complexity in net asset classification
- Transparency in reporting financial performance measures
- Consistency in reporting expenses by function and nature
- Clarity of information relating to liquidity and availability of cash

ASU No. 2016-14 is effective for fiscal years beginning after December 15, 2017, and for interim periods within fiscal years beginning after December 15, 2018. Application to interim financial statements is permitted but not required in the initial year of application. Early application is permitted. In the year of implementation, entities presenting comparative financial statements are permitted, but not required, to present certain newly required (that is as required by ASU No. 2016-14) financial information and disclosures on a comparative basis.

Key changes in ASU No. 2016-14

ASU No. 2016-14 changes only what information is required to be reported by not-for-profit entities in their external general purpose financial statements prepared on the GAAP basis of accounting. Key areas where the current financial reporting model changed are

- net asset classes and underwater endowments,
- statement of cash flows,
- liquidity and availability of financial assets,
- expense information,
- investment return, and
- placed-in-service approach.

The changes may have a significant effect on some not-for-profit entities whereas other not-for-profit entities may need to make little change to their current financial statements and related notes.

Net asset classes and underwater endowments

Net asset classes

Prior to ASU No. 2016-14, not-for-profit entities reported three classes of net assets at the end of a period — unrestricted net assets, temporarily restricted net assets, and permanently restricted net assets. To address the perceived complexity with these three classes of net assets, ASU No. 2016-14 requires the presentation of two classes of net assets, which are based on the existence or absence of donor-imposed restrictions:

- Net assets with donor restrictions
- Net assets without donor restrictions

A not-for-profit entity may choose to further disaggregate the two classes of net assets in its general purpose external financial statements. For example, a not-for-profit entity may wish to separate net assets with donor restrictions which are to be maintained in perpetuity (similar to former permanently restricted net assets) from net assets with donor restrictions expected to be spent over time and/or for a particular purpose (similar to former temporarily restricted net assets). Likewise, a not-for-profit entity may wish to report board-designated endowment funds separate from other net assets without donor restrictions. Regardless of the level of disaggregation within the two classes of net assets, ASU No. 2016-14 requires the amounts for each of the two classes of net assets and the total net assets to be reported in the statement of financial position.

ASU No. 2016-14 maintains the requirements to present total net assets as well as the total in each class of net assets. Additionally, the requirement to report the change in total net assets and in each class of net assets on the face of the statement of activities is retained in ASU No. 2016-14.

Additional or enhanced disclosures relating to the two new classes of net assets are also required under ASU No. 2016-14. These disclosure requirements relate to

- information about the nature and amounts of different types of donor-imposed restrictions (this may be presented on the face of the statement of financial position or in the notes to the financial statements).
- amounts and purposes of governing board designations of net assets without donor restrictions.
- appropriations and similar actions, which result in self-imposed limits on the use of net assets without donor restrictions.
- composition of net assets with donor restrictions at the end of the period and how the restrictions affect the use of resources (that is, net assets with donor restrictions).

Illustrative note disclosures for classes of net assets

Examples of note disclosures for net asset information included in the summary of significant accounting policies are outlined as follows.

Net Assets Without Donor Restrictions — Net assets available for use in general operations and not subject to donor (or certain grantor) restrictions. The governing board has designated, from net assets without donor restrictions, net assets for an operating reserve and board-designated endowment.

Net Assets With Donor Restrictions — Net assets subject to donor- (or certain grantor-) imposed restrictions. Some donor-imposed restrictions are temporary in nature, such as those that will be met by the passage of time or other events specified by the donor. Other donor-imposed restrictions are perpetual in nature, where the donor stipulates that resources be maintained in perpetuity. Gifts of long-lived assets and gifts of cash restricted for the acquisition of long-lived assets are recognized as revenue when the assets are placed in service. Donor-imposed restrictions are released when a restriction expires; that is, when the stipulated time has elapsed, when the stipulated purpose for which the resource was restricted has been fulfilled, or both.

Alternative when the not-for-profit has adopted a policy relating to restrictions expiring in the reporting period the contribution revenue is recognized

We report contributions restricted by donors as increases in net assets without donor restrictions if the restrictions expire (that is, when a stipulated time restriction ends or purpose restriction is accomplished) in the reporting period in which the revenue is recognized. All other donor-restricted contributions are reported as increases in net assets with donor restrictions, depending on the nature of the restrictions. When a restriction expires, net assets with donor restrictions are reclassified to net assets without donor restrictions and reported in the statements of activities as net assets released from restrictions.

Underwater endowments

Prior to ASU No. 2016-14, underwater endowments were typically reported as unrestricted net assets. However, under ASU No. 2016-14, not-for-profit entities will report donor-imposed underwater endowments as net assets with donor restrictions rather than net assets without donor restrictions.

Enhanced disclosures relating to both donor-imposed and board-designated underwater endowments required under ASU No. 2016-14 include

- the not-for-profit entity's endowment policy and any actions taken during the period concerning appropriation from underwater endowment funds;
- aggregate fair value of underwater endowment funds;
- aggregate original gift amounts (or level required by the donor or law) to be maintained; and
- aggregate amount by which endowment funds are underwater, which are classified as part of net assets with donor restrictions (donor-imposed endowment funds only).

Illustrative note disclosures for underwater endowments

An example of note disclosure for underwater endowments is outlined as follows.

Underwater Endowment Funds — From time to time, certain donor-restricted endowment funds may have fair values less than the amount required to be maintained by donors or by law (underwater endowments). We have interpreted the Uniform Prudent Management of Institutional Funds Act to permit spending from underwater endowments in accordance with prudent measures required under law. At December 31, 20X0, funds with original gift values of $19,883,738, fair values of $19,841,061, and deficiencies of $42,677 were reported in net assets with donor restrictions. These amounts were fully recovered during 20X1 due to favorable market fluctuations.

Knowledge check

1. ASU No. 2016-14 requires a not-for-profit entity to report net assets in which classifications?

    a. Net assets with donor restrictions and net assets without donor restrictions.
    b. Unrestricted net assets, temporarily restricted net assets, permanently restricted net assets.
    c. Board-designated net assets.
    d. Expendable net assets and nonexpendable net assets.

Statement of cash flows

ASU No. 2016-14 does not change the option not-for-profit entities have to present the statement of cash flows using the direct or indirect method. However, not-for-profit entities using the direct method of reporting cash flows from operations are no longer required to provide a reconciliation of the change in net assets to net cash flow from operating activities.

<table>
<tr><td align="center">**Key point**</td></tr>
<tr><td>ASU No. 2016-14 does not eliminate the option of presenting the statement of cash flows using either the direct or indirect method. However, not-for-profit entities are no longer required to provide a reconciliation of the change in net assets to net cash flow from operating activities under ASU No. 2016-14.</td></tr>
</table>

Liquidity and availability of financial assets

Perhaps one of the more challenging areas of ASU No. 2016-14 for not-for-profit entities is the requirement to provide qualitative and quantitative information about their liquidity. Prior to ASU No. 2016-14, liquidity information was limited to presenting assets in order of liquidity and liabilities in order of liquidation. The additional note disclosures required under ASU No. 2016-14 may prove challenging for some not-for-profit entities.

Specific qualitative information should communicate how the not-for-profit entity manages its liquid resources available to meet cash needs for general expenditures *within one year of the date of the statement of financial position*. Quantitative and additional qualitative information should be communicated relating to the availability of the entity's financial assets[1] at the date of the statement of financial position to meet cash needs for general expenditures[2] *within one year* of such date. This information may be presented in two separate notes to the financial statements or the information may be combined into one note. The ASU provides three significantly different examples of how to present the required information.

Quantitative information may be reported on the face of the statement of financial position or in the notes with the additional qualitative information reported in the notes as necessary.

Availability of financial assets may be affected by the following:

- Its nature (cash in demand accounts versus investments in long-term debt instruments)
- External limits imposed by donors, grantors, laws, and contracts with others (that is, funds on deposit to construct a new facility in the future)
- Internal limits imposed by governing board decisions (that is, internal liquidity reserve funds)

---

[1] Examples of financial assets as defined in GAAP include cash, contracts to receive cash (receivables, debt securities), and evidence of equity ownership in another entity (equity securities).
[2] ASU No. 2016-14 does not define "general expenditures."

An example of how the required liquidity information might be presented in the notes to the financial statements is as follows.

Note X — Liquidity and Availability

Financial assets available for general expenditure, that is, without donor or other restrictions limiting their use, within one year of the balance sheet date, include the following:

Cash and cash equivalents	$ 4,851,231
Accounts receivable	312,216
Operating investments	723,006
Promises to give	965,846
Distributions from assets held under split-interest agreements	145,000
Distributions from beneficial interests in assets held by others	180,110
Endowment spending-rate distributions and appropriations	1,115,664
	$ 8,293,073

Our endowment funds consist of donor-restricted endowments and funds designated by the board as endowments. Income from donor-restricted endowments is restricted for specific purposes, with the exception of the amounts available for general use. Donor-restricted endowment funds are not available for general expenditure.

Our board-designated endowment of $15,511,186 is subject to an annual spending rate of 4.5% as described in Note Y. Although we do not intend to spend from this board-designated endowment (other than amounts appropriated for general expenditure as part of our board's annual budget approval and appropriation), these amounts could be made available if necessary.

As part of our liquidity management plan, we invest cash in excess of daily requirements in short-term investments, CDs, and money market funds. Occasionally, the board designates a portion of any operating surplus to its operating reserve, which was $300,000 as of December 31, 201X.

Knowledge check

2. What is **not** accurate of the liquidity information required to be disclosed under the requirements of ASU No. 2016-14?

    a. Not-for-profit entities are required to present a classified statement of financial position.
    b. The period of time for which liquidity information is communicated is the period within one year of the date of the statement of financial position.
    c. Quantitative information may be presented on the face of the statement of financial position.
    d. Qualitative information about how the entity manages its liquid resources is required.

Expense information

Functional and natural expenses

Prior to ASU No. 2016-14, voluntary health and welfare organizations were required to present a statement of functional expenses as part of their general purpose external financial statements prepared in accordance with GAAP. This statement presents expenses by both their functional and natural classifications. Also, prior to ASU No. 2016-14, all not-for-profit entities were required to report expenses by function either on the face of the statement of activities or in the notes to the financial statements.

ASU No. 2016-14 requires all not-for-profit entities to report expenses by both their functional and natural classification. This analysis of expenses is required to be provided in one location using one of the following presentation options:

- Face of the statement of activities
- Separate statement of functional expenses
- In the notes to the financial statements

Regardless of the location, the presentation of functional and natural expenses should report all expenses including those netted with revenues in the statement of activities. For example, the direct benefits to donors attending a special event or expenses in cost of goods sold would need to be included in the presentation of functional and natural expenses. However, external investment expenses and direct internal investment expenses netted with investment return are not required to be included in the presentation of functional and natural expenses.

An additional requirement relating to allocation of management and general expenses is included in ASU No. 2016-14 as codified in 958-720-45-2A as follows:

> Activities representing *direct conduct or direct supervision* [emphasis added] of program or other supporting activities require allocation from management and general activities. Additionally, certain costs benefit more than one function and, therefore, shall be allocated. For example, information technology generally can be identified as benefiting various functions, such as management and general (for example, accounting and financial reporting and human resources), fundraising, and program delivery. Therefore, information technology costs generally would be allocated among the functions receiving the benefit.

To provide for more comparability between not-for-profit entities, ASU No. 2016-14 provides improved guidance to assist not-for-profit entities in understanding what activities constitute management and general expenses. For example, the current list of management and general activities in 958-720-45-7 expands "general recordkeeping" to include "payroll" and adds "employee benefits management and oversight (human resources)" to the list of management and general activities. In addition, the ASU reclassifies contract administration expenses from the cost of "soliciting funds other than contributions and membership dues" to its own activity. The revised and reclassified activity is identified as "administering government, foundation, and similar customer-sponsored contracts, including billing and collecting fees and grant and contract financial reporting."

Cost allocation disclosures

ASU No. 2016-14 requires not-for-profit entities to provide a qualitative description of the methods used to allocate expenses among program and support functions. An illustrative note describing this information is as follows:

> Note X — Functionalized Expenses
>
> The financial statements report certain categories of expenses that are attributed to more than one program or supporting function. Therefore, expenses require allocation on a reasonable basis that is consistently applied. Allocated expenses include occupancy, depreciation, and amortization, which are allocated on a square footage basis, as well as salaries and wages, benefits, payroll taxes, professional services, office expenses, information technology, interest, insurance, and other, which are allocated on the basis of estimates of time and effort.

Investment return

Prior to the effective date of ASU No. 2016-14, not-for-profit entities were required to disclose the components of investment return including investment income, gains and losses, and any netting investment expenses. In addition, GAAP provided a not-for-profit entity with the following two options for presenting investment expenses in the statement of activities:

- Net investment expenses with investment return
- Present investment expenses as a component of expenses

ASU No. 2016-14 eliminates the requirement to disclose the composition of investment return and the amount of investment expenses. Additionally, the ASU requires only presentation of net investment return in endowment fund roll forward disclosures. A major change made with ASU No. 2016-14 is the requirement that not-for-profit entities net all external and direct internal investment expenses against investment return in the statement of activities.

Direct internal investment expenses are defined as those involving the direct conduct or direct supervision of the strategic and tactical activities involved in generating investment return. Such expenses do not include items associated with generating investment return. However, direct internal investment expenses include but are not limited to *both* of the following:

- Salaries, benefits, travel, and other costs associated with the officer and staff responsible for the development and execution of investment strategy
- Allocable costs associated with internal investment management and supervising, selecting, and monitoring of external investment management firms

In the statement of activities, not-for-profit entities are permitted to present separate amounts of net investment return from portfolios that may be managed differently or derived from different sources. In such cases, the separate line items on the statement of activities are to be appropriately labeled (such as interest and dividends, realized gains and losses, and unrealized gains and losses). Net investment return appropriated for spending may be presented separately from net investment return in excess of amounts appropriated for spending in the statement of activities as long as such amounts are appropriately labeled.

Changes to the determination of investment return are expected to make the measurement of such more comparable across all not-for-profit entities. Additionally, it will provide more comparable measurement of investments such as mutual and hedge funds where the management fees are embedded within the investment return.

Key point
Under ASU No. 2016-14, direct internal investment expenses include costs associated with supervising, selecting, and monitoring external investment management firms. Upon implementation of the ASU, not-for-profit entities will need to determine the amount of time internal staff spend in these functions to fully reflect the amount of direct internal investment expenses.

Knowledge check

3. Which is **not** a potential direct internal investment expense when incurred in the development and execution of an entity's investment strategy?

   a. Salaries.
   b. Depreciation.
   c. Benefits.
   d. Travel.

Placed-in-service approach

Before and after the implementation of ASU No. 2016-14, gifts of long-lived assets received without donor stipulations about how long the asset must be used are required to be reported as contribution revenue without donor restrictions. However, prior to ASU No. 2016-14 not-for-profits were allowed to adopt a policy relating to implied time restrictions when donors of long-lived assets did not explicitly stipulate how long the asset must be used.

ASU No. 2016-14 eliminates the option for a not-for-profit to adopt a policy relating to implied time restrictions. Consequently, any long-lived assets currently accounted for under such a policy are to be reclassified as net assets without donor restrictions upon implementation of ASU No. 2016-14.

Additionally, ASU No. 2016-14 requires all gifts of cash or other assets restricted to acquire long-lived assets to be reported as donor-restricted support. As such, these assets are required to be released from restrictions and *reclassified to net assets without donor restrictions when the asset is acquired and placed in service* unless the donor has placed a time restriction on the use of the long-lived asset.

The placed-in-service approach required under ASU No. 2016-14 may affect how some not-for-profit entities currently release donor support restricted for the acquisition or construction of capital assets. For example, some not-for-profit entities consider donor restrictions met when payments are made to the contractor constructing a new facility rather than when the facility is actually completed and placed in service. As such, net assets with donor restrictions (temporarily restricted net assets prior to implementation of ASU No. 2016-14) are reclassified to net assets without donor restrictions (unrestricted net assets prior to implementation of ASU No. 2016-14) in the amount incurred or in the amount paid to the contractor when the payment is made.

Knowledge check

4. Which method relating to the acquisition/construction of long-lived assets with donor resources for such assets is required under ASU No. 2016-14?

    a. Placed-in-service approach.
    b. Pay-as-you-use approach.
    c. Pay-as-you-go approach.
    d. ASU No. 2016-14 does not specify any method of accounting for the acquisition/construction of long-lived assets.

Initial implementation and subsequent application considerations

Implementing and subsequently applying the requirements of ASU No. 2016-14 may affect not-for-profit entities differently due to differences in size, mission, stakeholders, staff expertise, and other things. However, all not-for-profit entities and their stakeholders should *understand the requirements* of the ASU and how the changes have affected them. Management and auditors will need to work closely during implementation as well as in subsequent years. As with any standard having far reaching effects, it is expected that not-for-profit entities may continue to refine amounts and disclosures required by ASU 2016-14.

ASU 2016-14 likely required some not-for-profit entities to update some of their policies and have them approved by the governing board whereas other entities may not have found it necessary to develop and then adopt new policies. For example, entities having a policy implying time restrictions on contributions of long-lived assets need to rescind the policy as ASU No. 2016-14 requires the placed-in-service approach for such assets.

Auditors of small- and medium-sized not-for-profit entities may have assisted or been asked to assist their clients in implementing the required changes. In addition, this assistance may also be needed in continued application of the requirements in subsequent years. This can be problematic when personnel at the entity do not have adequate knowledge or experience to understand and or implement the requirements of ASU. In such cases, auditors need to evaluate the effect of this assistance on their independence. Government Auditing Standards and the AICPA *Code of Professional Conduct* require the auditor to consider the effect providing nonaudit/nonattest services has on independence *before they agree to accept the nonaudit/nonattest services engagement*.

Common implementation and ongoing application considerations are discussed in the following sections.

Financial statement presentation

The requirements of ASU No. 2016-14 are applied on a retrospective basis in the year of implementation. However, entities presenting comparative statements are permitted, but not required, to present comparative information for the following:

- Analysis of expenses by nature and function
- Liquidity and availability of resources disclosures

Not-for-profit entities that normally present comparative statements may not have done so in the year of implementation. In years subsequent to the implementation of ASU 2016-14, these not-for-profit entities will need to determine if they will present comparative statements. Things to consider in making this decision would include stakeholder and user expectations and whether an external requirement to present comparative statements exists. This is an important determination at implementation because ASU No. 2016-14 requires the following to be restated for all prior periods presented:

- Amounts previously reported for classes of net assets
- Investment return
- Contributions accounted for under an implied time restriction policy

In addition to determining if comparative financial statements will be presented in the year of implementation and years subsequent to implementation, a number of other financial statement presentation decisions a not-for-profit entity may need to make. These decisions relate to the following:

- Presentation of financial information in columns versus presenting information using a "stacked" approach. Reducing the number of classes of net assets to two from three may allow entities previously presenting information using a columnar approach to consider a "stacked" presentation.
- Level of detail to be included on the face of the statements rather than in the notes to the financial statements. Enhanced and additional disclosure requirements relating to net asset classes, investment return, and expenses may affect how entities previously presented this information.

Key point

Not-for-profit entities may face challenges implementing the requirements of ASU 2016-14 not only in the year of initial implementation but also in applying the requirements of the ASU in subsequent years.

Net assets

Upon initial implementation of ASU No. 2016-14, not-for-profit entities need to determine what amounts previously reported as temporarily or permanently restricted net assets meet the requirements to be classified as net assets with donor restrictions. An entity cannot simply assume all amounts previously reported as temporarily or permanently restricted net assets will be reported as net assets with donor restrictions.

As stated previously, the requirement to use the placed-in-service approach eliminates the use of policies relating to implied restrictions for contributions of long-lived assets. Additionally, the requirement to report underwater endowments as net assets with donor restrictions necessitates reclassification of any such amounts currently reported as unrestricted net assets. In some cases, these changes may initially and in subsequent years adversely affect required ratios or debt covenants.

Another area of concern relates to policies that may be needed to determine board-designated amounts. In addition, policies relating to spending from underwater endowments may require modification upon initial implementation or in years subsequent to implementation.

Statement of cash flows

Entities using the direct method to present changes in operating cash flows are not required to reconcile the change in net assets to net cash flow from operation activities under the requirements of ASU No. 2016-14. This change may affect expectations of the users of the financial statements.

Not-for-profit entities not using the direct method to present changes in operating cash flows may decide providing information on this basis is more useful to the users of their financial statements. The decision to use the direct method over the indirect method may not have been made in the year of initial implementation but may be considered in subsequent years. However, the need for any system or process changes as well as any additional preparation or audit costs may affect this decision.

Liquidity and availability of financial assets

A number of not-for-profit entities report the requirement to include information about liquidity and the availability of financial assets was a significant implementation challenge. Not-for-profit entities who presented liquidity and availability information prior to the implementation of ASU No. 2016-14 spent less time and effort changing their disclosures to meet the requirements of ASU No. 2016-14. Liquidity information may be presented only in text form or in text and tabular form. The method of presenting this information in the year of initial implementation may need to be reconsidered in subsequent years based on stakeholder feedback.

In some cases, the new disclosure requirements revealed some entities do not have adequate financial assets to fund activities over the next 12 months. Commingling cash with and without donor restrictions in one bank account and not maintaining other internal records of the different balances and using cash restricted for grants or capital construction purposes for current period expenses appear to be the major reasons for this situation. In these circumstances, an entity could decide to eliminate or loosen any internal designations restricting the use of financial assets to lessen the impact of the required liquidity disclosures.

Expense information

ASU No. 2016-14 requires all entities to present an analysis of expenses by function and natural classifications in a separate statement, in the statement of activities, or in the notes to the financial statements. The method chosen to present this information in the year of initial implementation may need to be reconsidered based on stakeholder feedback in subsequent years.

Enhanced disclosures relating to how expenses are allocated between program and management and general expenses are also required under ASU No. 2016-14. Examples of management and general expenses have been expanded and enhanced with ASU No. 2016-14. The ASU clarifies management and general activities are only allocable to program activities when such activities represent direct conduct or direct supervision of program activities. As such, not-for-profit entities will need to review management and general activities allocated to program activities in the year of initial implementation as well as in subsequent years.

ASU 2016-14 also requires disclosure of cost allocation methodologies. In the year of initial implementation and in subsequent years, entities will need to ensure their actual cost allocation methodologies are consistent with the related adopted policies. The level of detail at which functional expenses are reported as well as determining if functional classifications are accurately captured in the financial statements is a concern in the year of initial implementation as well as in subsequent years.

Investment return

All not-for-profit entities will report investment return net of related external and direct internal investment expenses under ASU No. 2016-14. Direct internal investment expenses are defined as those involving the direct conduct or direct supervision of the strategic and tactical activities involved in generating investment return. Therefore, it is likely all entities will need to determine the amount of direct internal investment expenses incurred even those entities engaging external money managers. This determination will be necessary in the year of initial implementation as well as in subsequent years. All not-for-profit entities will need to evaluate which costs are appropriate to net with investment return under ASU No. 2016-14 in the year of initial implementation as well as in subsequent years.

Netting direct internal investment expenses with investment returns may result in investment returns not meeting established performance benchmarks or stakeholder expectations. Entities may need to routinely evaluate the need to change current investment policies and or performance benchmarks to address the concept of direct internal investment expenses. In some cases, continued education of board members, financial statement users, or other stakeholders may be necessary.

Some not-for-profit entities may provide management, the board, committees, and others with additional investment information or reports outside of the basic financial statements. These reports may or may not present investment return in accordance with GAAP. When these reports present investment return in accordance with GAAP, the entity will need to decide if such information will be consistent with the requirements of ASU No. 2016-14 in the year of initial implementation and in subsequent years.

Auditors of not-for-profit entities need to be aware of the effect the requirements of ASU No. 2016-14 may have on reported financial statement amounts as well as internal processes and systems in the year of initial implementation and in subsequent years. The auditor may need to determine how any changes made to processes, controls, and or systems, affect the audit each year. The auditor may need to allocate more time to understanding any changes made to determine what, if any, effect the changes may have on the audit approach or audit procedures. Small- or medium-sized entities may ask their auditor for assistance in understanding and implementing the investment return requirements of ASU No. 2016-14 in the year of implementation and in subsequent years. In such cases, the auditor will need to evaluate the level of assistance provided and its effect on his or her independence.

Placed-in-service approach

ASU No. 2016-14 eliminates the option for a not-for-profit entity to adopt a policy relating to implied time restrictions and requires all such assets to be accounted for using the placed-in-service approach. Consequently, any long-lived assets currently accounted for under such a policy are reclassified as net assets without donor restrictions upon implementation of ASU No. 2016-14. It is not likely this will be a costly change to make nor is it expected to affect an entity's overall financial position.

All gifts of cash or other assets restricted to acquire long-lived assets are required to be reported as donor-restricted support under ASU No. 2016-14. As such, these assets are required to be released from restrictions and *reclassified to net assets without donor restrictions when the asset is acquired and placed in service* unless the donor has placed a time restriction on the use of the long-lived asset.

Not-for-profit entities holding cash or other financial assets restricted for the acquisition or construction of long-lived assets need to initially and periodically review their policy relating to the release of such amounts. In the initial year of implementation, these entities need to determine what amounts may have been previously released relating to long-lived assets which are not yet in service at the implementation date.

Some not-for-profit entities may have a policy whereby assets with donor restrictions for the construction of a long-lived asset are released when the contractor is paid or when costs are incurred. This accounting treatment is not permitted under ASU No. 2016-14 as the placed-in-service approach for long-lived assets is required. Upon implementation, entities using the aforementioned approach need to determine what amount of net assets with donor restrictions have been released and reclassified as net assets without donor restrictions in prior years. Additionally, these entities will need to ensure the acquired asset is actually in service at the implementation date. If the acquired long-lived asset was not placed in service at the implementation date, any amounts previously reclassified from net assets with donor restrictions to net assets without donor restrictions needed to be reversed. This requirement would apply retrospectively if comparative financial statements are presented in the year of initial implementation.

Summary

This chapter provides a high-level discussion of FASB's financial reporting model for not-for-profit entities. The chapter emphasizes the major areas that change upon implementation of the ASU and provides examples of newly required or enhanced disclosures. In addition, this chapter discusses a number of initial and ongoing implementation considerations associated with the ASU and how not-for-profit entities might address these challenges.

Practice questions

1. What is the effective date of ASU No. 2016-14?

2. What are the major areas where ASU No. 2016-14 changed previous reporting?

3. How many classes of net assets are required under ASU No. 2016-14 and what are they?

4. How did ASU No. 2016-14 change the reporting of investment return?

5. What qualitative liquidity information is required to be communicated under ASU No. 2016-14?

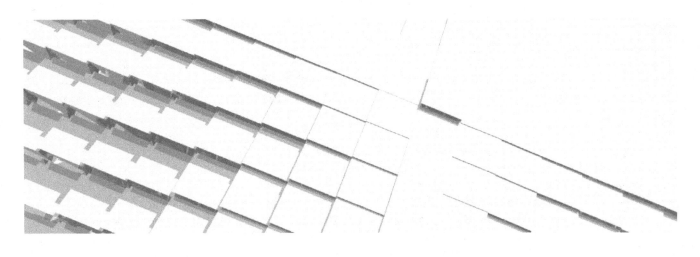

Chapter 8

Government Auditing Standards — Independence, Competence, and Continuing Professional Education

---

Learning objectives

- Identify when the auditor is required to be independent when performing audit services under the 2018 *Government Auditing Standards* (GAGAS).

- Identify when the auditor is required to evaluate the effect of nonaudit services on independence under the 2018 GAGAS.

- Identify threats to independence using the framework in the 2018 GAGAS.

- Identify the documentation requirements relating to nonaudit services and independence in the 2018 GAGAS.

- Identify the changes to competence and continuing professional education (CPE) in the 2018 GAGAS.

Major areas of inquiry

Auditors have numerous questions relating to changes made to the independence and competence standards in the 2018 Revision of GAGAS. These questions relate primarily to financial audits and to the following areas:

- Period for which independence is required under GAGAS
- How and when to apply the conceptual framework approach
- Threats to independence under GAGAS
- Safeguards available to eliminate threats or reduce them to an acceptable level
- What level of assistance can the auditor provide with respect to nonaudit services under GAGAS
- Nonaudit services that impair independence
- Nonaudit services that do not impair independence
- Extent of required documentation relating to nonaudit services and independence considerations
- Level of competence required for audit team members as well as the audit team

Overview

In July 2018, the U.S. Government Accountability Office (GAO) issued *Government Auditing Standards, 2018 Revision.*[1] Upon its effective date, the 2018 revision supersedes the December 2011 revision of the standards. The effective dates of the 2018 revision are

- for financial audits, attestation engagements, and reviews of financial statements for periods ending on or after June 30, 2020,
- for performance audits for periods beginning on or after July 1, 2019.

Therefore, the first full fiscal year audits performed under the 2018 revision will be for June 30, 2020, year-ends. Access to the 2018 revision is available on the GAO website at www.gao.gov/products/GAO-18-568G. Following are some of the major changes the 2018 revision makes to the 2011 revision.

Format and organization. The 2018 revision reorganizes the format in order to present all requirements within a box, with the application guidance following. This allows for clear identification of the requirements versus application guidance. Furthermore, two chapters were added, and content within chapters has been reorganized. Application guidance has been added to a number of topics. In addition, content that previously was in the appendixes to the 2011 revision or the GAO *Guidance on GAGAS Requirements for Continuing Professional Education* (GAO-05-568G) has either been incorporated into the 2018 revision or removed.

Independence. This area has some of the more significant changes, particularly as it relates to nonaudit services. For example, the 2018 revision states that auditors should conclude that preparing financial statements in their entirety from a client-provided trial balance or underlying accounting records creates significant threats to an auditor's independence. The 2018 revision also requires auditors to identify certain other services relating to preparing accounting records and financial statements as threats to independence. These changes are discussed in detail later in this chapter.

> ### *Government Auditing Standards, 2018 Revision* – Independence alert
>
> An auditor must be independent from the audited entity for the entire period under audit. Therefore, for a June 30, 2020, fiscal year-end (the first fiscal year required to be audited under the 2018 revision) an auditor is required to comply with the 2018 Yellow Book independence requirements beginning on July 1, 2019.

CPE. Application guidance for CPE emphasizes the need to obtain CPE related to GAGAS, particularly in a year where the standards have been revised. As noted previously, certain guidance found in GAO's 2005 document, "Guidance on GAGAS Requirements for Continuing Professional Education," has been included as application guidance in the 2018 revision. This document is superseded upon the effective

---

[1] The AICPA has a course on the 2018 revision titled: The New Yellow Book: *Government Auditing Standards, 2018 Revision.*

date of the 2018 revision. In addition, the 2018 revision expands and clarifies requirements relating to the competence of the audit team individuals as well as the audit team as a whole.

Peer review. Content related to peer review has been expanded and includes a listing of recognized peer review organizations. The 2018 revision notes that audit organizations affiliated with a recognized peer review organization should comply with their requirements and certain other requirements found in the 2018 revision.

Waste and abuse. The 2011 revision of GAGAS included auditor requirements related to abuse. The 2018 revision moves the concept of abuse to application guidance and adds the concept of waste.

Reviews of financial statements. The 2018 revision adds guidance relating to reviews of financial statements.

Performance audits. Content relating to performance audits in the 2018 revision includes considerations for when internal control is significant to the audit objectives.

A full discussion of the 2018 revision to GAGAS is outside the scope of this course; however, this chapter focuses on the requirements relating to independence and competence.

Independence

The importance of independence
In all matters relating to the GAGAS audit, auditors and audit organizations must be independent from an audited entity.
Auditors and audit organizations should avoid situations that could lead reasonable and informed third parties to conclude that the auditors and audit organizations are not independent and thus are not capable of exercising objective and impartial judgment on all issues associated with conducting the audit and reporting on the work.

Like the 2011 revision to GAGAS, standards relating to independence are in chapter 3 of the 2018 GAGAS. However, chapter 3 of the 2011 revision discussed all of the general standards although chapter 3 of the 2018 GAGAS discusses ethics and professional judgment in addition to independence.

Under GAGAS, independence includes independence of mind and independence of appearance.

- *Independence of mind* — The state of mind that permits the conduct of an audit without being affected by influences that compromise professional judgment, thereby allowing an individual to act with integrity and exercise objectivity and professional skepticism
- *Independence in appearance* — The absence of circumstances that would cause a reasonable and informed third party[2] to reasonably conclude that the integrity, objectivity, or professional skepticism of an audit organization or member of the audit team had been compromised

As can be seen previously, the 2018 GAGAS add a specific component to the independence standard to address the independence in appearance aspect of auditor independence. Independence is necessary to ensure that the opinions, findings, conclusions, judgments, and recommendations of the auditor will be impartial and viewed as impartial by reasonable and informed third parties. Therefore, GAGAS require auditors to avoid situations that could lead reasonable and informed third parties to conclude that they are not independent (that is, not capable of exercising objective and impartial judgment on all issues associated with conducting the audit and reporting on the work).

Except under limited circumstances, auditors and audit organizations should be independent from an audited entity during

---

[2] The concept of a reasonable and informed third party is a test involving an evaluation by a hypothetical person. Such person possesses skills, knowledge, and experience to objectively evaluate the appropriateness of the auditor's judgments and conclusions. This evaluation entails weighing all the relevant facts and circumstances, including any safeguards applied, that the auditor knows, or could reasonably be expected to know, at the time the evaluation is made.

- any period of time that falls within the period covered by the financial statements or subject matter of the audit; and
- the *period of professional engagement* is described in the application material of the 2018 GAGAS as
  - beginning when the auditors either sign an initial engagement letter or other agreement to conduct an audit or begin to conduct an audit, whichever is earlier; and
  - lasting for the duration of the professional relationship (that, for recurring audits, could cover many periods) and ends with the formal or informal notification, either by the auditors or the audited entity, of the termination of the professional relationship or by the issuance of a report, whichever is later.

The 2018 GAGAS provide the following four interrelated sections for the practical consideration of independence:

1. General requirements and application guidance
2. Requirements for and guidance on a conceptual framework for making independence determinations based on facts and circumstances that are often unique to specific environments
3. Requirements for and guidance on independence for auditors providing nonaudit services, including indication of specific nonaudit services that always impair independence and others that would not normally impair independence
4. Requirements for and guidance on documentation necessary to support adequate consideration of auditor independence

Key point
Auditors should be independent during (*a*) any period of time that falls within the period covered by the financial statements or subject matter of the audit and (*b*) the period of the professional engagement.

Knowledge check

1. *Government Auditing Standards* require auditors to be independent in

    a. Mind and appearance.
    b. Appearance of mind.
    c. Mind.
    d. Appearance.

GAGAS conceptual framework approach to independence

General

Many different circumstances, or combinations of circumstances, are relevant in evaluating threats to independence. Therefore, GAGAS establishes a conceptual framework that auditors use to identify, evaluate, and apply safeguards to address threats to independence.

The conceptual framework assists auditors in maintaining both independence of mind and independence in appearance. It can be applied to many variations in circumstances that create threats to independence and allows auditors to address threats to independence that result from activities that are not specifically prohibited by GAGAS.

Auditors should apply the conceptual framework at three levels:

1. Audit organization
2. Audit team
3. Individual auditor

The identification and evaluation of threats to independence

Threats to independence are circumstances that could impair independence and represent conditions that need to be evaluated using the conceptual framework. They may be created by a wide range of relationships and circumstances but threats to independence do not necessarily impair independence.

Whether independence is impaired depends on

- the nature of the threat,
- whether the threat is of such significance that it would compromise an auditor's professional judgment or create the appearance that the auditor's integrity, objectivity, or professional skepticism may be compromised, and
- the specific safeguards applied to eliminate the threat or reduce it to an acceptable level[3].

---

[3] A threat is not at an acceptable level if it either (*a*) could affect the auditors' ability to conduct an engagement without being affected by influences that compromise professional judgment or (*b*) could expose the auditors or audit organization to circumstances that would cause a reasonable and informed third party to conclude the integrity objectivity, or professional skepticism of the audit organization, or an auditor, had been compromised.

At a minimum, auditors should evaluate the following broad categories of threats to independence when applying the GAGAS conceptual framework:

Self-interest threat	The threat that a financial or other interest will inappropriately influence an auditor's judgment or behavior
Self-review threat	The threat that an auditor or audit organization that has provided nonaudit services will not appropriately evaluate the results of previous judgments made or services provided as part of the nonaudit services when forming a judgment significant to a GAGAS audit
Bias threat	The threat that an auditor will, as a result of political, ideological, social, or other convictions, take a position that is not objective
Familiarity threat	The threat that aspects of a relationship with management or personnel of an audited entity, such as a close or long relationship, or that of an immediate or close family member, will lead an auditor to take a position that is not objective
Undue influence threat	The threat that influences or pressures from sources external to the audit organization will affect an auditor's ability to make objective judgments
Management participation threat	The threat that results from an auditor's taking on the role of management or otherwise performing management functions on behalf of the audited entity, which will lead an auditor to take a position that is not objective
Structural threat	The threat that an audit organization's placement within a government entity, in combination with the structure of the government entity being audited, will affect the audit organization's ability to perform work and report results objectively

Circumstances that result in a threat to independence in one of the preceding categories may result in other threats as well. For example, a circumstance resulting in a structural threat to independence may also expose auditors to undue influence and management participation threats.

Examples of threats to independence

The 2018 GAGAS provide the following examples of circumstances that create threats for the auditor. In prior revisions of GAGAS, these types of examples were included in the appendix information of the respective revision. Circumstances listed below are not the only examples of threats to the auditors' independence.

Self-interest threat

- Audit organization having undue dependence on income from a particular audited entity
- Member of the audit team entering into employment negotiations with an audited entity
- Audit organization discovering a significant error when evaluating the results of a previous professional service provided by the audit organization
- Member of the audit team having a direct financial interest in the audited entity. This would not preclude auditors from auditing pension plans they participate in if the auditors
  - have no control over the investment strategy, benefits, or other management issues associated with the pension plan, and

- belong to such pension plan as part of their employment with the audit organization or prior employment with the audited entity, provided that the plan is normally offered to all employees in equivalent employment positions.

Self-review threat

- Audit organization issuing a report on the effectiveness of the operation of financial or performance management systems after designing or implementing the systems
- Audit organization having prepared the original data used to generate records that are the subject matter of the audit
- Audit organization providing a service for an audited entity that directly affects the subject matter information of the audit
- Member of the audit team being, or having recently been, employed by the audited entity in a position to exert significant influence over the subject matter of the audit

Bias threat

- Member of the audit team having preconceptions about the objectives of a program under audit that are strong enough to affect the auditor's objectivity
- Member of the audit team having biases associated with political, ideological, or social convictions that result from membership or employment in, or loyalty to, a particular type of policy, group, entity, or level of government that could affect the auditor's objectivity

Familiarity threat

- Member of the audit team having a close or immediate family member who is a principal or senior manager of the audited entity
- Member of the audit team having a close or immediate family member who is an employee of the audited entity and is in a position to exert significant influence over the subject matter of the audit
- Principal or employee of the audited entity having recently served on the audit team in a position to exert significant influence over the subject matter of the audit
- An auditor accepting gifts or preferential treatment from an audited entity, unless the value is trivial or inconsequential
- Senior audit personnel having a long association with the audited entity

Undue influence threat

- External interference or influence that could improperly limit or modify the scope of an audit or threaten to do so, including exerting pressure to inappropriately reduce the extent of work performed in order to reduce costs or fees
- External interference with the selection or application of audit procedures or in the selection of transactions to be examined
- Unreasonable restrictions on the time allowed to complete an audit or issue the report
- External interference over assignment, appointment, compensation, and promotion
- Restrictions on funds or other resources provided to the audit organization that adversely affect the audit organization's ability to carry out its responsibilities
- Authority to overrule or to inappropriately influence the auditors' judgment as to the appropriate content of the report

- Threat of replacing the auditor or the audit organization based on a disagreement with the contents of an audit report, the auditors' conclusions, or the application of an accounting principle or other criteria
- Influences that jeopardize the auditors' continued employment for reasons other than incompetence, misconduct, or the audited entity's need for GAGAS audits

Management participation threat

- Member of the audit team being, or having recently been, a principal or senior manager of the audited entity
- Auditor serving as a voting member of an entity's management committee or board of directors, making policy decisions that affect future direction and operation of an entity's programs, supervising entity employees, developing or approving programmatic policy, authorizing an entity's transactions, or maintaining custody of an entity's assets
- Auditor or audit organization recommending a single individual for a specific position that is key to the audited entity or program under audit, or otherwise ranking or influencing management's selection of the candidate
- Auditor preparing management's corrective action plan to deal with deficiencies detected in the audit

Structural threat

- For both external and internal audit organizations
  - structural placement of the audit function within the reporting line of the areas under audit
- For internal audit organizations
  - administrative direction from the audited entity's management

---

Applying safeguards to eliminate or reduce threats

Safeguards are actions or other measures, individually or in combination, that auditors and audit organizations take that effectively eliminate threats to independence or reduce them to an acceptable level. Under the conceptual framework, the auditor applies safeguards that address the specific facts and circumstances under which specific threats to independence exist. Multiple safeguards may be necessary to effectively eliminate a threat or reduce it to an acceptable level.

Chapter 3 of the 2018 GAGAS provide examples of safeguards that may be effective under certain circumstances. These examples cannot provide safeguards for all circumstances but may provide a starting point. Auditors who have identified significant threats to independence are required to apply safeguards as necessary to eliminate those threats or reduce them to an acceptable level.

Potential safeguards

The following lists the examples of safeguards in paragraph 3.50 of chapter 3 of the 2018 GAGAS.

Examples of safeguards

1	Consulting an independent third party, such as a professional organization, a professional regulatory body, or another auditor to discuss audit issues or assess issues that are highly technical or that require significant judgment
2	Involving another audit organization to perform or reperform part of the audit
3	Having an auditor who was not a member of the audit team review the work performed
4	Removing an auditor from an audit team when that auditor's financial or other interests or relationships pose a threat to independence

Potential safeguards relating to nonaudit services

The following lists the examples of safeguards in paragraph 3.69 of chapter 3 of the 2018 GAGAS.

Examples of safeguards relating to nonaudit services

1	Not including individuals who provided the nonaudit service as audit team members
2	Having another auditor, not associated with the audit, review the audit and nonaudit work as appropriate
3	Engaging another audit organization to evaluate the results of the nonaudit service
4	Having another audit organization reperform the nonaudit service to the extent necessary to enable that other audit organization to take responsibility for the service.

Application of the conceptual framework

Auditors should apply the conceptual framework to identify threats to independence and to evaluate the significance of the identified both individually, and in the aggregate. In addition, the auditor should apply safeguards as necessary to eliminate the threats or reduce them to an acceptable level=.

Facts and circumstances that create threats to independence can result from events such as

- the start of a new audit,
- assigning new staff to an ongoing audit, and
- acceptance of a nonaudit service for an audited entity.

In some situations, the audit organization or the auditors may become aware of new information or changes in facts and circumstances that could affect whether a threat has been eliminated or reduced to an acceptable level. Auditors should reevaluate threats to independence, including any safeguards applied, in such circumstances in accordance with the conceptual framework.

Auditors should determine whether identified threats to independence are at an acceptable level or have been eliminated or reduced to an acceptable level. Both qualitative and quantitative factors should be considered in determining the significance of a threat. In cases where threats to independence are not at an acceptable level, the auditor should determine whether appropriate safeguards can be applied to eliminate the threats or reduce them to an acceptable level. In cases where auditors determine threats to independence require the application of safeguards, auditors should document the threats identified and the safeguards applied to eliminate or reduce the threats to an acceptable level.

Certain conditions may lead to threats that are so significant that they cannot be eliminated or reduced to an acceptable level through the application of safeguards. In these circumstances, the auditor should conclude independence is impaired and should decline to accept an audit or should terminate an audit in progress.

If auditors conclude an individual auditor's independence is impaired, it may be necessary to terminate the audit or it may be possible to take action that satisfactorily addresses the effect of the individual auditor's independence impairment. Factors that are relevant in evaluating whether the independence of the audit team or the audit organization is impaired by an individual auditor's independence impairment include

- nature and duration of the individual auditor's impairment
- number and nature of any previous impairments with respect to the current audit
- whether a member of the audit team had knowledge of the interest or relationship that caused the individual auditor's impairment
- whether the individual auditor whose independence is impaired is
  - a member of the audit team or
  - another individual for whom there are independence requirements
- role of the individual auditor on the audit team whose independence is impaired
- effect of the service, if any, on the accounting records or audited entity's financial statements if the individual auditor's impairment was caused by the provision of a nonaudit service
- whether a partner or director of the audit organization had knowledge of the individual auditor's impairment and failed to ensure the individual auditor's impairment was promptly communicated to an appropriate individual within the audit organization
- extent of the self-interest, undue influence, or other threats created by the individual auditor's impairment.

Threats initially identified after the audit report is issued

If a threat to independence is initially identified after the audit report is issued, the auditor should evaluate the threat's effect on the audit and on GAGAS compliance. The auditor may determine the newly identified threat had an impact on the audit and would have resulted in the audit report being different from the report issued had the auditor been aware of it. In this circumstance, the auditor should communicate in the same manner as used to originally distribute the report to those charged with governance, the appropriate officials of the audited entity, the appropriate officials of the audit organization requiring or arranging for the audits, and other known users, so that they do not continue to rely on findings or conclusions that were affected by the threat to independence.

If the report was previously posted to the auditor's publicly accessible website, the auditor should remove the report and post a public notification that the report was removed. The auditor should then determine whether to perform additional audit work necessary to reissue the report, including any revised findings or conclusions, or repost the original report if the additional audit work does not result in a change in findings or conclusions.

Key point
The auditor should evaluate both qualitative and quantitative factors when determining the significance of a threat.

Figure 1: GAGAS conceptual framework for independence

Figure 1 in chapter 3 of the 2018 Yellow Book includes the following flowchart to assist auditors in the application of the conceptual framework for independence. (**Note:** figure 2, referenced in figure 1, is presented later in this chapter.)

Knowledge check

2. What event can create threats to independence?

    a. Rotation of partners on an audit after three years.
    b. Termination of a member of the audited entity for work performance issues.
    c. Assigning new staff to an ongoing audit.
    d. Rotation of staff on an audit after five years.

Provision of nonaudit services to audited entities

Overall, there is increased emphasis in the 2018 GAGAS regarding the consideration of nonaudit services by the auditor. This is an area that needs to be considered early on because an auditor is required to be independent from an audited entity during any period of time that falls within the period covered by the financial statements or subject matter of the audit and the period of the professional engagement. For example, an auditor performing nonaudit services relating to a June 30, 2020, financial statement audit (the first full fiscal year required to be audited under the 2018 GAGAS) is required to be independent beginning July 1, 2019.

General requirements for performing nonaudit services

Before auditors agree to provide a nonaudit service to an audited entity, they should determine whether providing such a service would create a threat to independence, either by itself or in aggregate with other nonaudit services provided, with respect to any GAGAS audit they conduct. A critical component of this determination is consideration of management's ability to effectively oversee the nonaudit service to be provided. The auditor should determine that the audited entity has designated an individual who possesses suitable skill, knowledge, or experience, and that the individual understands the services to be provided sufficiently to oversee them. The individual is not required to possess the expertise to perform or reperform the services.

The 2018 GAGAS provide indicators of management's ability to effectively oversee the nonaudit service that include management's ability to

- Determine the reasonableness of the results of the nonaudit services provided.
- Recognize a material error, omission, or misstatement in the results of the nonaudit services provided.

Key point
The auditor should document consideration of management's ability to effectively oversee nonaudit services to be provided.

Management responsibilities

Management responsibilities involve leading and directing an entity, including making decisions regarding the acquisition, deployment, and control of human, financial, physical, and intangible resources. Therefore, auditors should conclude management responsibilities the auditors perform for an audited entity are impairments to independence. If the auditors were to assume management responsibilities for an audited entity, the management participation threats created would be so significant that no safeguards could reduce them to an acceptable level.

Whether an activity is a management responsibility depends on the facts and circumstances and the auditor exercises professional judgment in identifying these activities. The 2018 GAGAS provide the following examples of activities that are considered management responsibilities and therefore impair independence if performed for an audited entity.

Examples of activities considered a management responsibility and therefore impair independence if performed for an audited entity
Setting policies and strategic direction for the audited entity
Directing and accepting responsibility for the actions of the audited entity's employees in the performance of their routine, recurring activities
Having custody of an audited entity's assets
Reporting to those charged with governance on behalf of management
Deciding which of the audit organization's or outside third party's recommendations to implement
Accepting responsibility for the management of an audited entity's project
Accepting responsibility for designing, implementing, or maintaining internal control
Providing services that are intended to be used as management's primary basis for making decisions that are significant to the subject matter of the audit
Developing an audited entity's performance measurement system when that system is material or significant to the subject matter of the audit
Serving as a voting member of an audited entity's management committee or board of directors

Auditors providing nonaudit services to entities should obtain agreement from audited entity management that audited entity management performs the following functions in connection with the nonaudit services:

- Assumes all management responsibilities
- Oversees the services by designating an individual, preferably within senior management, who possesses suitable skill, knowledge, or experience
- Evaluates the adequacy and results of the services provided
- Accepts responsibility for the results of the services

In cases where the audited entity is unable or unwilling to assume these responsibilities, auditors should conclude the provision of these services is an impairment to independence.

Routine activities

Routine activities performed by auditors relating directly to conducting an audit, such as providing advice and responding to questions as part of an audit, are not considered nonaudit services under the 2018 GAGAS. Such routine activities generally involve providing advice or assistance to the audited entity on an informal basis as part of an audit.

Routine activities typically are

- insignificant in terms of time incurred or resources expended, and
- generally do not result in a specific project or engagement or in the auditors producing a formal report or other formal work product.

Key point
Activities such as financial statement preparation, cash-to-accrual conversions, and reconciliations are considered nonaudit services under GAGAS. Because they are not routine activities relating to the performance of an audit, they are evaluated using the conceptual framework.

Routine activities directly relating to an audit may include the following:

- Providing advice to the audited entity on an accounting matter as an ancillary part of the overall financial audit
- Providing advice to the audited entity on routine business matters
- Educating the audited entity about matters within the technical expertise of the auditor
- Providing information to the audited entity that is readily available to the auditors, such as best practices and benchmarking studies

Impact of previously provided nonaudit services on independence

Auditors who previously provided nonaudit services for an entity that is a prospective subject of an audit should evaluate the effect of those nonaudit services on independence before agreeing to conduct a GAGAS audit. If the nonaudit services were performed in the period to be covered by the audit, the auditors should

- determine if GAGAS expressly prohibits the nonaudit service;
- if audited entity management requested the nonaudit service, determine whether the skills, knowledge, and experience of the individual responsible for overseeing the nonaudit service were sufficient; and,
- determine whether a threat to independence exists and address any threats noted in accordance with the conceptual framework.

Auditors may also need to consider the impact of nonaudit services they provide beyond the period in which they initially provided the nonaudit service. For example, if auditors have designed and implemented an accounting and financial reporting system that is expected to be in place for many years, a threat to independence in appearance for future engagements performed by those auditors may exist in future periods.

For recurring audits, having another independent audit organization perform an audit of the areas affected by the nonaudit service may provide a safeguard that allows the audit organization that provided the nonaudit service to mitigate the threat to its independence. Auditors use professional judgment to determine whether the safeguards adequately mitigate the threats.

> ### Key point
>
> Auditors may also need to consider the impact of nonaudit services they provide beyond the period in which they initially provided the nonaudit service.

Auditors in a government entity

An auditor in a government entity may be required to perform a nonaudit service that impairs the auditors' independence with respect to a required audit. If, because of constitutional or statutory requirements over which they have no control, the auditors can neither implement safeguards to reduce the resulting threat to an acceptable level, nor decline to provide or terminate a nonaudit service that is incompatible with audit responsibilities, auditors should disclose the nature of the threat that could not be eliminated or reduced to an acceptable level and modify the GAGAS compliance statement in the auditor's report accordingly. Determining how to modify the GAGAS compliance statement in these circumstances is a matter of professional judgment.

Knowledge check

3. What is a routine activity under *Government Auditing Standards*?

    a. Preparing the audited entity's financial statements.
    b. Providing advice to the audited entity on routine business matters.
    c. Performing bookkeeping services to adjust the audited entity's cash basis records to the accrual basis of accounting.
    d. Reconciling control accounts to subsidiary ledgers.

Consideration of specific nonaudit services

By their nature, certain nonaudit services directly support an entity's operations and, if provided to an audited entity, create a threat to the auditor's ability to maintain independence in mind and appearance. Some aspects of these services will impair auditors' ability to conduct GAGAS audits for the entities to which the services are provided.

The 2018 GAGAS discuss some aspects of specific nonaudit services that will impair an auditor's ability to audit the entities for whom the services are provided. However, the specific services indicated in the 2018 GAGAS are not the only nonaudit services that would impair an auditors' independence.

Auditors may be able to provide nonaudit services in the broad areas indicated in this section without impairing independence if

- the nonaudit services are not expressly prohibited by GAGAS requirements,
- the auditors have determined the requirements for providing nonaudit services have been met, and
- any significant threats to independence have been eliminated or reduced to an acceptable level through the application of safeguards.

Key point
Auditors should use the conceptual framework to evaluate independence given the facts and circumstances of individual services not specifically prohibited in this section.

For financial audits, examination or review engagements, and reviews of financial statements, a nonaudit service otherwise prohibited by GAGAS and provided during the period covered by the financial statements may not threaten independence with respect to those financial statements if the

- nonaudit service was provided prior to the period of professional engagement;
- nonaudit service relates only to periods prior to the period covered by the financial statements; and,
- financial statements for the period to which the nonaudit service did relate were audited by other auditors (or in the case of an examination, review, or review of financial statements, examined, reviewed, or audited by other auditors as appropriate).

The nonaudit services discussed in the following pages are among those the GAO believes are frequently requested of auditors working in a government environment. Some aspects of these services will impair an auditor's ability to perform audits for the entities for which the services are provided. The specific services indicated here are not the only nonaudit services that would impair an auditor's independence.

Preparing accounting records and financial statements	Auditors should conclude the following services involving preparation of accounting records impair independence with respect to an audited entity:

Auditors should conclude the following services involving preparation of accounting records impair independence with respect to an audited entity:

- Determining or changing journal entries, account codes or classifications for transactions, or other accounting records for the entity without obtaining management's approval
- Authorizing or approving the entity's transactions
- Preparing or making changes to source documents without management approval (for example, purchase orders, payroll time records, customer orders, and contracts) — Such records also include an entity's general ledger and subsidiary records or equivalent.

Auditors should conclude preparing financial statements in their entirety from a client-provided trial balance or underlying accounting records creates significant threats to auditors' independence. Threats and safeguards applied to eliminate and reduce threats to an acceptable level should be documented. If threats cannot be eliminated or reduced to an acceptable level, the auditors should decline to provide the services. Management is responsible for the preparation and fair presentation of the financial statements in accordance with the applicable financial reporting framework, even if the auditor assisted in drafting those financial statements. Consequently, an auditor's acceptance of responsibility for the preparation and fair presentation of financial statements that the auditor will subsequently audit or that will otherwise be the subject matter of an engagement would impair the auditor's independence.

Auditors should identify as threats to independence any services relating to preparing accounting records and financial statements including the following:

- Recording transactions for which management has determined or approved the appropriate account classification, or posting coded transactions to an audited entity's general ledger
- Preparing certain line items or sections of the financial statements based on information in the trial balance
- Posting entries that an audited entity's management has approved to the entity's trial balance
- Preparing account reconciliations that identify reconciling items for the audited entity management's evaluation

Factors relevant to evaluating the significance of any threats[4] created by providing services relating to preparing accounting records and financial statements include
- extent to which the outcome of the service could have a material effect on the financial statements
- degree of subjectivity involved in determining the appropriate amounts or treatment for those matters reflected in the financial statements
- extent of the audited entity's involvement in determining significant matters of judgment

---

[4] Providing clerical assistance, such as typing, formatting, printing, and binding financial statements, is unlikely to be a significant threat.

Internal audit assistance services provided by external auditors	Internal audit assistance services involve assisting an entity in the performance of its internal audit activities. Auditors should conclude that the following internal audit assistance activities impair an external auditor's independence with respect to an audited entity. These activities include • setting internal audit policies or the strategic direction of internal audit activities; • performing procedures that form part of the internal control, such as reviewing and approving changes to employee data access privileges; and • determining the scope of the internal audit function and resulting work.
Internal control evaluation as a nonaudit service	Auditors should conclude that providing or supervising ongoing monitoring procedures over an entity's system of internal control impairs independence because the management participation threat created is so significant that no safeguards could reduce the threat to an acceptable level. Separate evaluations are sometimes provided as a nonaudit service. When providing separate evaluations as nonaudit services, auditors should evaluate the significance of the threat created by performing separate evaluations and apply safeguards when necessary to eliminate the threat or reduce it to an acceptable level. Accepting responsibility for designing, implementing, or maintaining internal control includes accepting responsibility for designing, implementing, or maintaining monitoring procedures. Monitoring involves the use of either ongoing monitoring procedures or separate evaluations to gather and analyze persuasive information supporting conclusions about the effectiveness of the internal control system. Ongoing monitoring procedures performed on behalf of management are built into the routine, recurring operating activities of an entity. Factors relevant to evaluating the significance of any threats created by providing separate evaluations as a nonaudit service include (*a*) the frequency of the separate evaluations and (*b*) the scope or extent of the controls (in relation to the scope of the audit conducted) being evaluated. A separate evaluation provided as a nonaudit service is not a substitute for audit procedures in a GAGAS audit.

Information technology systems services	Auditors should conclude that providing information technology (IT) services to and audited entity that relate to the period under audit impairs independence if those services include • designing or developing an audited entity's financial information or other IT system that will play a significant role in the management of an area of operations that is or will be the subject matter of an audit; • making other than insignificant modifications to source code underlying an audited entity's existing financial information system or other IT system that will play a significant role in the management of an area of operations that is or will be the subject matter of an audit; • supervising audited entiy personnel in the daily operation of an audited entity's information system; or • operating an audited entity's network, financial information system, or other IT system that will play a significant role in the management of an area of operations that is or will be the subject matter of an engagemnet. Services related to IT systems include the design or implementation of hardware or software systems. The systems may aggregate source data, form part of the internal control over the subject matter of the audit, or generate information that affects the subject matter of the audit.
Appraisal, Valuation, and Actuarial services	Auditors should conclude that independence is impaired if an audit organization provides appraisal, valuation, or actuarial services to an audited entity when (1) the services involve a significant degree of subjectivity and (2) the results of the service, individually or when combined with other valuation, appraisal, or actuarial services, are material to the audited entity's financial statements or other information on which the audit organization is reporting. A valuation comprises the making of assumptions with regard to future developments, the application of appropriate methodologies and techniques, and the combination of both to compute a certain value, or range of values, for an asset, a liability, or an entity as a whole.

Other nonaudit services	Auditors should conclude providing certain other nonaudit services impairs an external auditor's independence with respect to an audited entity. These activities include the following:
	
	 • Advisory service
	  – Assuming any management responsibilities
	 • Benefit plan administration
	  – Making policy decisions on behalf of management
	  – Interpreting the provisions in a plan document for a plan participant on behalf of management without first obtaining management's concurrence
	  – Making disbursements on behalf of the plan
	  – Having custody of a plan's assets
	  – Serving in a fiduciary capacity, as defined by the Employee Retirement Income Security Act of 1974
	 • Executive or employee recruiting
	  – Committing the audited entity to employee compensation or benefit arrangements
	  – Hiring or terminating the audited entity's employees
	 • Business risk consulting
	  – Making or approving business risk decisions
	  – Presenting business risk considerations to those charged with governance on behalf of management
	 • Investment advisory or management
	  – Making investment decisions on behalf of management or otherwise having discretionary authority over an audited entity's investments
	  – Executing a transaction to buy or sell an audited entity's investment
	  – Having custody of an audited entity's assets, such as taking temporary possession of securities

GAGAS provides a flowchart to assist auditors in the independence considerations for preparing accounting records and financial statements. This flowchart is used for services not expressly prohibited by GAGAS.

Figure 2: Independence Consideration for Preparing Accounting Records and Financial Statements

---

Knowledge check

4. What service would **not** impair the auditor's ability to maintain independence in an audit performed under *Government Auditing Standards*?

    a. Determining or changing journal entries, account codes or classifications for transactions, or other accounting records for the entity without obtaining management's approval.

    b. Preparing or changing an entity's subsidiary records without management's approval.

    c. Determining or changing journal entries, account codes or classifications for transactions, or other accounting records for the entity after obtaining management's approval.

    d. Preparing or making changes to an audited entity's source documents without management's approval.

Documentation

Documentation of independence considerations provides evidence of the auditor's judgments in forming conclusions regarding compliance with independence requirements. As with other revisions to GAGAS, the 2018 revision includes specific requirements for documentation relating to nonaudit services and to independence.

Although insufficient documentation of an auditor's compliance with the independence standard does not impair independence, auditors should prepare appropriate documentation under the GAGAS quality control and assurance requirements. Audit organizations using "canned" audit software products may need to review the documentation the product produces to determine if it meets the requirements of GAGAS.

Nonaudit services

For nonaudit services, auditors should establish and document their understanding with the audited entity's management or those charged with governance, as appropriate, regarding the following:

- Objectives of the nonaudit service
- Services to be provided
- Audited entity's acceptance of its responsibilities
- Auditors' responsibilities
- Any limitations on the provision of nonaudit services

Audit services

The independence standard includes the following documentation requirements:

- Threats to independence that require the application of safeguards, along with safeguards applied, in accordance with the conceptual framework for independence
- Safeguards required if an audit organization is structurally located within a government entity and is considered structurally independent based on those safeguards
- Consideration of audited entity management's ability to effectively oversee a nonaudit service to be provided by the auditor
- Auditor's understanding with an audited entity for which the auditor will provide nonaudit services
- Evaluation of the significance of the threats created by providing any services relating to preparing accounting records and financial statements

Nonaudit versus nonattest services

Nonaudit services is the term used by the GAO to define professional services other than audits or attestation engagements. GAGAS require the audit organization providing nonaudit services to entities for which they also provide audits conducted in accordance with GAGAS to assess the impact that providing the nonaudit services may have on the auditor's and audit organization's independence.

The "Scope and Applicability of Nonattest Services" interpretation (AICPA, *Professional Standards*, ET sec. 1.295.010) of the "Independence Rule" provides guidance regarding nonattest services as it relates to independence. Paragraphs .05–.06 of this interpretation reinforce the guidance found in GAGAS. It states the following:

> However, the member should exercise judgment in determining whether his or her involvement has become so extensive that it would constitute performing a separate service that would be subject to the "General Requirements for Performing Nonattest Services" interpretation [1.295.040]. For example, activities such as financial statement preparation, cash-to-accrual conversions, and reconciliations are considered outside the scope of the attest engagement and, therefore, constitute a nonattest service. Such activities would not impair independence if the requirements of the interpretations of the "Nonattest Services" subtopic [1.295] are met.

Competence and CPE

This section discusses the major changes made to the competence and CPE guidance in the 2018 GAGAS. Chapter 4 of the 2018 GAGAS, *Competence and Continuing Professional Education*, establishes GAGAS requirements for competence and CPE. In the 2011 revision to GAGAS, requirements for the general standards, including competency and CPE, were found in chapter 3.

Competence includes being knowledgeable about the specific GAGAS requirements and having the skills and abilities to proficiently apply that knowledge on GAGAS audits. As such, competence is derived from a combination of education and experience and enables auditors to make sound professional judgments.

Competence

In the 2011 revision, the unconditional requirement relating to competency was as follows

> The staff assigned to perform the audit must collectively possess adequate professional competence needed to address the audit objectives and perform the work in accordance with GAGAS.

The 2018 revision of GAGAS states the following requirements.

Paragraphs 4.02–4.04 of GAGAS	Requirements: General
	4.02 The audit organization's management must assign auditors to conduct the engagement who before beginning work on the engagement collectively possess the competence needed to address the engagement objectives and perform their work in accordance with GAGAS.
	4.03 The audit organization's management must assign auditors who before beginning work on the engagement possess the competence needed for their assigned roles.
	4.04 The audit organization should have a process for recruitment, hiring, continuous development, assignment, and evaluation of personnel so that the workforce has the essential knowledge, skills, and abilities necessary to conduct the engagement. The nature, extent, and formality of the process will depend on various factors, such as the size of the audit organization, its structure, and its work.

As can be seen previously, the 2018 GAGAS unconditional requirement relating to competency has been expanded. Unlike prior revisions of GAGAS, the 2018 GAGAS identify the roles of members of the audit team and define the typical functions performed by audit team members.

Roles on the audit, as identified in the 2018 GAGAS, generally include the following:

- Nonsupervisory auditors
  - Auditors in these roles plan or perform audit procedures
  - Work situations for these auditors are characterized by low levels of ambiguity, complexity, and uncertainty
  - Nonsupervisory auditor role necessitates at least a basic level of proficiency
- Supervisory auditors
  - Auditors in these roles plan audits, perform audit procedures, or direct audits
  - Work situations for these auditors are characterized by moderate levels of ambiguity, complexity, and uncertainty
  - Supervisory auditor role necessitates at least an intermediate level of proficiency
- Partners and directors
  - Auditors in these roles plan audits, perform audit procedures, or direct or report on audits
  - Partners and directors may also be responsible for reviewing audit quality prior to issuing the report, for signing the report, or both
  - Work situations for these auditors are characterized by high levels of ambiguity, complexity, and uncertainty
  - Partner and director role necessitates an advanced level of proficiency

Key terms defined in the 2018 GAGAS are as follows:

- Planning (his definition excludes auditors whose role is limited to gathering information used in planning the engagement)
  - Determining engagement objectives, scope, and methodology
  - Establishing criteria to evaluate matters subject to audit
  - Coordinating the work of the other audit organizations
- Directing
  - Supervising the efforts of others who are involved in accomplishing the objectives of the engagement or reviewing engagement work to determine whether those objectives have been accomplished
- Performing engagement procedures
  - Performing tests and procedures necessary to accomplish the engagement objectives in accordance with GAGAS
- Reporting
  - Determining the report content and substance or reviewing reports to determine whether the engagement objectives have been accomplished and the evidence supports the report's technical content and substance prior to issuance (this includes signing the report)

CPE

Paragraph 4.16 of GAGAS	Requirements: General
	4.16 Auditors who plan, direct, perform engagement procedures for, or report on an engagement conducted in accordance with GAGAS should develop and maintain their professional competence by completing at least 80 hours of CPE in every 2-year period as follows.

CPE hours	Subject matter categories of CPE
24 hours	Subject matter directly related to the government environment, government auditing, or the specific or unique environment in which the audited entity operates
56 hours	Subject matter that directly enhance auditors' professional expertise to conduct engagements

4.17 Auditors should complete at least 20 hours of CPE in each year of the 2-year periods.

4.18 The audit organization should maintain documentation of each auditor's CPE.

The continuing competence of the audit organization's personnel depends, in part, on an appropriate level of CPE so that auditors maintain the knowledge, skills, and abilities necessary to conduct the GAGAS audit. Obtaining CPE specifically on GAGAS, particularly during years in which there are revisions to the standards, may assist auditors in maintaining the competence necessary to conduct GAGAS audits.

Although the 2018 GAGAS do not make major changes to the CPE requirements, a number of examples of subject matter categories of CPE are included in the application material. As mentioned earlier in this chapter, these examples are in a separate 2005 GAO report (GAO-05-568G) that will be superseded upon the effective date of the 2018 GAGAS.

Determining what subjects are appropriate for individual auditors to satisfy the CPE requirements is a matter of professional judgment to be exercised by auditors in consultation with appropriate officials in their audit organization. When determining what specific subjects qualify for the CPE requirement, the auditors may consider the types of knowledge, skills, and abilities, and the level of proficiency necessary, in order to be competent for their assigned roles. Auditors may consider probable future audits to which they may be assigned when selecting specific CPE subjects to satisfy the 24-hour and the 56-hour CPE requirements. The audit organization is ultimately responsible for determining whether a subject or topic qualifies as acceptable for its auditors.

Examples of CPE subjects that may qualify for 24-hour and the 56-hour categories enumerated in the 2018 GAGAS are listed below.

- Subject matter directly related to the government environment, government auditing, or the specific or unique environment in which the audited entity operates (24-hour requirement) may include, but is not limited to, the following:
  - GAGAS and related topics, such as internal control as addressed in GAGAS
  - Applicable AICPA Statements on Auditing Standards
  - Applicable AICPA Statements on Standards for Attestation Engagements and Statements on Standards for Accounting and Review Services
  - Applicable auditing standards issued by the Institute of Internal Auditors, the Public Company Accounting and Oversight Board, the International Auditing and Assurance Standards Board, or other auditing standard-setting body
  - U.S. generally accepted accounting principles, or the applicable financial reporting framework being used, such as those issued by the Federal Accounting Standards Advisory Board, the Governmental Accounting Standards Board, or the Financial Accounting Standards Board
  - *Standards for Internal Control in the Federal Government*
  - *Internal Control — Integrated Framework*, as applicable
  - Requirements for recipients of federal contracts or grants, such as Single Audits under the *Uniform Administrative Requirements, Cost Principles, and Audit Requirements for Federal Awards*
  - Requirements for federal, state, or local program audits
  - Relevant or applicable audit standards or guides, including those for IT auditing and forensic auditing
  - IT auditing topics applicable to the government environment
  - Fraud topics applicable to a government environment
  - Statutory requirements, regulations, criteria, guidance, trends, risks, or topics relevant to the specific and unique environment in which the audited entity operates
  - Statutory requirements, regulations, criteria, guidance, trends, risks, or topics relevant to the subject matter of the audit, such as scientific, medical, environmental, educational, or any other specialized subject matter
  - Topics directly related to the government environment, such as the nature of government (structures, financing, and operations), economic or other conditions and pressures facing governments, common government financial management issues, appropriations, measurement or evaluation of government financial or program performance, and application of general audit methodologies or techniques to a government environment or program
  - Specialized audit methodologies or analytical techniques, such as the use of complex survey instruments, actuarial estimates, statistical analysis tests, or statistical or nonstatistical sampling
  - Performance auditing topics, such as obtaining evidence, professional skepticism, and other applicable audit skills
  - Government ethics and independence
  - Partnerships between governments, businesses, and citizens
  - Legislative policies and procedures
  - Topics related to fraud, waste, abuse, or improper payments affecting government entities
  - Compliance with laws and regulations

- Subject matter that directly enhances auditors' professional expertise to conduct audits (56-hour requirement) may include, but is not limited to, the following:
  - Subject matter categories for the 24-hour requirement listed in the previous section
  - General ethics and independence
  - Topics related to accounting, acquisitions management, asset management, budgeting, cash management, contracting, data analysis, program performance, or procurement
  - Communicating clearly and effectively, both orally and in writing
  - Managing time and resources
  - Leadership
  - Software applications used in conducting audits
  - IT
  - Economics, human capital management, social and political sciences, and other academic disciplines that may be applied in audits, as applicable

Summary

This chapter discusses the major changes to the independence, competence, and CPE guidance in the 2018 GAGAS. In addition, the conceptual framework established by the GAO in the 2011 GAGAS, which should be applied in every GAGAS audit is discussed. The chapter identifies safeguards the auditor may have in place that the audit organization can apply to eliminate, or reduce to an acceptable level, significant threats to independence. This chapter includes a discussion of nonaudit services and their effect on independence in a GAGAS audit and a detailed discussion of specific nonaudit services that impair independence. A summary of the documentation required in a GAGAS audit relating to nonaudit services and independence is also discussed in this chapter. Nonattest services identified in the AICPA professional standards are also discussed in this chapter in light of GAGAS standards for nonaudit services. This chapter concludes with a discussion of the changes to the competence of the auditor and audit organization and CPE.

8-34

Practice questions

1. How do the 2018 GAGAS define independence of mind?

2. How do the 2018 GAGAS define independence in appearance?

3. List the seven threats to independence included in the GAGAS conceptual framework.

4. As noted in paragraph 3.50 in chapter 3, what safeguards do the 2018 GAGAS include?

5. List five activities noted as management responsibilities in the 2018 GAGAS.

6. What are the six categories of specific nonaudit services identified in the 2018 GAGAS that, because of their nature, impair the auditors' ability to maintain independence in mind and appearance?

7. List three specific nonaudit services in the "Preparing Accounting Records and Financial Statements" category of the 2018 GAGAS that impair independence.

Appendix A

ASU No. 2014-09: Revenue from Contracts with Customers (Topic 606)

ASU No. 2014-09: Revenue from Contracts with Customers, as Amended[1]

Why was this ASU issued?

The objective of ASU No. 2014-09, as amended, is to address a number of concerns regarding the complexity and lack of consistency surrounding the accounting for revenue transactions. In addition, ASU No. 2014-09, as amended, provides a framework for revenue recognition and eliminates the transaction- and industry-specific revenue recognition guidance under current GAAP. The intent is to avoid inconsistencies of accounting treatment across different geographies and industries.

Who is affected by this update?

This ASU, as amended, affects any entity either entering into contracts

- with customers to transfer goods or services
- for the transfer of nonfinancial assets unless those contracts are within the scope of other standards (for example, lease or insurance contracts).

Not-for-profit entities classifying government and other grants as exchange transactions will likely need to account for those agreements using the guidance in ASU No. 2014-09, as amended.

What are the main provisions of this ASU?[2]

The core principle of the revised revenue recognition standard is an entity should recognize revenue to depict the transfer of goods or services to customers in an amount reflecting the consideration to which the entity expects to be entitled in exchange for those good or services.

ASU No. 2014-09, as amended, states an entity should follow these five steps in recognizing revenue from contracts with customers:

1. Identify the contract(s) with a customer.
2. Identify the performance obligations in the contract.
3. Determine the transaction price.
4. Allocate the transaction price to the performance obligations in the contract.
5. Recognize revenue when (or as) the entity satisfies a performance obligation.

---

[1] The effective date of this ASU was amended upon issuance of ASU 2015-14, *Revenue from Contracts with Customers (Topic 606): Deferral of the Effective Date.*

[2] The Financial Accounting Standards Board (FASB) and the International Accounting Standards Board (IASB) periodically deliberate and make changes to this standard. The most current status of this project may be found at www.fasb.org.

<table>
<tr><td align="center">**Key point**</td></tr>
<tr><td>Under ASU No. 2014-09, as amended, revenue is recognized when an entity satisfies a performance obligation by transferring a promised good or service to a customer (which is when the customer obtains control of the good or service).</td></tr>
</table>

Understanding the five-step process

Step 1: Identify the contract(s) with a customer

ASU No. 2014-09, as amended, defines a contract as "an agreement between two or more parties that creates enforceable rights and obligations." This update affects contracts with a customer meeting the following criteria:

- Approval (in writing, orally, or in accordance with other customary business practices) and commitment of the parties is in place.
- Rights of the parties are identified.
- Payment terms are identified.
- Contract has commercial substance.
- It is probable the entity will collect the consideration to which it will be entitled in exchange for the goods or services transferred to the customer.

A contract does not exist if each party to the contract has the unilateral enforceable right to terminate a wholly unperformed contract without compensating the other party (parties).

Step 2: Identify the performance obligations in the contract

A *performance obligation* is a promise in a contract with a customer to transfer a good or service to the customer.

At contract inception, an entity should assess the goods or services promised in a contract with a customer and should identify as a performance obligation (possibly multiple performance obligations) each promise to transfer to the customer either

- a good or service (or bundle of goods or services) which is distinct, or
- a series of distinct goods or services which are substantially the same and have the same pattern of transfer to the customer.

A good or service which is not distinct should be combined with other promised goods or services until the entity identifies a bundle of goods or services which is distinct. In some cases, this would result in the entity accounting for all the goods or services promised in a contract as a single performance obligation.

Step 3: Determine the transaction price

The transaction price is the amount of consideration (fixed or variable) the entity expects to receive in exchange for transferring promised goods or services to a customer, excluding amounts collected on behalf of third parties. To determine the transaction price, an entity should consider the effects of

- variable consideration,
- constraining estimates of variable consideration,
- the existence of a significant financing component,
- noncash considerations, and
- consideration payable to the customer.

If the consideration promised in a contract includes a variable amount, then an entity should estimate the amount of consideration to which the entity will be entitled in exchange for transferring the promised goods or services to a customer. An entity would then include in the transaction price some or all of an amount of variable consideration only to the extent it is probable a significant reversal in the amount of cumulative revenue recognized will not occur when the uncertainty associated with the variable consideration is subsequently resolved.

An entity should consider the terms of the contract and its customary business practices to determine the transaction price.

Step 4: Allocate the transaction price to the performance obligations in the contract

The transaction price is allocated to separate performance obligations in proportion to the standalone selling price of the promised goods or services. If a standalone selling price is not directly observable, then an entity should estimate it. Reallocation of the transaction price for changes in the standalone selling price is not permitted. When estimating the standalone selling price, entities can use various methods including the adjusted market assessment approach, expected cost plus a margin approach, and residual approach (only if the selling price is highly variable and uncertain).

ASU No. 2014-09, as amended, specifies when an entity should allocate any discount or variable consideration relating to one performance obligation to this (or some other) performance obligation rather than to all of the performance obligations in the contract.

Step 5: Recognize revenue when (or as) the entity satisfies a performance obligation

The amount of revenue recognized when transferring the promised good or service to a customer is equal to the amount allocated to the satisfied performance obligation, which may be satisfied at a point in time (goods) or over time (services).

> **Key point**
>
> In the context of ASU No. 2014-09, as amended, control of an asset refers to the ability to direct the use of, and obtain substantially all of the remaining benefits from, the asset. Control also includes the ability to prevent other entities from directing the use of, and obtaining the benefits from, an asset.

When performance obligations are satisfied over time, the entity should select an appropriate method for measuring its progress toward complete satisfaction of the performance obligation. ASU No. 2014-09, as amended, discusses methods of measuring progress including input and output methods, and how to determine which method is appropriate.

Additional guidance under this ASU

ASU No. 2014-09 also addresses the following areas:

- Accounting for incremental costs of obtaining a contract, as well as costs incurred to fulfill a contract
- Licenses
- Warranties.

Lastly, ASU No. 2014-09, as amended, enhances disclosure requirements to include more information about specific revenue contracts entered into by the entity, including performance obligations and the transaction price.

> A thorough discussion of the full text of ASU No. 2014-09, as amended, is beyond the scope of this course and this course. Readers are strongly encouraged to read the full update, which is available at www.fasb.org.

When is this ASU effective?

For nonpublic entities, including not-for-profit entities, this ASU, as amended, is effective for annual reporting periods beginning after December 15, 2017, and interim periods within annual periods beginning after December 15, 2018. Nonpublic business entities and other entities may elect to adopt the standard earlier but no earlier than the annual periods beginning after December 15, 2017.

Implementation issues

Generally, to successfully implement the requirements of this standard, entities will first need to evaluate how the standard will affect the entity overall. This will include consideration of the effects not only on the financial statements but other information systems, processes, compensation, and other contractual commitments, and tax planning strategies.[3] All entities affected by this ASU need to develop an implementation plan as soon as possible. At a minimum, an implementation plan will need to include

- key actions for implementation
- time estimated for each implementation action
- mechanism to track the progress and timing of the implementation plan.

This ASU, as amended, is likely to affect not-for-profit entities accounting for government and other grants or membership dues in whole or in part as exchange transactions. It is very likely a government grant agreement will meet the definition of a "contract" delineated in ASU No. 2014-09, as amended. Not-for-profit entities may not use "formal" contracts for memberships especially when membership dues are accounted for, in whole or part, as contributions (rather than exchange transactions). On the other hand, other not-for-profit organizations may use formal membership contracts and it is likely these contracts would meet the definition of a "contract" under ASU No. 2014-09, as amended.

To prepare for transition, not-for-profit entities accounting for grants as exchange transactions may wish to re-evaluate this accounting treatment. Using the indicators in FASB ASC 958, *Not-for-Profit Entities*, many government grants are actually contributions rather than exchange transactions. In the event a not-for-profit entity believes government grants are exchange transactions, the entity will need to apply the guidance of ASU No. 2014-09, as amended. Not-for-profit entities may wish to discuss this decision with their auditors well in advance of the deferred effective date of ASU No. 2014-09, amended.

Even though the deferred effective date of ASU No. 2014-09 as amended, is several years in the future for most not-for-profit entities, it is important to begin the implementation process as early as possible. In the case of government grants accounted for as exchange transactions, not-for-profit entities will likely want to review their existing contracts to see what modifications, if any, need be made to the contract. Likewise, not-for-profit entities using membership contracts need to begin to review them for any modifications necessary to recognize revenue under ASU No. 2014-09, as amended.

Many not-for-profit entities enter into multiple year grants or membership contracts, or both. Any grant agreements or membership contracts signed prior to the effective date of ASU No. 2014-09, as amended, will require retrospective restatement upon the deferred effective date of ASU No. 2014-09, as amended. This could have significant negative consequences if revenue has been recognized prior to transition which does not meet the requirements for recognition under ASU No. 2014-09, as amended. If performance obligations are not clearly delineated in the grant agreement or membership contract, revenue is not recognized until the contract terminates.

---

[3] For more information, see "Tips for Successful Revenue Recognition Implementation" by Ken Tyslac available at www.aicpa.org.

Appendix B

ACCOUNTING STANDARDS UPDATE NO. 2018-08: NOT-FOR-PROFIT ENTITIES (TOPIC 958): CLARIFYING THE SCOPE AND THE ACCOUNTING GUIDANCE FOR CONTRIBUTIONS RECEIVED AND CONTRIBUTIONS MADE

In June 2018, FASB issued Accounting Standards Update (ASU) No. 2018-08, *Not-for-Profit Entities (Topic 958): Clarifying the Scope and the Accounting Guidance for Contributions Received and Contributions Made*. The ASU was issued to clarify and improve the scope and accounting guidance for contributions received and contributions made. As such, it clarifies when transactions should be accounted for as contributions subject to the requirements in FASB Accounting Standards Codification (ASC) 958, *Not-for-Profit Entities*, or as exchange transactions under FASB ASC 606, *Revenue from Contracts with Customers*. Additionally, the standard provides guidance to determine when a contribution is conditional. Information in this appendix summarizes the major areas of the ASU.

> Readers are strongly encouraged to read the entire ASU that can be found under the Standards tab at www.fasb.org.

To determine if FASB ASC 606 is applicable to grants or contracts of not-for-profit entities, the transaction should first be reviewed to determine if it is reciprocal (an exchange) or nonreciprocal (a contribution). Under the standard, an entity determines whether a resource provided is participating in an exchange transaction by evaluating whether the resource provider is "receiving commensurate value in return for the resources transferred." The type of resource provider does not factor into this determination. This determination is based on the agreement and the following:

- A resource provider is not synonymous with the general public. Benefits received by the public resulting from the assets transferred are not equivalent to commensurate value received by the resource provider.
- Execution of a resource provider's mission or positive sentiment a donor feels does not constitute commensurate value.
- Expressed intent asserted by both the recipient and resource provider relating to the assets transferred
- Discretion the resource provider has in determining the amount of the transferred assets—When both the recipient and resource provider agree on the amount, the transaction is an exchange transaction.
- Significance of penalties assessed on the recipient for failure to comply with the terms of the agreement—Economic forfeiture beyond the amount of assets transferred generally indicates the transaction is an exchange transaction. Penalties limited to returning unspent amounts or to delivery of assets/services previously provided generally indicate the transaction is a contribution.

Consistent with current GAAP, the ASU clarifies when a resource provider itself is not receiving commensurate value, the recipient entity must determine whether a transfer of assets represents a payment from a third-party payer on behalf of an existing exchange transaction between the recipient and an identified customer. In such cases, the transfer of assets is an exchange transaction and should be accounted for under FASB ASC 606 (or other guidance if applicable). If the donor or grantor does not receive commensurate value, the grant or contract is a contribution and accounted for under the guidance in FASB ASC 958-605.

As noted previously, the standard clarifies a resource provider is not synonymous with the general public, and, as such, the assets the resource provider transfers are not equivalent to commensurate value. Therefore, such transfers are not accounted for under FASB ASC 606 but rather under FASB ASC 958-605 as a contribution. For example, a not-for-profit entity with a mission to provide quality affordable child care to low-income families would account for a governmental grant, which subsidizes their programs as a contribution. Even though the governmental grant may further the mission of the government or granting agency, the not-for-profit's programs provide a societal benefit and the grantor does not receive commensurate reciprocal value.

Once it has been determined a transfer of assets (that is a grant, contract, or other donation) is a contribution, the next step is to determine if the contribution is conditional or unconditional. Similar to current guidance, conditional promises to give are not recognized and conditional contributions are recognized as liabilities. The ASU clarifies for a contribution to be conditional it must meet *both* of the following criteria:

- A barrier exists that the donee or grantee must overcome to gain rights to the resources provided and
  - a right of return of the assets transferred or
  - a right of release of the promisor from its obligation to transfer assets.

A number of indicators are included in the ASU to assist entities in determining if one or more barriers may exist in the agreement. Similar to current guidance, no single indicator is determinative of a barrier and facts and circumstances may make some indicators more significant than others. The following indicators of a barrier are included in the ASU:

- Inclusion of a measurable performance-related barrier or other measurable barrier
- Extent to which a stipulation limits discretion by the recipient on the conduct of the activity
- A stipulation in the agreement is related to the purpose of the agreement (This would generally exclude administrative tasks and trivial stipulations.)

A number of examples of contributions and exchange transactions, as well as barriers, are provided in the ASU. FASB expects the guidance will result in more grants and contracts being accounted for as contributions (often conditional contributions) than under previous standards. As such, recipients would be required to comply with current disclosures relating to conditional contributions in FASB ASC 958-310-50-4.

ASU No. 2018-08 should be applied on a modified prospective basis[1] (retrospective application is permitted) in the first set of financial statements following the effective date of the ASU to agreements that are either

- not completed[2] as of the effective date[3] or
- entered into after the effective date.

---

[1] No prior-period results are restated, and no cumulative-effect adjustment made to opening balances of net assets/retained earnings at the beginning of the year of adoption. However, retrospective application is permitted.
[2] A completed agreement is one for which all revenue (of a recipient) or expense (of a resource provider) has been recognized before the effective date of the ASU in accordance with current guidance.
[3] The ASU should only be applied to the portion of revenue or expense not yet recognized before the effective date of the ASU.

In the year of adoption, entities are required to disclose both

- the nature and reason for the accounting change; and
- an explanation of the reasons for significant changes in each financial statement line item in the current annual or interim period resulting from applying the proposed amendments compared with current practice.

Amendments in the ASU are effective based on the type of entity involved in the transaction and whether the entity is acting in the capacity of a resource recipient or a resource provider. The various effective dates are as follows:[4]

- Public business entities and not-for-profit entities that have issued, or are a conduit bond obligor for, securities traded, listed, or quoted on an exchange or over-the-counter market
  - Serving as a resource recipient
    - Annual periods beginning after June 15, 2018, including interim periods within this annual period
  - Serving as a resource provider
    - Annual periods beginning after December 15, 2018, including interim periods within this annual period
- All other entities
  - Serving as a resource recipient
    - Annual periods beginning after December 15, 2018, and interim periods within annual periods beginning after December 15, 2019
  - Serving as a resource provider
    - Annual periods beginning after December 15, 2019, and interim periods within annual periods beginning after December 15, 2020

---

[4] Early adoption is permitted.

Exempt Organizations Glossary

Governmental terminology

accounting system. The methods and records established to identify, assemble, analyze, classify, record, and report a government's transactions and to maintain accountability for the related assets and liabilities.

accrual basis of accounting. The recording of financial effects on a government of transactions and other events and circumstances that have consequences for the government in the periods in which those transactions, events, and circumstances occur, rather than only in the periods in which cash is received or paid by the government.

ad valorem tax. A tax based on value (such as a property tax).

advance from other funds. An asset account used to record noncurrent portions of a long-term debt owed by one fund to another fund within the same reporting entity. (See **due to other funds** and **interfund receivable/payable**).

appropriation. A legal authorization granted by a legislative body to make expenditures and to incur obligations for specific purposes. An appropriation is usually limited in the amount and time it may be expended.

assigned fund balance. A portion of fund balance that includes amounts that are constrained by the government's intent to be used for specific purposes, but that are neither restricted nor committed.

basis of accounting. A term used to refer to *when* revenues, expenditures, expenses, and transfers, and related assets and liabilities are recognized in the accounts and reported in the financial statements. Specifically, it relates to the timing of the measurements made, regardless of the nature of the measurement. (See **accrual basis of accounting**, **cash basis of accounting**, and **modified accrual basis of accounting**).

bond. A written promise to pay a specified sum of money (the face value or principal amount) at a specified date or dates in the future (the maturity dates[s]), together with periodic interest at a specified rate. Sometimes, however, all or a substantial part of the interest is included in the face value of the security. The difference between a note and bond is that the latter is issued for a longer period and requires greater legal formality.

business type activities. Those activities of a government carried out primarily to provide specific services in exchange for a specific user charge.

capital grants. Grants restricted by the grantor for the acquisition or construction, or both, of capital assets.

capital projects fund. A fund used to account for and report financial resources that are restricted, committed, or assigned to expenditures for capital outlays, including the acquisition or construction of capital facilities and other capital assets. Capital project funds exclude those types of capital-related outflows financed by proprietary funds or for assets that will be held in trust for individuals, private organizations, or other governments.

cash basis of accounting. A basis of accounting that requires the recognition of transactions only when cash is received or disbursed.

committed fund balance. A portion of fund balance that includes amounts that can only be used for specific purposes pursuant to constraints imposed by formal action of the government's highest level of decision-making authority.

consumption method. The method of accounting that requires the recognition of an expenditure or expense as inventories are used.

contributed capital. Contributed capital is created when a general capital asset is transferred to a proprietary fund or when a grant is received that is externally restricted to capital acquisition or construction. Contributions restricted to capital acquisition and construction and capital assets received from developers are reported in the operating statement as a separate item after nonoperating revenues and expenses.

custodial fund. A fiduciary fund used to account for financial resources not administered through a trust or equivalent arrangement meeting specified criteria, and that are not required to be reported in a pension (and other employee benefit) trust fund, investment trust fund, or private-purpose trust fund.

debt service fund. A fund used to account for and report financial resources that are restricted, committed, or assigned to expenditure for principal and interest. Debt service funds should be used to report resources if legally mandated. Financial resources that are being accumulated for principal and interest maturing in future years should also be reported as debt service funds.

deferred inflow of resources. An acquisition of net assets by a government that is applicable to a future reporting period.

deferred outflow of resources. A consumption of net asset by a government that is applicable to a future reporting period.

deficit. (*a*) The excess of the liabilities of a fund over its assets. (*b*) The excess of expenditures over revenues during an accounting period or, in the case of proprietary funds, the excess of expenses over revenues during an accounting period.

disbursement. A payment made in cash or by check. Expenses are only recognized at the time physical cash is disbursed.

due from other funds. A current asset account used to indicate an account reflecting amounts owed to a particular fund by another fund for goods sold or services rendered. This account includes only short-term obligations on an open account, not interfund loans.

due to other funds. A current liability account reflecting amounts owed by a particular fund to another fund for goods sold or services rendered. This account includes only short-term obligations on an open account, not interfund loans.

enabling legislation. Legislation that authorizes a government to assess, levy, charge, or otherwise mandate payment of resources from external resource providers and includes a legally enforceable requirement that those resources be used for the specific purposes stipulated in the legislation.

encumbrances. Commitments related to unperformed (executory) contracts for goods or services. Used in budgeting, encumbrances are not generally accepted accounting principles (GAAP) expenditures or liabilities but represent the estimated amount of expenditures that will ultimately result if unperformed contracts in process are completed.

enterprise fund. A fund established to account for operations financed and operated in a manner similar to private business enterprises (such as gas, utilities, transit systems, and parking garages). Usually, the governing body intends that costs of providing goods or services to the general public be recovered primarily through user charges.

expenditures. Decreases in net financial resources. Expenditures include current operating expenses requiring the present or future use of net current assets, debt service and capital outlays, intergovernmental grants, entitlements, and shared revenues.

expenses. Outflows or other consumption of assets or incurrences of liabilities, or a combination of both, from delivering or producing goods, rendering services, or carrying out other activities that constitute the entity's ongoing major or central operations.

fiduciary fund. A fund that reports fiduciary activities meeting the criteria in paragraphs 6–11 of GASB Statement No. 84, *Fiduciary Activities*. Financial reporting is focused on reporting net position and changes in net position.

fund. A fiscal and accounting entity with a self-balancing set of accounts in which cash and other financial resources, all related liabilities and residual equities, or balances, and changes therein, are recorded and segregated to carry on specific activities or attain certain objectives in accordance with special regulations, restrictions, or limitations.

fund balance. The difference between fund assets and fund liabilities of the generic fund types within the governmental category of funds.

fund financial statements. Each fund has its own set of self-balancing accounts and fund financial statements that focus on information about the government's governmental, proprietary, and fiduciary fund types.

fund type. The 11 generic funds that all transactions of a government are recorded into. The 11 fund types are as follows: general, special revenue, debt service, capital projects, permanent, enterprise, internal service, private-purpose trust, pension (and other employee benefit) trust, investment trust, and custodial.

GASB. The Governmental Accounting Standards Board (GASB), organized in 1984 by the Financial Accounting Foundation (FAF) to establish standards of financial accounting and reporting for state and local governmental entities. Its standards guide the preparation of external financial reports of those entities.

general fund. The fund within the governmental category used to account for all financial resources, except those required to be accounted for in another governmental fund.

general-purpose governments. Governmental entities that provide a range of services, such as states, cities, counties, towns, and villages.

governmental funds. Funds used to account for the acquisition, use, and balances of spendable financial resources and the related current liabilities, except those accounted for in proprietary funds and fiduciary funds. Essentially, these funds are accounting segregations of financial resources. Spendable assets are assigned to a particular government fund type according to the purposes for which they may or must be used. Current liabilities are assigned to the fund type from which they are to be paid. The difference between the assets and liabilities of governmental fund types is referred to as *fund balance*. The measurement focus in these fund types is on the determination of financial position and changes in financial position (sources, uses, and balances of financial resources), rather than on net income determination.

government-wide financial statements. Highly aggregated financial statements that present financial information for all assets (including infrastructure capital assets), liabilities, and net assets of a primary government and its component units, except for fiduciary funds. The government-wide financial statements use the economic resources measurement focus and accrual basis of accounting.

infrastructure assets. Long-lived capital assets that normally are stationary in nature and can be preserved for a significantly greater number of years than most capital assets. Examples of infrastructure assets are roads, bridges, tunnels, drainage systems, water and sewer systems, dams, and lighting systems. Buildings, except those that are an ancillary part of a network of infrastructure assets, are not considered infrastructure assets.

interfund receivable/payable. Activity between funds of a government reflecting amounts provided with a requirement for repayment, or sales and purchases of goods and services between funds approximating their external exchange value (also referred to as **interfund loans** or **interfund services provided and used**).

internal service fund. A generic fund type within the proprietary category used to account for the financing of goods or services provided by one department or agency to other departments or agencies of a government, or to other governments, on a cost-reimbursement basis.

investment trust fund. A generic fund type within the fiduciary category used by a government in a fiduciary capacity, such as to maintain its cash and investment pool for other governments.

major funds. A government's general fund (or its equivalent), other individual governmental type, and enterprise funds that meet specific quantitative criteria, and any other governmental or

---

enterprise fund that a government's officials believe is particularly important to financial statement users.

management's discussion and analysis. Management's discussion and analysis, or MD&A, is required supplementary information that introduces the basic financial statements by presenting certain financial information as well as management's analytical insights on that information.

measurement focus. The accounting convention that determines (*a*) which assets and which liabilities are included on a government's balance sheet and where they are reported, and (*b*) whether an operating statement presents information on the flow of financial resources (revenues and expenditures) or information on the flow of economic resources (revenues and expenses).

modified accrual basis of accounting. The basis of accounting adapted to the governmental fund type measurement focus. Revenues and other financial resource increments are recognized when they become both *measurable* and *available to finance expenditures of the current period. Available* means collectible in the current period or soon enough thereafter to be used to pay liabilities of the current period. Expenditures are recognized when the fund liability is incurred and expected to be paid from current resources, except for (*a*) inventories of materials and supplies that may be considered expenditures either when purchased or when used, and (*b*) prepaid insurance and similar items that may be considered expenditures either when paid for or when consumed. All governmental funds are accounted for using the modified accrual basis of accounting in fund financial statements.

modified approach. Rules that allow infrastructure assets that are part of a network or subsystem of a network not to be depreciated as long as certain requirements are met.

net position. The residual of all other elements presented in a statement of financial position.

nonspendable fund balance. The portion of fund balance that includes amounts that cannot be spent because they are either (*a*) not in spendable form or (*b*) legally or contractually required to be maintained intact.

pension (and other employee benefit) trust fund. A trust fund used to account for a public employees retirement system, OPEB plan, or other employee benefits other than pensions that are administered through trusts that meet specified criteria. Pension (and other employee benefit) trust funds use the accrual basis of accounting and the flow of economic resources measurement focus.

permanent fund. A generic fund type under the governmental category used to report resources that are legally restricted to the extent that only earnings, and not principal, may be used for purposes that support the reporting government's programs and, therefore, are for the benefit of the government or its citizenry. (Permanent funds do not include private-purpose trust funds, which should be used when the government is required to use the principal or earnings for the benefit of individuals, private organizations, or other governments).

private purpose trust fund. A general fund type under the fiduciary category used to report resources held and administered by the reporting government acting in a fiduciary capacity for individuals, other governments, or private organizations.

proprietary funds. The government category used to account for a government's ongoing organizations and activities that are similar to those often found in the private sector (these are enterprise and internal service funds). All assets, liabilities, equities, revenues, expenses, and transfers relating to the government's business and quasi-business activities are accounted for through proprietary funds. Proprietary funds should apply all applicable GASB pronouncements and those GAAP applicable to similar businesses in the private sector, unless those conflict with GASB pronouncements. These funds use the accrual basis of accounting in conjunction with the flow of economic resources measurement focus.

purchases method. The method under which inventories are recorded as expenditures when acquired.

restricted fund balance. Portion of fund balance that reflects constraints placed on the use of resources (other than nonspendable items) that are either (*a*) externally imposed by a creditor, such as through debt covenants, grantors, contributors, or laws or regulations of other governments or (*b*) imposed by law through constitutional provisions or enabling legislation.

required supplementary information. GAAP specify that certain information be presented as required supplementary information, or RSI.

special-purpose governments. Legally separate entities that perform only one activity or a few activities, such as cemetery districts, school districts, colleges and universities, utilities, hospitals and other health care organizations, and public employee retirement systems.

special revenue fund. A fund that must have revenue or proceeds from specific revenue sources that are either restricted or committed for a specific purpose other than debt service or capital projects. This definition means that in order to be considered a special revenue fund, there must be one or more revenue sources upon which reporting the activity in a separate fund is predicated.

interfund transfers. All transfers, such as legally authorized transfers from a fund receiving revenue to a fund through which the resources are to be expended, where there is no intent to repay. Interfund transfers are recorded on the operating statement.

unassigned fund balance. Residual classification for the general fund. This classification represents fund balance that has not been assigned to other funds and has not been restricted, committed, or assigned to specific purposes within the general fund. The general fund should be the only fund that reports a positive unassigned fund balance amount. In other funds, if expenditures incurred for specific purposes exceeded the amounts restricted, committed, or assigned to those purposes, it may be necessary to report a negative unassigned fund balance.

unrestricted fund balance. The total of committed fund balance, assigned fund balance, and unassigned fund balance.

Not-for-profit terminology

board-designated endowment fund. An endowment fund created by a not-for-profit entity's governing board by designating a portion of its net assets without donor restrictions to be invested to provide income for a long, but not necessarily specified, period. In rare circumstances, a board-designated endowment fund also can include a portion of net assets with donor restrictions. For example, if a not-for-profit is unable to spend donor-restricted contributions in the near term, then the board sometimes considers the long-term investment of these funds.

board-designated net assets. Net assets without donor restrictions subject to self-imposed limits by action of the governing board. Board-designated net assets may be earmarked for future programs, investment, contingencies, purchase or construction of fixed assets, or other uses. Some governing boards may delegate designation decisions to internal management. Such designations are considered to be included in board-designated net assets.

charitable lead trust. A trust established in connection with a split-interest agreement in which the not-for-profit entity receives distributions during the agreement's term. Upon termination of the trust, the remainder of the trust assets are paid to the donor or to third-party beneficiaries designated by the donor.

charitable remainder trust. A trust established in connection with a split-interest agreement in which the donor or a third-party beneficiary receives specified distributions during the agreement's term. Upon termination of the trust, a not-for-profit entity receives the assets remaining in the trust.

collections. Works of art, historical treasures, or similar assets that are (*a*) held for public exhibition, education, or research in furtherance of public service, rather than financial gain; (*b*) protected, kept unencumbered, cared for, and preserved; and (*c*) subject to an organizational policy that requires the proceeds of items that are sold to be used to acquire other items for collections.

conditional promise to give. A promise to give that is subject to a donor-imposed condition.

contribution. An unconditional transfer of cash or other assets, as well as unconditional promises to give, to an entity or a reduction, settlement, or cancellation of its liabilities in a voluntary nonreciprocal transfer by another entity acting other than as an owner.

costs of joint activities. Costs incurred for a joint activity. Costs of joint activities may include joint costs and costs other than joint costs. *Costs other than joint costs* are costs that are identifiable with a particular function, such as program, fund-raising, management and general, and membership development costs.

donor-imposed restriction. A donor stipulation (*donors* include other types of contributors, including makers of certain grants) that specifies a use for the contributed asset that is more specific than broad limits resulting from the nature of the organization, the environment in which it operates, and the purposes specified in its articles of incorporation or bylaws, or comparable documents for an unincorporated association. A restriction on an organization's use of the asset contributed may be temporary in nature or perpetual in nature.

donor-restricted endowment fund. An endowment fund that is created by a donor stipulation (*donors* include other types of contributors, including makers of certain grants) that requires investment of the gift in perpetuity or for a specified term. Some donors or laws may require that a portion of income, gains, or both be added to the gift and invested subject to similar restrictions.

donor-restricted support. Donor-restricted revenues or gains from contributions that increase net assets with donor restrictions (*donors* include other types of contributions, including makers of certain grants).

economic interest. A not-for-profit entity's interest in another entity that exists if any of the following criteria are met: (*a*) The other entity holds or uses significant resources that must be used for the purposes of the not-for-profit entity, either directly or indirectly, by producing income or providing services, or (*b*) the not-for-profit entity is responsible for the liabilities of the other entity.

endowment fund. An established fund of cash, securities, or other assets that provides income for the maintenance of a not-for-profit entity. The use of the assets of the fund may be with or without donor-imposed restrictions. Endowment funds generally are established by donor-restricted gifts and bequests to provide a source of income.

functional expense classification. A method of grouping expenses according to the purpose for which the costs are incurred. The primary functional classifications of a not-for-profit entity are program services and supporting activities.

funds functioning as endowment. Net assets without donor restrictions (*donors* include other types of contributors, including makers of certain grants) designated by an entity's governing board to be invested to provide income for generally a long, but not necessarily specified, period.

joint activity. An activity that is part of the fund-raising function and has elements of one or more other functions, such as programs, management and general, membership development, or any other functional category used by the entity.

joint costs. The costs of conducting joint activities that are not identifiable with a particular component of the activity.

management and general activities. Supporting activities that are not directly identifiable with one or more programs, fund-raising activities, or membership development activities.

natural expense classification. A method of grouping expenses according to the kinds of economic benefits received in incurring those expenses. Examples of natural expense classifications include salaries and wages, employee benefits, professional services, supplies, interest expense, rent, utilities, and depreciation.

net assets. The excess or deficiency of assets over liabilities of a not-for-profit entity, which is divided into two mutually exclusive classes according to the existence or absence of donor-imposed restrictions.

net assets with donor restrictions. The part of net assets of a not-for-profit entity that is subject to donor-imposed restrictions (*donors* include other types of contributors, including makers of certain grants).

net assets without donor restrictions. The part of net assets of a not-for-profit entity that is not subject to donor-imposed restrictions (*donors* include other types of contributors, including makers of certain grants).

programmatic investing. The activity of making loans or other investments that are directed at carrying out a not-for-profit entity's purpose for existence, rather than investing in the general production of income or appreciation of an asset (for example, total return investing). An example of programmatic investing is a loan made to lower-income individuals to promote home ownership.

promise to give. A written or oral agreement to contribute cash or other assets to another entity. A promise to give may be either conditional or unconditional.

underwater endowment fund. A donor-restricted endowment fund for which the fair value of the fund at the reporting date is less than either the original gift amount or the amount required to be maintained by the donor or by law that extends donor restrictions.

Single audit and Yellow Book terminology

attestation engagements. Attestation engagements concern examining, reviewing, or performing agreed-upon procedures on a subject matter or an assertion about a subject matter and reporting on the results.

compliance supplement. A document issued annually in the spring by the OMB to provide guidance to auditors.

data collection form. A form submitted to the Federal Audit Clearinghouse that provides information about the auditor, the auditee and its federal programs, and the results of the audit.

federal financial assistance. Assistance that nonfederal entities receive or administer in the form of grants, loans, loan guarantees, property, cooperative agreements, interest subsidies, insurance, food commodities, direct appropriations, or other assistance, but does not include amounts received as reimbursement for services rendered to individuals in accordance with guidance issued by the director.

financial audits. Financial audits are primarily concerned with providing reasonable assurance about whether financial statements are presented fairly, in all material respects, in conformity with GAAP or with a comprehensive basis of accounting other than GAAP.

GAGAS. Generally accepted government auditing standards issued by the GAO. They are published as *Government Auditing Standards*, also commonly known as the Yellow Book.

GAO. The United States Government Accountability Office. Among its responsibilities is the issuance of GAGAS.

OMB. The Office of Management and Budget. The OMB assists the President in the development and implementation of budget, program, management, and regulatory policies.

pass-through entity. A nonfederal entity that provides federal awards to a subrecipient to carry out a federal program.

performance audits. Performance audits entail an objective and systematic examination of evidence to provide an independent assessment of the performance and management of a program against objective criteria as well as assessments that provide a prospective focus or that synthesize information on best practices or cross-cutting issues.

program-specific audit. A compliance audit of one federal program.

single audit. An audit of a nonfederal entity that includes the entity's financial statements and federal awards.

single audit guide. This AICPA Audit Guide, formally titled Government Auditing Standards *and Single Audits*, is the former Statement of Position (SOP) 98-3, *Audits of States, Local Governments, and Not-for-Profit Organizations Receiving Federal Awards*. The single audit guide provides guidance on the auditor's responsibilities when conducting a single audit or program-specific audit in accordance with the Single Audit Act, GAGAS, and the Uniform Guidance.

subrecipient. A nonfederal entity that receives federal awards through another nonfederal entity to carry out a federal program but does not include an individual who receives financial assistance through such awards.

Uniform Guidance. Formally known as Title 2 U.S. *Code of Federal Regulations* Part 200, *Uniform Administrative Requirements, Cost Principles, and Audit Requirements for Federal Awards*. The Uniform Guidance sets forth the requirements for the compliance audit portion of a single audit.

Index

Annual Update: Top Governmental and Not-for-Profit Accounting and Auditing Issues Facing CPAs

By Lynda Dennis, Ph.D., CPA, CGFO

Solutions

The AICPA publishes *CPA Letter Daily*, a free e-newsletter published each weekday. The newsletter, which covers the 10-12 most important stories in business, finance, and accounting, as well as AICPA information, was created to deliver news to CPAs and others who work with the accounting profession. Besides summarizing media articles, commentaries, and research results, the e-newsletter links to television broadcasts and videos and features reader polls. *CPA Letter Daily*'s editors scan hundreds of publications and websites, selecting the most relevant and important news so you don't have to. The newsletter arrives in your inbox early in the morning. To sign up, visit smartbrief.com/CPA.

Do you need high-quality technical assistance? The AICPA Auditing and Accounting Technical Hotline provides non-authoritative guidance on accounting, auditing, attestation, and compilation and review standards. The hotline can be reached at 877.242.7212.

Solutions

Chapter 1

Knowledge check solutions

1.
   a. Incorrect. Requirements of GASB Statement No. 87 are mostly consistent with the requirements business entities use to account for leases. However, GASB Statement No. 87 also makes accounting for leases by governments consistent with GASB Concepts Statement No. 4, *Elements of Financial Statements*.
   b. Correct. GASB Statement No. 87 makes accounting and reporting of leases by state and local governments consistent with GASB Concept Statement No. 4 and updates lease accounting for the approaches considered by FASB and IASB.
   c. Incorrect. GASB Statement No. 87 addresses accounting and reporting of leases by lessees and lessors.
   d. Incorrect. GASB Statement No. 87 addresses accounting and reporting of leases by lessees and lessors.

2.
   a. Incorrect. Leases of intangible assets are not within the scope of GASB Statement No. 87.
   b. Incorrect. Supply contracts are not within the scope of GASB Statement No. 87.
   c. Incorrect. Leases of biological assets are not within the scope of GASB Statement No. 87.
   d. Correct. Leases of tangible capital assets are within the scope of GASB Statement No. 87 if the arrangement meets the definition of a lease as defined in the statement.

3.
   a. Incorrect. The lease term considers periods covered by a lessor's option to terminate a lease if it is reasonably certain (not reasonably possible) the lessor will not exercise that option.
   b. Incorrect. The lease term considers periods covered by a lessor's option to extend a lease if it is reasonably certain (not reasonably possible) the lessor will exercise that option.
   c. Incorrect. The lease term considers periods covered by a lessee's option to extend a lease if it is reasonably certain (not reasonably possible) the lessee will exercise that option .
   d. Correct. The lease term considers periods covered by a lessee's option to terminate a lease if it is reasonably certain the lessee will not exercise that option.

4.

a. Incorrect. Fixed payments are included in the initial measurement of a lease liability.

b. Incorrect. Variable payments that are fixed in substance are included in the initial measurement of a lease liability.

c. Correct. The exercise price of a purchase option is included in the initial measurement of a lease liability when the lessee is reasonably certain to exercise the option.

d. Incorrect. Lease incentives due from the lessor are included in the initial measurement of a lease liability.

5.

a. Correct. Commitments under leases before the commencement of the lease term are required to be disclosed by the lessee.

b. Incorrect. A lessee is required to disclose a general description of its leasing arrangements.

c. Incorrect. The amount of lease assets by major classes of underlying assets is required to be disclosed separately from other capital assets.

d. Incorrect. Principal and interest requirements to maturity are required to be presented separately for the lease liability for each of the five subsequent fiscal years and in five-year increments thereafter.

6.

a. Incorrect. Fixed payments are included in the initial measurement of a lease receivable.

b. Incorrect. Variable payments that are fixed in substance are included in the initial measurement of a lease receivable.

c. Correct. The exercise price of a purchase option is not included in the initial measurement of a lease receivable. Revenue from the exercise of a purchase option is recognized when the option is exercised.

d. Incorrect. Lease incentives due to the lessee are included in the initial measurement of a lease receivable.

7.
- a. Incorrect. Disclosing the amount of lease assets by major classes of underlying assets, disclosed separately from other capital assets is a requirement of lessees.
- b. Correct. Lessors are required to disclose the total amount of revenues (inflows of resources such as lease revenue, interest revenue, and any other lease-related revenues) recognized in the reporting period from leases, if the amount cannot be determined based on amounts displayed on the face of the financial statements.
- c. Incorrect. This disclosure is required of a lessor for all of its leases (including leases of assets that are investments) other than regulated leases.
- d. Incorrect. A lessor is only required to disclose future payments included in the lease receivable with principal and interest presented separately for each of the five subsequent fiscal years and in five-year increments thereafter if its principal ongoing operations consist of leasing assets to other entities.

8.
- a. Correct. Lease incentives decrease rather than increase the amount a lessee is required to pay for a lease.
- b. Incorrect. In the context of GASB Statement No. 87, lease incentives are payments made to or on behalf of the lessee for which the lessee has a right of offset with its obligation to the lessor.
- c. Incorrect. In the context of GASB Statement No. 87, lease incentive payments provided after the commencement of the lease term are not included in the initial measurement.
- d. Incorrect. Lease incentive payments provided before the commencement of the lease term are included in the initial measurement.

9.
- a. Incorrect. Identifying existing leases is discussed as a potential implementation challenge.
- b. Incorrect. Determining if identified leases will terminate before the effective date of the statement is discussed as a potential implementation challenge.
- c. Correct. The effect of recording leases on total net position is not discussed as a potential implementation challenge. The section discusses the effect of recording leases on financial condition, debt covenants, and debt limits.
- d. Incorrect. Measurement of lease receivables and corresponding deferred inflows of resources is discussed as a potential implementation challenge.

Chapter 2

Case study solution

Contribution based on what is known of the agreement between the state and the not-for-profit entity and the following indicators enumerated in FASB ASC 958:

1. As the resource provider, the state is not synonymous with the general public. Benefits received by the qualifying families and the areas in which they live are not equivalent to commensurate value received by the state as the resource provider.
2. Execution of the state's mission or positive sentiment grantor staff or elected officials feel does not constitute commensurate value.
3. Expressed intent asserted by both the recipient and resource provider relating to the purpose of the grant being to subsidize low- or no-cost day care programs for low income individuals.
4. As the resource provider, the state has discretion in determining the amount of the grant and the amount of each reimbursement. The not-for-profit and the state do not appear to have "agreed" on the amount.
5. There is no mention in the case of penalties. However, if the not-for-profit discontinues, the program reimbursement is limited to the actual amounts spent rather than the grant amount approved.

The grant appears to be a conditional contribution because spending the funds in accordance with the state procurement policies is a barrier to be overcome before the not-for-profit can be reimbursed (that is, access the resources promised). In addition to the barrier, the state is released from its obligation to fund the program if the not-for-profit entity discontinues the program (right of release) and costs not in accordance with the state's procurement policies will not be reimbursed (right of return or right of release).

Practice question solutions

1. FASB ASC 958 defines an exchange transaction as a *reciprocal transfer* (emphasis added) in which each party receives and sacrifices approximately commensurate value.

2. FASB ASC 958 defines contribution as an *unconditional transfer* (emphasis added) of cash or other assets, as well as unconditional promises to give, to an entity or a reduction, settlement, or cancellation of its liabilities in a voluntary nonreciprocal transfer by another entity acting other than as an owner. In a contribution transaction, the resource provider often receives value indirectly by providing a societal benefit although the benefit is not considered to be of commensurate value. In an exchange transaction, the potential public benefits are secondary to the potential direct benefits to the resource provider.

3. A not-for-profit entity is required to report gifts of long-lived assets received without stipulations (about how long they must be used) as donor-restricted support.

4. *Variance power* is defined in FASB ASC as

. . . the unilateral power to redirect the use of the transferred assets to another beneficiary. A donor *explicitly grants* [emphasis added] variance power if the recipient entity's [not-for-profit entity's] unilateral power [emphasis added] to redirect the use of the assets is *explicitly referred to* [emphasis added] in the instrument transferring the assets. Unilateral power means the recipient entity [not-for-profit entity's] can override the donor's instructions without approval from the donor, specified beneficiary, or any other interested party.

5. When determining if grants, awards, sponsorships, or membership dues represent exchange transactions, the terms of the agreement should be considered in addition to the following:

- A resource provider is not synonymous with the general public. Benefits received by the public resulting from the assets transferred are not equivalent to commensurate value received by the resource provider.
- Execution of a resource provider's mission or positive sentiment a donor feels does not constitute commensurate value.
- If the expressed intent asserted by both the recipient and resource provider relating to the assets transferred is to exchange goods or services of commensurate value, then the transaction is indicative of an exchange transaction. If the recipient solicits assets from the resource provider without the intent of exchanging goods or services, then the transaction is indicative of a contribution.
- If the resource provider has full discretion in determining the amount of the transferred assets, the transaction is indicative of a contribution. When both the recipient and resource provider agree on the amount of assets transferred in exchange for goods or services of commensurate value, the transaction is indicative of an exchange transaction.
- If penalties assessed on the recipient for failure to comply with the terms of the agreement are limited to the delivery of assets or services already provided and the return of the unspent amount, the transaction is indicative of a contribution. The existence of contractual provisions for economic forfeiture beyond the amount of assets transferred generally indicates the transaction is an exchange transaction.

6. Indicators membership dues represent exchange transactions include the following:

a. The membership solicitation materials indicate the dues provide economic benefits to members or to other entities or individuals designated by or related to members.

b. Substantive member benefits (such as publications, admissions, reduced admissions, educational programs, special events, and so on) may be available to nonmembers for a fee.

c. Benefits provided by the not-for-profit entity are provided only to members.

d. Benefits are provided to members for a defined period of time and additional payment of dues is required to extend benefits.

e. The dues payment is fully or partially refundable if the member terminates his or her membership.

f. Membership is available only to individuals that meet certain criteria (such as living in a certain area, possessing a particular professional certification, and so on).

7. Indicators membership dues are contributions include the following:
   a. The membership solicitation materials indicate that the dues provide benefits to the general public or to service beneficiaries of the not-for-profit entity.
   b. Member benefits are negligible.
   c. Benefits provided by the not-for-profit entity to members and nonmembers.
   d. Duration of the benefit period is not specified.
   e. The dues payment is not refundable if the member terminates his or her membership.
   f. Membership is available to the general public.

Knowledge check solutions

1.
   a. Incorrect. Exchange transactions are reciprocal transfers.
   b. Incorrect. Restrictions are associated with contributions but not exchange transactions.
   c. Correct. Parties in an exchange give up and receive something of commensurate value.
   d. Incorrect. In an exchange transaction, the potential public benefits are secondary to the potential proprietary benefits to the resource provider.

2.
   a. Incorrect. Conditional contributions are not recognized when any restrictions have been met. Restrictions relate only to the class of net asset in which contributions are recognized.
   b. Correct. Unconditional contributions are recognized when received or promised, and conditional promises are recognized when all conditions have been substantially met or explicitly waived by the donor.
   c. Incorrect. Conditional contributions are recognized when the conditions have been substantially met.
   d. Incorrect. Conditional contributions are not recognized when both restrictions and conditions have been substantially met. Restrictions relate only to the class of net asset in which contributions are recognized.

3.
   a. Incorrect. Accepting assets from a donor is not the only requirement.
   b. Incorrect. Using the assets received from a donor on behalf of a beneficiary specified by the donor is not the only requirement.
   c. Incorrect. Transferring the assets received to a beneficiary specified by the donor is not the only requirement.
   d. Correct. The items in a–c must all be present for the not-for-profit entity to be considered an agent.

4.

    a. Incorrect. One entity must have more than the ability to influence the operating and financial decisions of the other entity.

    b. Incorrect. One entity must have more than an ongoing economic interest in the net assets of the other entity.

    c. Correct. A not-for-profit entity is financially interrelated to a donor-specified beneficiary when either the not-for-profit entity or the beneficiary have both the ability to influence the operating and financial decisions of the other entity and an ongoing economic interest in the net assets of the other entity.

    d. Incorrect. There are requirements related to a not-for-profit entity's ability to influence and ongoing economic interest.

Chapter 3

Practice question solutions

1. Risk assessment procedures include inquiries of management and others within the entity, analytical procedures, and observation and inspection.

2. Tests of details and analytical procedures are the two types of substantive procedures defined in professional standards.

3. Audit risk is defined in professional standards as the risk the auditor may unknowingly fail to appropriately modify his or her opinion on the financial statements when they are materially misstated.

4. A significant risk is one requiring special audit consideration.

5. Control risk is the risk a material misstatement (individually or in the aggregate) could occur in a relevant assertion and not be prevented or detected on a timely basis by the entity's internal control.

6. When identifying significant risks, the auditor should consider the following:

    a. Nature of the risk
    b. Likely magnitude of the potential misstatement (including the possibility the risk might give rise to multiple misstatements)
    c. Likelihood of the risk occurring

7. Inherent risk is the susceptibility of a *relevant assertion* to a material misstatement (individually or in the aggregate) assuming there are not related controls.

Knowledge check solutions

1.

    a. Correct. Industry risk is not a component of audit risk.

    b. Incorrect. Control risk is a component of audit risk.

    c. Incorrect. Detection risk is a component of audit risk.

    d. Incorrect. Inherent risk is a component of audit risk.

2.

    a. Correct. Substantive tests of details are a type of further audit procedure.

    b. Incorrect. Observation and inspection are risk assessment procedures.

    c. Incorrect. Inquiries of management are a risk assessment procedure.

    d. Incorrect. Analytical procedures are a risk assessment and further audit procedure.

3.

    a. Correct. An entity's hiring policies may be a part of its control environment, but it is not an individual component of internal control.

    b. Incorrect. The control environment is a component of internal control.

    c. Incorrect. An entity's risk assessment process is a component of internal control.

    d. Incorrect. An entity's information system along with its communication system is a component of internal control.

4.

    a. Incorrect. Tests of controls may reduce the amount of substantive tests, but they do not eliminate the need for substantive tests of details.

    b. Incorrect. Tests of controls may be performed on every audit engagement but should be performed in certain circumstances as identified in professional standards.

    c. Incorrect. Substantive tests of details provide evidence recorded amounts are correct.

    d. Correct. Tests of controls provide evidence of their operating effectiveness.

Chapter 4

Knowledge check solutions

1.
   a. Incorrect. The definition of *contamination* does relate to an event or condition normally involving a substance.
   b. Incorrect. The definition of *contamination* does relate to substances deposited in, on, or around a tangible capital asset.
   c. Correct. The definition of *contamination* does not relate to substances deposited that may harm animals.
   d. Incorrect. The definition of *contamination* does relate to substances deposited that may harm people, equipment, or the environment.

2.
   a. Correct. At least annually a government is required to adjust the current value of an ARO for price increases or decreases due to general inflation or deflation.
   b. Incorrect. Changes in technology are an example of a factor that may lead to a significant change in the estimated outlays.
   c. Incorrect. Changes in legal or regulatory requirements resulting from changes in laws, regulations, contracts, or court judgments are an example of a factor that may lead to a significant change in the estimated outlays.
   d. Incorrect. Changes in the type of equipment, facilities, or services that will be used to meet the obligations to retire the tangible capital asset are an example of a factor that may lead to a significant change in the estimated outlays.

3.
   a. Incorrect. A general description of the ARO and associated tangible capital assets are required to be disclosed.
   b. Correct. Assets available for payment of ARO liabilities are not required to be disclosed. However, any assets restricted for payment of ARO liabilities are required to be disclosed.
   c. Incorrect. Methods and assumptions used to measure the liabilities are required to be disclosed.
   d. Incorrect. How any legally required funding and assurance provisions associated with AROs are being met are required to be disclosed.

4.

    a. Incorrect. Changes resulting from the requirements of GASB Statement No. 83 should be applied retroactively by restating all prior periods presented.

    b. Incorrect. The cumulative effect of applying the requirements of GASB Statement No. 83 is required to be reported when restatement of prior periods is not practicable.

    c. Incorrect. Reasons for not restating prior periods when it is not practicable to do so are required to be disclosed.

    d. Correct. Governments are not required to disclose the cost of implementing the requirements of GASB Statement No. 83 in the first year of application or in any subsequent year.

5.

    a. Incorrect. Solid waste treatment facilities are an example of a tangible capital asset typically subject to legal requirements requiring asset retirement activities.

    b. Incorrect. X-ray equipment is an example of a tangible capital asset typically subject to legal requirements requiring asset retirement activities.

    c. Incorrect. Wind turbines are an example of a tangible capital asset typically subject to legal requirements requiring asset retirement activities.

    d. Correct. Fossil fuel power plants are not an example of a tangible capital asset typically subject to legal requirements requiring asset retirement activities.

Chapter 5

Practice question solutions

1. In the statement of activities, a special event that is ongoing or central to the operations of a not-for-profit entity is recognized as *revenue and expense(s)*.

2. Special events incidental or peripheral to operations are recognized as a *net gain or loss* in the statement of activities. Net losses on special events are not required to be reported by functional classification in the (*a*) statement of activities, (*b*) notes to the financial statements, or (*c*) reporting of functional and natural expenses.

3. Events representing *ongoing major and central activities* are those that either (*a*) are normally part of a not-for-profit entity's strategy and it normally carries on such activities, or (*b*) generate gross revenues or incur expenses that are significant in relation to the not-for-profit entity's annual budget.

4. GAAP define *incidental or peripheral* events as those that are either (*a*) not an integral part of a not-for-profit entity's usual activities or (*b*) not significant in relation to a not-for-profit entity's annual budget.

5. For ongoing major *joint activities not meeting the purpose, audience, and content criteria*, only costs associated with direct benefits to donors or attendees would be reported as special event costs. Any other direct costs are recognized as fundraising expenses (and expensed in the period incurred) because the criteria to allocate joint costs are not met.

6. Direct and indirect costs of special events conducted as ongoing major *joint activities meeting the purpose, audience, and content criteria* are recognized as special event costs (including direct benefits received by donors or attendees).

7. When the *receipts* of a special event represent *both an exchange transaction and a contribution*, a not-for-profit entity may choose to bifurcate the receipts to reflect the duality of the transaction. For special event receipts accounted for as a bifurcated transaction, the portion of the receipts relating to an *exchange transaction* is not recognized as revenue until the identified obligations have been satisfied (the event is held). Therefore, the exchange transaction portion of special event receipts received in one year for an event to be held in the subsequent period should be reported as a contract liability.

   Accounting for special event receipts representing *contributions* in whole or part depends on whether the contribution is conditional or unconditional. Special event receipts received in one year for an event to be held in the subsequent period related to *unconditional contributions* should be reported as *donor-restricted support* in the year they are received or promised. The portion of special event receipts relating to *conditional contributions* is not recognized as contributions until the conditions have been substantially met or explicitly waived by the donor. Therefore, special event receipts received in one year for an event to be held in the subsequent period relating to conditional contributions are recognized as *refundable advances* (that is, until the conditions have been substantially met — the event held)—or the requirement to hold the event explicitly waived by the donor.

Knowledge check solutions

1.
   a. Incorrect. Events that are incidental or peripheral to operations are not reported as revenues and expenses.
   b. Incorrect. Events that are ongoing major or central to operations are reported as revenues and expenses.
   c. Incorrect. Events that are incidental or peripheral to operations are not considered extraordinary items.
   d. Correct. Events that are incidental or peripheral to operations are reported as net gains or losses.

2.

    a. Correct. The purpose, audience, and content criteria must be met to allocate costs of joint activities.

    b. Incorrect. There are other requirements besides purpose and audience to allocate costs of joint activities.

    c. Incorrect. There are other requirements besides purpose and content criteria to allocate costs of joint activities.

    d. Incorrect. There are requirements that must be met to allocate costs of joint activities.

3.

    a. Incorrect. Revenues from exchange transactions are not recognized when the ticket to the event is purchased.

    b. Incorrect. Revenues from exchange transactions are not recorded when a promise to buy a ticket is given.

    c. Correct. Revenues from exchange transactions are recorded when identified performance obligations have been satisfied (that is, when the event is held).

    d. Incorrect. The purchaser of the ticket need not attend the event for revenue to be recognized as a result of the transaction.

4.

    a. Incorrect. Unconditional donations of goods and services meeting the recognition criteria are recognized when received or promised.

    b. Correct. Goods and services donated with no donor-imposed conditions are recorded as support with or without donor restrictions at fair value when received or promised.

    c. Incorrect. Donated goods and services are not recorded at the donor's cost, billing rate, or salary.

    d. Incorrect. All donated services must meet the recognition criteria.

Chapter 6

Practice question solutions

1. Sampling risk is the risk that the auditor's conclusions based on a sample might have been different if the entire population (for example, account balance or class of transaction) had been tested (for example, risk of incorrect acceptance/rejection for substantive tests of details or risk of assessing control risk too low/high for tests of controls).

2. AU-C section 530, *Audit Sampling* (AICPA, *Professional Standards*), provides guidance for planning, performing, and evaluating audit samples using either a nonstatistical or statistical approach.

3. Both sampling approaches require the use of professional judgment in planning, performing, and evaluating an audit sample. However, judgment is also required to relate the audit evidence from the sample to other audit evidence when forming a conclusion about an account balance or class of transactions.

Statistical sampling is based on probability theory and allows the auditor to

- design an efficient sample,
- measure sufficiency of the audit evidence obtained, and
- quantitatively evaluate sample results.

The auditor generally relies on professional judgment as well as statistical training and experience to determine a nonstatistical sample. Factors considered when determining the size of a nonstatistical sample need not be quantified as is necessary for a statistical sample. *Any sampling procedure that does not permit the numerical measurement of sampling risk is a nonstatistical sampling procedure*. Regardless of the rigor an auditor uses in randomly selecting items for a nonstatistical sample, it remains a nonstatistical sampling application.

4. The auditor uses judgment in determining the technique to use in selecting items for a sample and also considers the efficiency to be gained by choosing one selection technique over another. Random-based selection techniques include the following:

- *Random sampling* — Every combination of sampling units has an equal probability of being selected.
- *Stratified random sampling* — Every combination of sampling units within each individual stratum has an equal probability of being selected.
- *Systematic sampling with one or more random starts* — After a random start items are selected based on a uniform interval (calculated by dividing the number of units in the population being tested by the sample size).
- *Sampling with probability proportional to size (PPS)* — This method is used *only for substantive tests* using monetary unit sampling where items are selected for such a sample in proportion to their relative size (dollar amount).

5. Professional standards identify the following three types of audit tests:

- *Tests of controls* — These tests provide evidence about the *effectiveness* of the design, implementation, or operation of a control in preventing or detecting material misstatements in a financial statement assertion.
- *Substantive tests* — These tests provide evidence about the *validity and propriety* of the accounting treatment of transactions and balances as well as misstatements.
- *Dual-purpose tests* — Such tests are designed to provide evidence about the operating effectiveness of a control as well as whether a recorded balance or class of transactions is materially misstated.

6. Generally, the auditor would consider (*a*) his or her knowledge of statistical concepts, (*b*) the availability of sampling software, and (*c*) whether the population to be sampled is in electronic format when determining a sampling approach. More specific considerations include the

   - auditing procedures to be applied.
   - appropriateness of the audit evidence obtained (with respect to individual items in the sample).
   - actions that might be taken in light of the nature and cause of particular misstatements.

7. Factors influencing the size of a sample for a substantive test of details include the following:

   - *Assessment of inherent risk* — A low assessed level of inherent risk results in a *smaller* sample size.
   - *Assessment of control risk* — A low assessed level of control risk also results in a *smaller* sample size.
   - *Assessment of risk related to other substantive procedures directed at the same assertion* — A low assessment of risk associated with other relevant substantive procedures results in a *smaller* sample size.
   - Tolerable misstatement for the specific account balance/class of transactions being tested — A small amount of tolerable misstatement results in a larger sample size.
   - *Expected size and frequency of misstatement* — Smaller expected misstatements or lower frequency rates result in a *smaller* sample size.

8. Factors influencing the size of a sample for a test of controls include the following:

   - *Assessed level of control risk* — Assurance or confidence level is the complement of control risk.
   - *Assessment of risk of over reliance on controls* — This is generally set at a low level (10% or less based on the population, nature of transactions, and significance of control being tested) because a test of controls is the primary source of evidence about their effectiveness. Assurance or confidence level is the complement of the risk of over reliance. The lower the acceptable risk of over reliance, the *larger* the sample that is needed.
   - *Tolerable rate* — In tests of controls this is the maximum rate of deviation from a control that the auditor is willing to accept without altering the planned assessed level of control risk. A higher tolerable rate results in a *smaller* sample size.
   - *Expected population deviation rate (also known as the expected rate of occurrence)* — There is a direct relationship between the expected population deviation rate and sample size. As the expected rate nears the tolerable rate, more precise information is needed from the sample and a *larger* sample size is needed.
   - *Desired level of assurance provided by the test* — High levels of desired assurance result in *larger* sample sizes.

9. Three common methods used to project sample errors to the population in a financial statement audit include the following:

- Applying the misstated rate of dollar misstatements observed in the sample to the population
- Projecting the average difference between the audited and recorded amounts of each item in the sample to all items in the population
- Use of a point estimator for nonstatistical samples when sample selection approximated a probability proportional to size selection

10. For a given test of controls, the auditor is concerned the actual rate of deviation in the population does not exceed the tolerable rate in a sample. An unacceptably high level of sampling risk is generally indicated when the actual deviation rate for a tested control, plus the allowance for sampling risk, exceeds the tolerable rate. The same holds true when the actual deviation rate exceeds the expected deviation rate used to design the sample. In these cases, the auditor will need to increase the assessed level of control risk or consider whether to rely on the control at all.

Knowledge check solutions

1.
   a. Incorrect. The guide assists auditors in designing and performing sampling in a financial statement audit conducted in accordance with generally accepted auditing standards.
   b. Incorrect. The guide provides guidance on the application of nonstatistical and statistical sampling techniques to tests of controls and substantive tests of details.
   c. Correct. The guide provides guidance on the application of nonstatistical and statistical sampling techniques, not just nonstatistical sampling, to tests of controls and substantive tests of details.
   d. Incorrect. The guide does provide guidance on the determination of sample size and evaluating sample results.

2.
   a. Incorrect. Tests of controls are defined in professional standards.
   b. Correct. Single-purpose tests are not defined in professional standards.
   c. Incorrect. Tests of details of transactions and balances are defined in professional standards.
   d. Incorrect. Dual-purpose tests are defined in professional standards.

3.

    a. Incorrect. Sample size does not depend only on the objectives of the sample.

    b. Incorrect. Sample size does not depend only on the efficiency of the sample.

    c. Correct. Sample size depends on both the objectives and efficiency of the sample.

    d. Incorrect. Sample size does not depend on the dollar amount of the population being tested.

4.

    a. Incorrect. Whether a sample was stratified or not does affect the method selected to project the misstatement.

    b. Correct. The number of items in a sample does affect the method selected to project the misstatement.

    c. Incorrect. The method of sample selection does affect the method selected to project the misstatement.

    d. Incorrect. The auditor's understanding of the magnitude and distribution of misstatements in the population does affect the method used to project the misstatement.

Chapter 7

Practice question solutions

1. ASU No. 2016-14 is effective for fiscal years beginning after December 15, 2017, so calendar year 2018 and fiscal year 2019 financial statements.

2. ASU No. 2016-14 made changes in the following major areas.

    a. Net asset classes and underwater endowments
    b. Statement of cash flows
    c. Liquidity and availability of financial assets
    d. Expense information
    e. Investment return
    f. Placed-in-service approach

3. ASU requires the use of two classes of net assets — net assets with donor restrictions and net assets without donor restrictions.

4. ASU No. 2016-14 changed the reporting of investment return in the following manner:

   a. Eliminates the requirement to disclose the composition of investment return and the amount of investment expenses
   b. Requires only the presentation of net investment return in endowment fund roll forward disclosures
   c. All external and direct internal investment expenses are required to be netted with investment return.

5. Qualitative liquidity information required to be communicated under ASU No. 2016-14 includes information about

   a. How the entity manages liquid resources available to meet cash needs for general expenditures within one year of the date of the statement of financial position
   b. Availability of the entity's financial assets at the date of the statement of financial position to meet cash needs for general expenditures within one year of the date of the statement of financial position

Knowledge check solutions

1.

   a. Correct. ASU No. 2016-14 requires the use of two classes of net assets — net assets with donor restrictions and net assets without donor restrictions.
   b. Incorrect. These are the classes of net assets prior to the effective date of ASU No. 2016-14.
   c. Incorrect. Board designations are a subset of net assets without donor restrictions under ASU No. 2016-14.
   d. Incorrect. Expendable and nonexpendable may be used to identify an intermediate measure of operations on the statement of activities.

2.

   a. Correct. ASU No. 2016-14 does not require the presentation of a classified statement of financial position. It is an option entities may elect.
   b. Incorrect. ASU No. 2016-14 does identify the period of time for liquidity information as the period within one year of the date of the statement of financial position.
   c. Incorrect. ASU No. 2016-14 does permit the presentation of quantitative liquidity information on the face of the statement of financial position.
   d. Incorrect. ASU No. 2016-14 does require disclosure of qualitative information relating to how the entity manages its liquid resources.

3.

   a. Incorrect. Direct internal investment expenses do include salaries of personnel involved in the direct conduct or direct supervision of the strategic and tactical activities of generating the entity's investment return.

   b. Correct. Direct internal investment expenses involve the direct conduct or direct supervision of the strategic and tactical activities of generating the entity's investment return. Depreciation does not fall within this definition.

   c. Incorrect. Direct internal investment expenses do include benefits relating to salaries of personnel involved in the direct conduct or direct supervision of the strategic and tactical activities of generating the entity's investment return.

   d. Incorrect. Direct internal investment expenses do include travel if it is related to the direct conduct or direct supervision of the strategic and tactical activities of generating the entity's investment return.

4.

   a. Correct. ASU No. 2016-14 requires the use of the placed-in-service approach to account for long-lived assets acquired/constructed with donor resources for such assets.

   b. Incorrect. The pay-as-you-use approach refers to financing the acquisition/construction of long-lived assets with long-term debt.

   c. Incorrect. The pay-as-you-go approach refers to accumulating financial resources to provide funding for the acquisition/construction of long-lived assets without the use of long-term debt.

   d. Incorrect. ASU No. 2016-14 does specify a method to account for long-lived assets acquired/constructed with donor resources for such assets.

Chapter 8

Practice question solutions

1. GAGAS define independence of mind as the state of mind that permits the conduct of an audit without being affected by influences that compromise professional judgment, thereby allowing an individual to act with integrity and exercise objectivity and professional skepticism.

2. GAGAS define independence in appearance as the absence of circumstances that would cause a reasonable and informed third party to reasonably conclude that the integrity, objectivity, or professional skepticism of an audit organization or member of the audit team had been compromised.

3. The seven threats to independence included in the GAGAS conceptual framework are as follows:

    a. Self-interest threat
    b. Self-review threat
    c. Bias threat
    d. Familiarity threat
    e. Undue influence threat
    f. Management participation threat
    g. Structural threat

4. Safeguards noted in paragraph 3.50 of chapter 3 include the following:

    a. Consulting an independent third party, such as a professional entity, a professional regulatory body, or another auditor to discuss engagement issues or assess issues that are highly technical or that require significant judgment
    b. Involving another audit organization to perform or reperform part of the audit
    c. Having an auditor who was not a member of the audit team review the work performed
    d. Removing an auditor from an audit team when the auditor's financial or other interests or relationships pose a threat to independence

5. Management responsibilities addressed in GAGAS include the following:

    a. Setting policies and strategic direction for the audited entity
    b. Directing and accepting responsibility for the actions of the audited entity's employees in the performance of their routine, recurring activities
    c. Having custody of an audited entity's assets
    d. Reporting to those charged with governance on behalf of management
    e. Deciding which of the audit organization's or outside third party's recommendations to implement
    f. Accepting responsibility for the management of an audited entity's project
    g. Accepting responsibility for designing, implementing, or maintaining internal control
    h. Providing services intended to be used as management's primary basis for making decisions significant to the subject matter of the audit
    i. Developing an audited entity's performance measurement system when the system is material or significant to the subject matter of the audit
    j. Serving as a voting member of an audited entity's management committee or board of directors

6. The specific services indicated in the 2018 GAGAS listed as follows are not the *only* nonaudit services that would impair an auditor's independence. The following specific services are identified in GAGAS as those impairing independence:

    a. Preparing accounting records and financial statements
    b. Internal audit assistance services provided by external auditors
    c. Internal control evaluation as a nonaudit service
    d. Information technology systems services
    e. Appraisal, valuation, and actuarial services
    f. Other nonaudit services

7. Specific "Preparing Accounting Records and Financial Statements" services that impair independence are

   a. determining or changing journal entries, account codes or classifications for transactions, or other accounting records for an entity without obtaining management's approval;
   b. authorizing or approving the entity's transactions; and
   c. preparing or making changes to source documents without management approval (for example, purchase orders, payroll time records, customer orders, and contracts). Such records also include an audited entity's general ledger and subsidiary records or equivalent.

Knowledge check solutions

1.

   a. Correct. *Government Auditing Standards* require government auditors to be independent in mind and appearance.

   b. Incorrect. *Government Auditing Standards* do not require government auditors to be independent in appearance of mind.

   c. Incorrect. *Government Auditing Standards* require government auditors to be independent in areas other than mind.

   d. Incorrect. *Government Auditing Standards* require government auditors to be independent in areas other than appearance.

2.

   a. Incorrect. Rotation of partners on an audit may help to mitigate threats to independence.

   b. Incorrect. *Government Auditing Standards* do not include termination of a member of the audited entity as a threat to independence.

   c. Correct. *Government Auditing Standards* state threats to independence can occur when new staff are assigned to an ongoing audit.

   d. Incorrect. Rotation of staff on an audit may help to mitigate threats to independence.

3.

   a. Incorrect. Preparing an audited entity's financial statements is not a routine activity under *Government Auditing Standards*.

   b. Correct. Providing advice on routine business matters is a routine activity under *Government Auditing Standards*.

   c. Incorrect. Performing bookkeeping services to adjust the audited entity's cash basis records to the accrual basis of accounting is not a routine activity under the *Government Auditing Standards*.

   d. Incorrect. Reconciling control accounts to subsidiary ledgers is not a routine activity under *Government Auditing Standards*.

4.

a. Incorrect. Determining or changing journal entries, account codes or classifications for transactions, or other accounting records for the entity without obtaining management's approval impairs auditor independence.

b. Incorrect. Preparing or changing an entity's subsidiary records without management's approval impairs auditor independence.

c. Correct. Determining or changing journal entries, account codes or classifications for transactions, or other accounting records for the entity after obtaining management's approval would not impair auditor independence.

d. Incorrect. Preparing or making changes to an audited entity's source documents without obtaining management's approval impairs auditor independence.

The AICPA publishes *CPA Letter Daily*, a free e-newsletter published each weekday. The newsletter, which covers the 10-12 most important stories in business, finance, and accounting, as well as AICPA information, was created to deliver news to CPAs and others who work with the accounting profession. Besides summarizing media articles, commentaries, and research results, the e-newsletter links to television broadcasts and videos and features reader polls. *CPA Letter Daily*'s editors scan hundreds of publications and websites, selecting the most relevant and important news so you don't have to. The newsletter arrives in your inbox early in the morning. To sign up, visit smartbrief.com/CPA.

Do you need high-quality technical assistance? The AICPA Auditing and Accounting Technical Hotline provides non-authoritative guidance on accounting, auditing, attestation, and compilation and review standards. The hotline can be reached at 877.242.7212.

Learn More

Continuing Professional Education

Thank you for selecting the Association of International Certified Professional Accountants as your continuing professional education provider. We have a diverse offering of CPE courses to help you expand your skill set and develop your competencies. Choose from hundreds of different titles spanning the major subject matter areas relevant to CPAs and CGMAs, including

- governmental and not-for-profit accounting, auditing, and updates;
- internal control and fraud;
- audits of employee benefit plans and 401(k) plans;
- individual and corporate tax updates; and
- a vast array of courses in other areas of accounting and auditing, controllership, management, consulting, taxation, and more!

Get your CPE when and where you want

- Self-study learning options that include on-demand, webcasts, and text formats with superior quality and a broad portfolio of topics, including bundled products like –
  - ➢ CPExpress® online learning for immediate access to hundreds of one- to four-credit hour online courses for just-in-time learning at a price that is right.
  - ➢ Annual Webcast Pass offering live Q&A with experts and unlimited access to the scheduled lineup, all at an incredible discount.
- Staff training programs for audit, tax and preparation, compilation, and review.
- Certificate programs offering comprehensive curriculums developed by practicing experts to build fundamental core competencies in specialized topics.
- National conferences presented by recognized experts.
- Affordable courses on-site at your organization – visit **aicpalearning.org/on-site** for more information.
- Seminars sponsored by your state society and led by top instructors. For a complete list, visit **aicpalearning.org/publicseminar**.

Take control of your career development

The Association's Competency and Learning website at **https://competency.aicpa.org** brings together a variety of learning resources and a self-assessment tool, enabling tracking and reporting of progress toward learning goals.

Visit www.AICPAStore.com to browse our CPE selections.

AICPA®

Your strategic learning partner
Let us help prepare your staff for the future.

What is your current approach to learning? One size does not fit all. Your organization is unique, and your approach to learning and competency should be, too. But where do you start? Choose a strategic partner to help you assess competencies and gaps, design a customized learning plan, and measure and maximize the ROI of your learning and development initiatives.

We offer a wide variety of learning programs for finance professionals at every stage of their career.

AICPA Learning resources can help you:
- Create a learning culture to attract and retain talent
- Enrich staff competency and stay current on changing regulations
- Sharpen your competitive edge
- Capitalize on emerging opportunities
- Meet your goals and positively impact your bottom line
- Address CPE/CPD compliance

Flexible learning options include:
- On-site training
- Conferences
- Webcasts
- Certificate programs
- Online self-study
- Publications

An investment in learning can directly impact your bottom line. Contact an AICPA learning consultant to begin your professional development planning.

Call: 800.634.6780, option 1
Email: AICPALearning@aicpa.org